EVERYTHING YOU NEED TO KNOW

Permission-Based E-Mail Marketing
That Works!

Kim MacPherson

DEARBORN™
TRADE
A **Kaplan Professional** Company

Publisher: Cynthia A. Zigmund
Acquisitions Editor: Jean Iversen
Managing Editor: Jack Kiburz
Project Editor: Trey Thoelcke
Interior Design: Lucy Jenkins
Cover Design: Design Alliance, Inc.
Typesetting: the dotted i

Library of Congress Cataloging-in-Publication Data

MacPherson, Kim.
    Permission-based E-mail marketing that works / Kim MacPherson.
       p.   cm.
    Includes index.
    ISBN 0-7931-4295-4 (pbk.)
    1. Telemarketing. 2. Electronic mail messages. 3. Customer relations. I. Title.
HF5415.1265 .M324 2001
658.8′4—dc21

                         00-012907

Dearborn Trade books are available at special quantity discounts to use as premiums and sales promotions, or for use in corporate training programs. For more information, please call the Special Sales Manager at 800-621-9621, ext. 4514, or write to Dearborn Financial Publishing, Inc., 155 N. Wacker Drive, Chicago, IL 60606-1719.

PRAISE FOR *PERMISSION-BASED E-MAIL MARKETING THAT WORKS!*

"Kim MacPherson's book is a great next step for anyone who is sold on permission marketing. Exactly the sort of nuts and bolts details you'll need to implement a permission marketing campaign of your own."
Seth Godin
Author, *Permission Marketing*

"Kim MacPherson has long been the goddess of e-mail marketing. Here—collected in one place—is evidence why. What you are holding is a must-have reference for anyone launching an e-mail campaign worth its salt."
Ann Handley
President/Chief Content Officer
The ClickZ Network

"Kim MacPherson's informative book goes a long way towards educating both novice and veteran marketers about the dos and don'ts of e-mail marketing. By following her road-tested advice, you will avoid the pitfalls and learn the best practices of a marketing discipline that is only beginning to formulate hard and fast rules. And who knows? The next e-mail marketing success story could be yours."
Rosalind Resnick
CEO, NetCreations, Inc.

"Finally, a how-to manual that walks through each step involved in building and executing a successful e-mail campaign. This book is just what the permission e-mail marketing industry needed and belongs on every serious Internet marketer's desk."
Robbin Zeff
President, Zeff Group
Coauthor, *Advertising on the Internet*

"Before even reading the first page, I knew that Kim would overdeliver bigtime in this book. It's her nature. And I was right. Whether you're new to e-mail marketing or you're a seasoned professional looking for a few extra percentage points, you'll find what you need right here. Which part did I like best? The numerous interviews with experienced e-mail marketers. Getting honest feedback from senior people who are out in the trenches right now is pure gold."
Nick Usborne
Marketing Specialist

"Kim MacPherson has written the ultimate how-to guide for e-mail marketing. *Permission-Based E-mail Marketing That Works!* is a thoroughly comprehensive tour of the exploding e-mail marketing revolution. No one should attempt to conceive, create, or deploy an e-mail marketing campaign without reading this book."
Geoffrey Ramsey
Cofounder, CEO
eMarketer

"Our own firm has done much research on the best practices and ROI effectiveness of permission e-mail marketing. Kim has done an excellent job translating those proven principals into the day-to-day tactics that make those strategies pay off. A great handbook."
Rick E. Bruner
VP of Interactive Marketing Research of IMT Strategies
Author, *Net Results.2: Best Practices for Web Marketing*

"The first book that explains not only the why but the how of using e-mail to acquire new customers and cement relationships with existing ones. Indispensable reading for business owners, managers, and webmasters at firms of all sizes."
Roger C. Parker
Author, *The Streetwise Guide to Relationship Marketing on the Internet*

DEDICATION

To all of the hard-working marketers out there who have helped to shape and create the following "best practices" for e-mail marketing.

And to my late Aunt Lauree, who—had she been born thirty years later—would have been certain to embrace the Internet, as she did all great, exciting, and worthy things. She passed away during the writing of this book, just four months shy of her fiftieth wedding anniversary to my Uncle Ross. This book is dedicated to her memory.

CONTENTS

Foreword   xi
Acknowledgments   xiii
Introduction   xv

PART ONE | E-mail as a Promotional Device

1. The Power of E-mail   3
The Benefits of E-mail Marketing   3
The E-mail Customer Contact Cycle   5

2. E-mail Terms You Should Know   8

3. Opt-In versus Opt-Out—Permission and Privacy   14
Defining Opt-In and Opt-Out   15
The Four-Letter Word That Is Spam   15
Getting New Customers with Opt-In Lists   18
Collecting E-mail Addresses in an Opt-In Manner   19
Your Prospects Have Signed On—Now What?   21

PART TWO | Reeling 'Em In (Acquiring New Customers That Stay)

4. Creating Your Budget   25
Back to Basics   25
Identifying Your Campaign's Goals   27
Budget Building for E-mail Marketing Newbies   29
Short-Term Budgeting   30
Budgeting for a Paid Campaign   30
Summary   33

 5. **Brainstorming the Offer 35**
    Finding the Cream   36
    Your Audience   36
    The All-Important Offer   39
    Types of Offers   41
    Pulling It All Together   45
    GolfCoachConnection.com Develops an Offer   46

 6. **All about Lists   49**
    Opt-In Lists Further Defined   49
    Enhance with Selects   55
    The Datacard   56
    Datacard Components   60
    Top Three Questions to Ask Your Broker or Vendor   61
    Wrap Up   62
    GolfCoachConnection.com Picks a List   62

 7. **Acquisitions Testing Strategies   64**
    Setting Up Your Tests   66
    Creating Keycodes   67
    Tracking and Reporting Software   69
    More Variables, More Tests, More Codes   69
    Testing Rules 101   71
    GolfCoachConnection.com Tests and Reads Results   72

PART THREE | Creative Pointers and Tricks of the Trade

 8. **The Dialogue: How to Speak to Your Prospects and Customers   77**
    The Introduction   79
    As the Relationship Evolves   80

 9. **Copywriting for E-mail: Best Practices   82**
    How Good Copy Sells   83
    Know Thy Prospect   84
    How Good Copy Is Constructed   85
    Copy Details and Tricks of the Trade   87
    Copywriting for the E-mail Landscape   89
    The Subject Line   91
    The *From* Line (A.K.A., the Sender)   94

The Introduction 95
The Body 97
The Close 100
GolfCoachConnection.com Creates Some Copy 100

10. The Power of Design 105
Design 101 106
More Design Bits and Bytes 115
Designing an E-mail 116
A Few Words on Punctuation and Special Effects 124
One More Thing . . . 125
GolfCoachConnection.com Comes Up with a Winning HTML Design! 125
Rich Media E-mail 126

PART FOUR | Best E-mail Retention Practices

**11. Promoting to Your House List: The Other Side
of E-mail Marketing 133**
Creating an Opt-In House List 134
Retention Marketing 101 134
The Strategies 135
GolfCoachConnection.com Starts to Develop a Retention Strategy 140

12. Communications to Retain 142
How Much Is Enough? How Much Is Too Much? 142
What to E-mail? 144

13. Segmentation and Splits for Top Retention 150
Optimizing a Database 151
The RFM Model 153
What Makes a Customer Respond? 155
What to Test? 158
Next Steps 159
GolfCoachConnection.com Gets Its Results 160

14. Viral Marketing 162
How Many Eyeballs? 163
Viral Components 164
Types of Message 165
To Attach or Not to Attach? 165

What Makes a Viral *Virile*?   166
The Technology   166
GolfCoachConnection.com Adds a Viral Component to Its House Offers   167

PART FIVE | Back-End Necessities and Things to Be Mindful Of

15. Coming in for a Landing   171
What Is a Landing Page?   171
Importance of Custom Landing   172
Different Types of Landing Pages   173
Landing Page Must-Haves   176
The Form   177
A Last Word on Landings   178
GolfCoachConnection.com Creates Its Landing Page   178

16. More on Testing, Cookies, and Other Bits and Bytes   180
Setting Up Timing Tests   181
Make Assumptions   184
Remail Strategy   184
Cookies for Additional Tests and Enhancements   184
A Final Word on Testing   186

17. The Last Word: What It All Adds Up To—Tracking and Measuring Your Results   189
ROI: The Ultimate Measurement   190
The Future   193
GolfCoachConnection.com Looks toward the Future   195
Conclusion   195

Case Studies   197
Resources   237
Index   257

Back in February 1996 when my partner, Ryan Scott Druckenmiller, and I pioneered the concept of allowing Internet users to opt in to receive targeted offers by checking a box on our Web site, few people dreamed that the humble e-mail message would one day become the killer app that would revolutionize direct marketing as we know it.

Back then, direct marketing was all about blitzing consumers with junk mail that cost marketers many weeks and many dollars to get out the door, only to be discarded by most recipients unwanted and unread. Clearly, there had to be a better way for marketers to reach consumers who really wanted to get their offers and for consumers to let the marketers know what kind of offers they wanted to receive.

Thanks to the Internet, the dream of one-to-one marketing is fast becoming a reality. Opt-in e-mail marketing—the practice of putting consumers behind the wheel and allowing them to choose the products, services, and companies they wish to hear about—has exploded from a handful of tiny lists to an industry that Jupiter Research predicts will balloon to $7.3 billion by the year 2005.

To what does e-mail marketing owe its rapid rise? In my view, marketers are flocking to email for three main reasons:

1. *E-mail is better.* Unlike recipients of postal mail and telemarketing solicitations, most consumers who receive e-mail offers have voluntarily given marketers permission to send them offers about products and services of interest. In some cases, consumers have opted in not once, but twice, to receive these offers, a process known as double opt-in. This ensures that every person who joins an e-mail list has verified a request to receive the marketer's mailings. The net result: Response rates (on a click-through basis) of 5 to 15 percent on a typical opt-in e-mail marketing campaign versus 1 to 2 percent for postal mail.

2. *E-mail is faster.* Unlike postal mail campaigns that often take weeks to get out the door of the lettershop and months to tabulate responses, an e-mail campaign can go out right away and deliver results in minutes. That's because e-mail messages can be delivered via the Internet almost immedi-

ately. Marketers who seek to acquire new customers using e-mail can tap into Web-enabled databases that use cutting-edge technology, which gives them the power to create real-time campaigns on the fly, from selecting lists to placing orders to mailing out millions of messages in a single day. Real-time tracking systems allow marketers to automatically insert unique URLs (Web addresses) in their messages to capture clickstream data and monitor the success of their campaigns as the responses pour in.

3. *E-mail is cheaper.* Because e-mail marketing requires no paper, printing, or postage, a list of opt-in e-mail addresses can cost as little as 5 cents ($50 CPM) a name, including the cost of renting the list, delivering the message, and deduping the list against other lists in the database. This compares to an average cost of 50 cents to $1 ($500 to $1,000 CPM) to send out a catalog or credit card offer by postal mail. While ROI (return on investment) may vary depending on the copy, the product, and the offer, both consumer-oriented and business-to-business marketers have been able to lower their customer acquisition costs by using e-mail to retain existing customers and acquire new ones.

Kim MacPherson's informative book goes a long way towards educating both novice and veteran marketers about the dos and don'ts of e-mail marketing. By following her road-tested advice, you will avoid the pitfalls and learn the best practices of a marketing discipline that is only beginning to formulate hard and fast rules. And who knows? The next e-mail marketing success story could be yours . . .

Rosalind Resnick
CEO
NetCreations, Inc.
November 2000

ACKNOWLEDGMENTS

While I can't say it took an entire village to write this book, it certainly felt like it at times. I feel incredibly blessed to have so many people to thank. First, to my friends and members of my family, thanks for putting up with my "not being there" for a few months. I was definitely scarce during the time that I will forever refer to as "The Period of *The Book,*" and I'm afraid I didn't do a very good job of keeping in touch. Thanks for putting up with that and *remaining* in my life!

I also want to thank my mother and father and grandmother—the three people in my life who always drilled into my head that I could do anything I set my mind to. (Growing up an only child *did* have its advantages.) I'm not sure if I would have had the drive and tenacity to write this book—let alone start my company, Inbox Interactive, a few short years ago—without that unyielding guidance and confidence building. Thanks, Mom and Dad and Gam.

Andy Bourland and Ann Handley of The ClickZ Network also have my utmost appreciation and gratitude for giving me the opportunity to launch ClickZ's Email Marketing column. That column was the catalyst for a lot of great things. I also want to acknowledge ClickZ's Managing Editor Claudia Bruemmer, who so kindly offered to review and help edit this book. Another great help to me was Internet industry expert and author Robbin Zeff, for sharing her keen insights into the daunting book writing process.

I'd also like to thank a few key vendors and resources who contributed. The guys at MetaResponse—Jerry Whiteway, Larry Roth, and Al DiBlasi—are really more "partners" than vendors and helped shape the Resources section at the back of this book. Thanks also to Geoff Ramsey of eMarketer, who so generously shared eMarketer's latest industry research.

As far as the major players—those who played a big part in getting this book off the ground and then getting it done—there are many. I'd like to thank Jean Iversen Cook, my editor, for seeing the potential of this book and guiding me through it. It is definitely a better book because of her savvy input. I also want to thank Jack Scovil, my agent, for working so well with me and knowing *immediately* that he wanted to work on this project. Thanks also, Jack, for never failing to believe it would be successful.

Cindy Videto Samson, my "case study researcher extraordinaire": she was one of my heroes! Cindy spent countless hours calling and e-mailing and collecting some fantastic real-life research for this book from some of the industry's top online marketers. (And given the schedules of these busy people, the fact that she was able to gather such great stuff was an incredible feat!) Cindy, I couldn't have gotten this part of the book accomplished without you.

And to Jen Cosgrove, a very talented copywriter: thanks so much for creating our hypothetical company, GolfCoachConnection.com. A terrific company idea, to be sure, and a story that adds a lot to the book. Thanks also to Holli Rathman and Eleni Giannakopoulos—two very talented designers who helped the design come to life.

I also want to thank Inbox Interactive's Online Campaign Coordinator (*and my right arm*), Lindsey Singer, for holding the fort down at work when things became so insane. Same goes for Lynne Rolls and Mardith Buyer, who came on after the majority of the book was done, but who were invaluable members of the team.

And last, but certainly not least, I want to thank my wonderful husband, Paul Broni, without whom I definitely could not have had the will, stamina, energy, and good nature to continue with and complete this book. He is my best friend, and one of the smartest people I know . . . with one of the sharpest (and most sarcastic!) wits around (laughter definitely helped keep me sane). He also is one of my favorite writers—and my true "editor-at-home." Paul, this may sound trite, but words truly can't express how much your love and support meant to me . . . especially during the last few months of writing and revisions and craziness at work. It goes without saying—I share credit for this book with you.

Millions of people use e-mail. In fact, for many, it has replaced the telephone and postal mail as the preferred method of communication. Therefore, the projections for e-mail's stellar growth as a communications device are not surprising. As other forms of media have grown in worldwide acceptance in the past, e-mail is now an integral part of that same mainstream and the number of new users grows rapidly every day.

On a marketing level, an e-mail "pushes" a message directly into an individual user's inbox, and doesn't have to wait for a radio spot or a magazine issue or a television commercial in order to make its debut. It can read like great literature, or like a comic book. It can be completely interactive; a recipient of an e-mail can quickly and easily respond with a simple "point and click." Most importantly, e-mail allows the sender to communicate on a one-to-one basis through the use of personalized language, salutations, and other strategic methods.

All of this, of course, presents a tremendous opportunity for advertisers that want to reach people within a medium in which they truly "live" and work. A compelling and lively message, a strong presentation and offer, and a clear call to action is truly all it takes to induce a solid number people to respond. Once that goal is accomplished, and a clear-cut strategy is laid out for future regular communications with both prospects and existing customers, there's no stopping the success that marketing through e-mail can create for a business. Using the strategies in this book will help ensure that success.

WHAT THIS BOOK COVERS

First, this book focuses on the ins and the outs of what is commonly referred to as the *dedicated, permission-based e-mail campaign.* In other words, while "e-mail marketing" can encompass a wide array of various outlets, including e-mailed newsletter sponsorships, discussion lists, newsgroups, e-zines, message boards, and the like, those areas are decidedly *not* what this book is about.

However, that's not to say that those are not all fine venues. They certainly are. And they certainly have their place for the right companies at the right times. However, the fact is that one of e-mail's greatest strengths lies in its ability to communicate with prospects and customers on a one-to-one level, rather than "en masse." A *dedicated* e-mail—the format of which you'd use to write to a business associate, or cousin Sue—has the ability to sound like it has been written *directly for the recipient*. It has only *one* advertiser, rather than several.

A dedicated e-mail promotion of this nature works because it has the "space" to tease and tickle and woo. A compelling subject line and message can grab attention and captivate an audience like no other online medium. And it has the potential for those glorious click-through rates you've no doubt heard about come from dedicated, permission-based messages built with the goal of winning over prospects and customers. Not to mention the fact that a well-planned campaign that utilizes e-mail in this manner is extremely measurable—meaning it's easy to set up tracking in order for you to see where your best results come from for a given campaign, as far as lists go. That means that follow-up campaigns can be improved and developed quickly and easily. You can't say *all* of that about other e-mail–related opportunities.

Think of this book as a guide to the planning, execution, creative development, and management of this highly esteemed marketing tool—the *dedicated, permission-based e-mail campaign*—along with a step-by-step guide to creating specific promotions therein. It contains a practical "action plan" for you to create and build an effective e-mail marketing campaign from start to finish.

HOW TO USE THIS BOOK

Each section of this book contains chapters that will chronologically present the necessary steps to developing an effective e-mail campaign. And each chapter will outline those steps in an easy-to-follow format and will showcase examples of each step with graphics.

Part One

The chapters in this section will cover the necessary background for those completely new to the e-mail medium. (If you are already a practitioner, or even a veteran, of e-mail marketing, you may want to skip to Part Two, where we start getting into the nitty-gritty of crafting an e-mail campaign.) Included in Part One is background material such as the e-mail industry terminology that is used among those of us who actively work in this medium. We'll also review a few industry statistics on the effectiveness of e-mail, as well as projections for its future.

Also in this section, we will go over the often-heated issue of e-mail address privacy, as well as the debate over "opt-in" versus "opt-out." We'll answer the following questions: What does permission-based e-mail really mean? And how do we use it for maximum effectiveness?

Part Two

Starting here, we begin to lay the groundwork necessary to build a dynamic, effective, and results-driven e-mail marketing campaign. We will learn how to develop a campaign acquisitions strategy and set promotional goals in order to help you create the best potential offer(s) for your products and services. Part Two also will help you create testing strategies to maximize your results, and increase your much-needed knowledge for future efforts. There also will be plenty of information about e-mail lists for prospecting purposes—from pricing to negotiating to research.

Part Three

In this section, we will explore the creative side of e-mail marketing, beginning with details of the best relationship marketing practices and how to create an ongoing dialogue with your audience. We'll then get into copywriting and design tips for optimal results—in other words, what does and doesn't work online? Which tried-and-true copywriting principles are transferable to e-mail? And which are *not*? What do you and/or your copywriters and designers need to know before crafting a dedicated e-mail campaign? We'll also take a look at the quickly evolving world of rich media e-mail promotions and how this dynamic and colorful tool may very well be the wave of the future.

Part Four

This section outlines top customer retention strategies, including those related to offer, creative, personalization, and viral marketing. We'll also explore how to segment and communicate with your database of current customers through e-mail.

Part Five

Here we will take a look at how to "close the deal" with some traditional principles, as well as with a few advanced methodologies. For instance, the destination page, or the page that your e-mail promotion leads people to, is a crucial part of the dedicated e-mail promotion because it is where the final call to action takes place. The first chapter in Part Five (Chapter 15) includes tips on creating a dynamic, persuasive landing page. The rest of Part Five reviews key necessary items such as best days of the week to e-mail and other timing issues. There also are a few words about "cookies" as they relate to e-mail.

The final chapter discusses how to most accurately and effectively measure an e-mail campaign's results as it relates to the success of the campaign. We'll also review how to take those results to the next level so you can develop a top-notch plan for subsequent campaigns. This chapter delves into the various means of tracking click-through and conversion numbers, and demonstrates examples of helpful reports that you can apply to your own business.

Case Studies

After all the "rules" are laid out and applied, we revisit the plan in a compendium of real-life e-mail campaign case studies. Both acquisitions campaigns and retention campaigns will be explored and detailed. The strategies, insights, and experiences presented here come from those "in the trenches"—those lucky e-mail marketers who were ready, willing, and able to share their stories. Although permission-based e-mail marketing is now a standard and integral part of the online promotional mix, this is still relatively new territory and we're all learning new things every day.

WHO THIS BOOK IS FOR

Whether your business is consumer-oriented or business-to-business, you should have a game plan to take an e-mail campaign from conception through completion. From A–Z, this book will cover everything from the basic to the most critical steps that every e-mail marketer should know. In other words, *Permission-Based E-mail Marketing* has everything you need if you are

- completely new to any form of direct marketing—both online and offline.
- a seasoned direct marketer, yet new to the online or e-mail world.
- an online marketing professional who wants to expand into or strengthen your e-mail marketing program.
- an experienced executive or manager who heads a group or organization that needs a step-by-step guide for your staff to use as a guide or resource.

This also is the book for you if your goals include any or all of the following:

- Acquiring new prospects and/or customers to communicate with by e-mail
- Creating new sales and/or leads through e-mail

- Building a house e-mail list
- Retaining existing customers
- Cross-selling, upselling, reselling to your current database of customers
- Establishing a one-to-one communication and relationship with your customers
- Tracking, measuring, and testing various offers
- Improving or optimizing your existing outbound e-mail marketing efforts

In a nutshell, if you have products and/or services and you want to apply the core principles of one of the most cost-effective, response-generating ways to market them, then you hold in your hands the means to that end. By the time you have read this book, you will be well on your way to becoming a regular e-mail marketing practitioner, if you're not already. And from now through the foreseeable future, that is a very good place to be.

GOLFCOACHCONNECTION.COM—USING E-MAIL TO INCREASE "LOVE" AND SALES IN THE GOLF MARKET

To show you what is involved in planning, creating, and deploying an e-mail campaign, we'll follow the experience of a hypothetical company throughout this book, step-by-step, as it develops its first e-mail campaign.

Introducing GolfCoachConnection.com, an Online Marketer of Golf Instruction Services and Equipment

There are millions of golfers in the United States, and they all have a love-hate relationship with the game. Thousands of players give up the game every year, citing "frustration with poor play." So GolfCoachConnection.com has a two-fold mission:

1. Help golfers play better so they love the game more and stay in the market.
2. Build relationships with those players so that they spend more of their (ample) golf budgets in the GCC Pro Shop.

GCC uses a countrywide network of certified golf-teaching professionals to provide instructional content and expertise for its Web site. Visitors can browse generic game improvement tips, or fill out player profiles to view personalized "Golf Tips from Your Coach" on the Web or by e-mail, for free. Visitors also can submit videotapes of their swings and pay to have them analyzed by GCC teaching professionals.

The GCC Pro Shop offers a large selection of name-brand golf equipment and accessories that visitors can purchase online. It does not have a retail counterpart.

The GCC marketing team is anxious to launch its first e-mail promotion because it has heard what a powerful direct marketing tool e-mail can be. And besides, the team members ask themselves, "How hard can it be?"

Stay tuned for more on GolfCoachConnection.com in later chapters.

PART ONE

E-mail as a Promotional Device

CHAPTER 1

The Power
of E-mail

For direct response marketing, there is no faster, cheaper, or more effective current venue to reach your top prospects than e-mail. Of course, this is not news to those of us who have been practicing this "art" for the last few years. E-mail allows you to target an audience that is primed and ready to hear your message. You can slice and dice that particular audience by demographics, geographics—even psychographics at times—and e-mail each group a customized message in order to lift response. You can write salesworthy copy that is music to your audience's ears, and can craft a design that will make recipients stand up and take notice. You also can create campaigns around offers that allow you to cross-sell, upsell, and resell your products and services over and over again. And, instead of generating sales and leads over the course of weeks or even months after a promotion begins—as in the case of a postal mailing—an e-mail campaign is considered complete within just a matter of days.

THE BENEFITS OF E-MAIL MARKETING

Marketing with e-mail offers numerous benefits. They include:

- *Direct communication with prospects and customers.* E-mail allows direct business-to-consumer(s) or business-to-businessperson(s) messaging and also allows for two-way exchanges, if so desired or needed. Communications can be in the form of a letter, an electronic "postcard" complete with photographs, a colorful and dramatically-designed HTML advertisement, or streaming video and sound encased in a rich media message. The message can be light or serious, solicitous or informative, friendly or businesslike. If targeted properly, an e-mail promotion can reach your core audience right where they live. For business building purposes, of course, the goal is to increase the number of people that reads the e-mail, thereby increasing the likelihood that your *end* goal—whether it's to make a sale or capture a new lead—will be reached.

- *Interactivity.* Unlike a print ad, television commercial, radio spot, direct mail, or any other offline media, a promotion via e-mail encourages and facilitates *direct* and *immediate* interactivity. The request made of the prospect/recipient is made crystal clear—"Click here to get this" or "Visit here to see this." In a standard e-mail promotion, if the prospect follows the call to action, he or she is taken to a page on the advertiser's Web site where he or she can place an order, enter a credit card number, fill out a registration form, and more. Any response where a new lead is captured or a sale is made is to the benefit of the advertiser. Due to the fast interactive nature of an e-mail promotion, a sales or lead generation campaign can be completed within a matter of days of its initial deployment ("send") date.

- *Lower costs.* E-mail can be extremely inexpensive on a cost-per-piece, or cost-per-e-mail address basis, regardless of whether you're in acquisitions or retention mode, especially when you compare it to other forms of marketing media. A *dedicated* prospecting promotion—wherein the e-mail promotion is solely dedicated to one and only one advertiser—normally runs anywhere between $.20 and $.45 apiece, including all list and sending costs. A retention promotion, of course, is far less because the list is yours (hence, zero costs there) and the cost to send can be very inexpensive, whether or not you're using a software solution or the services of an outside e-mail solutions provider.

- *Targeting qualified leads on a one-to-one basis.* For acquisitions e-mailings, there are opt-in lists available for rental that span a variety of categories, so to reach an audience interested in a particular category is not difficult. For retention campaigns, the targeting is even more enhanced, and allows marketers to segment and pinpoint their house lists by a variety of criteria—including interest, previous transaction (whether that transaction was based on a purchase or simply a click-through on a particular product or service), geographic and demographic data, and more. This type of fine-tuned segmentation can help marketers create customized communications to enhance loyalty, brand building, and sales.

THE E-MAIL CUSTOMER CONTACT CYCLE

Essentially, successful e-mail marketing is developed through a multistep process—let's just call it the *e-mail customer contact cycle*—shown here boiled down to three core phases as shown in Figure 1.1.

1. *Acquisitions Phase.* This is the hunting and gathering phase. It is the time when you identify your market, create the best offer for your business, and search for and promote to your top prospects by e-mailing to your best potential target audience. It is the time to create salesworthy copy and design that will persuade these prospects to "sign up" for whatever you have deemed your offer to be. Of course, you can acquire new e-mail addresses to add to your house list by a means other than e-mail (e.g., direct mail postcards, and radio and television ads to lead people to sign up); but for purposes of this book, we will focus on *acquisitions* by e-mail only.

2. *Testing Phase.* This can be part of the acquisitions phase, of course, but should be viewed and treated as an ongoing part of your overall e-mail marketing plan. By regularly testing and retesting what works and what doesn't as far as offers, e-mail lists, creative and other components, you will hone in on and roll out with your best efforts possible from promotion to promotion, campaign to campaign.

3. *Retention Phase.* After you've gathered your prospects, and even converted some of them into customers or clients, it's time to develop a way

FIGURE 1.1   Customer Contact Points through E-Mail Marketing

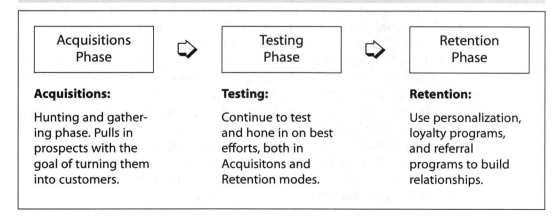

Acquisitions Phase	Testing Phase	Retention Phase
Acquisitions:	**Testing:**	**Retention:**
Hunting and gathering phase. Pulls in prospects with the goal of turning them into customers.	Continue to test and hone in on best efforts, both in Acquisitons and Retention modes.	Use personalization, loyalty programs, and referral programs to build relationships.

to keep them. This is the most profitable side of the business because now that those prospects/customers are a part of your house list, you don't bear the burden of often-weighty list acquisitions costs, such as outside e-mail lists. This also is the time when you build a true "relationship" with your customers by marketing to them individually, personalizing your messages, and only showcasing products that fit their wants and needs. By doing so, you can then ask for their endorsement of your products and services, thereby getting back to goal one—acquiring a new set of customers through the use of viral marketing and other loyalty and referral-type programs.

An e-mail campaign covers all three phases of the above cycle. And there are *methods* to develop and fine-tune the necessary critical steps within each phase. To acquire new customers, for instance, the lists you use should be dead-on as far as targeting goes, meaning your list research should be thorough and should be approached—at least in part—as a science. There are *hundreds* of prospecting lists out there; yet a number of them are completely ineffective or are suited for only the most select niche audiences. Finding the *right* lists is the key to e-mail marketing success. It's all a matter of doing your homework. (See Chapter 6.)

Additionally, you should be aware that in order to segment an audience properly for optimum results, you should be well versed in testing strategies. In other words, you should know the methodologies behind creating and executing tests that will identify winning promotions and campaigns you can utilize for months to come. I also should probably note here that e-mail is not for those only willing to take "baby steps"; to truly reap all of the potential rewards that marketing with e-mail has to offer, you must plan and test aggressively. For instance, I would not recommend e-mail to those who can send out only a one-time promotion to one very small, untested list of, for example, 2,000 or fewer names. Chances are, it's not going to get a good response. And if that happens, what's your gain? What can you learn? In a word: Nothing. By the same token, that doesn't mean that you have to mail to 100,000 e-mail addresses in order to achieve success. It simply means that you have to be a little aggressive (but smart); and at the same time, you need to be prepared to take a few hits. (See Chapter 7.) However, you need to make sure you have the backups in place to help leverage those hits. Those backups come from knowledge, and that knowledge comes from testing. We'll explore more details on *this* note later in the book.

Creativity certainly can go a long way in executing a promotional e-mail. However, compelling copy isn't just about laying out your features and benefits in one neat and tidy little package. It's about the art of selling. And rhythm. And tone. It's about giving your audience of readers all it needs to make that final buying decision.

Perhaps best of all is that e-mail allows you to create an ongoing rapport and dialogue with your prospects and customers; hence, it can help build those all-important customer relationships. I'm sure you've heard this before, but it bears repeating: The level of the relationship that you have with your customers (high or low) will, to a large extent, determine your business's success in future years; that is virtually guaranteed. Bottom line: Simply keep in mind that there are "rules" to this exciting medium. The path to great e-mail campaigns is not a difficult one to follow. It simply takes a little sure-footedness that comes from having a solid plan of action, following a few well-established rules, and reaping some guidance from those in-the-know.

CHAPTER 2

E-mail Terms You Should Know

Like any other widely reaching industry that involves a number of practitioners and players, there is a language to the Internet and all things tied to it, including e-mail. There are industry-specific words and phrases to describe technical terms, measurement tools, design aspects, and more.

To avoid getting too bogged down in *all* online-related terminology, for purposes of this chapter (and this book), we will focus only on the most common and relevant words within the e-mail marketing industry. Some, you'll find, have been used in other areas of marketing, such as direct mail and telemarketing, but are repeated here for those who may not know them *or* their place within the e-mail marketing world. As time goes on and you go through the process of launching and managing regular e-mail promotions, using the following terms no doubt will become second nature.

Audience. The group of people that an e-mail promotion or campaign targets. For example, an e-mail marketer promoting a jewelry site might select and target a list of people who have expressed an interest in buying diamonds online. That list would contain the "audience."

Clickable text. The links within an e-mail message that become "hyperlinks," meaning that they are executed when clicked on and take people directly to a Web site or page. Many text only e-mail programs will convert plain text to clickable text when they see "http://" in the message body.

Click-through rate. See CTR.

Compiled list. This is a list of e-mail addresses that has been gathered by a means other than response to a previous e-mail message. For example, these e-mail addresses can be part of a large database, and can typically be segmented by demographic information. A compiled list could consist of a list of people who have Social Security numbers beginning with the numbers 2423. A compiled e-mail list may not be one to promote to because the e-mail addresses within it are collected by methods such as customer warranty cards, purchase transactions, surveys, etc.—hence, the people have not "opted in" to receive promotions by e-mail. They have simply submitted their e-mail addresses to register for something else altogether.

Conversion. The number or percentage of recipients that complete a promotion's ultimate goal. Conversions could include the number of leads garnered from a lead generation campaign, or the number of actual sales derived from a promotional sales campaign. This is the final number and generally the most important measurement of a campaign's success. A conversion percentage or rate can refer to the percentage of people that clicked on the promotion or the percentage of all of the people that received the initial promotion.

Cookie. A small file stored or embedded within an e-mail promotion's HTML. It can track recipients' "open" rates (i.e., how many people actually opened the e-mail), as well as whether or not recipients forwarded the message. Cookies are very useful when it comes to reporting and measuring a campaign's overall success.

CPM (Cost Per Thousand). In e-mail marketing terms, it is one method for pricing e-mail lists. For example, a "$200 CPM" price for a list means that it costs $200 for every thousand e-mail addresses purchased (or $.20 per single address).

Cross-selling. When a company develops offers and promotions for its house list, and those offers are for other products that company offers, it is called cross-selling.

CTR (Click-Through Rate). The number of times that a standard e-mail's "call to action" link has been clicked. A promotion's goal is to garner a high CTR in order to drive as many people as possible to the promoting site. For example, if out of 10,000 e-mail promotions sent, 500 people clicked through, the CTR would be 5 percent. Obviously, the higher the CTR, the higher the chances of increasing your number of *converted* prospects. This is a key success measure of an e-mail campaign.

Database marketing. The discipline of enhancing a house e-mail list and promoting it, using a variety of database-related tools. For example, an e-mail marketer can use database marketing techniques to communicate with selected segments within its house list of customer e-mail addresses, such as those with certain incomes and prior purchase histories. The goal is to find that combination of offers, messages, and other components to optimize those selected areas of the database and achieve maximum response rates.

Deployment. The "sending" of an e-mail message.

Direct response marketing. Also known as direct marketing, a discipline designed for the advertiser to drive immediate sales, leads, or some other end goals. (Besides e-mail, a direct response ad can use television, radio, print, telemarketing, and postal mail.)

Domain name. A registered Web site name or address.

Download. Copying information or files from a server or other source to a computer or network.

Dynamic content marketing. Sending targeted messages to small customer segments from a house file, based on a set of database criteria, or rules. For example, you may send out a message where people east of the Mississippi receive a promotion for products offered with free shipping and, due to higher costs, people west of the Mississippi receive a promotion requiring payment for shipping. Dynamic content can segment a house file into hundreds of thousands of segments, all dynamically generated during the delivery of the e-mail campaign.

GIF (Graphical Interchange Format). An electronic image file format. Many of the graphics that you see on the Web and in e-mail promotions are GIF files.

Hard versus soft bounces. Undeliverable e-mail addresses within a campaign. A *hard bounce* represents an specifically addressed e-mail that, for whatever reason, either never left the transmitting server or never made it to the destined server. A *soft bounce* represents an e-mail that made it to the destined server but couldn't find the designated e-mail address that resides there.

HTML (HyperText Markup Language). A standard presentation tool for many e-mail marketers that is graphically rich with color and images. Like viewing a Web page within an e-mail program, graphics and other images are most often "served" from the advertiser's site. HTML often pulls a higher response than plain text messages; however, it generally requires a longer download time, particularly for those recipients who have 56K or less modem access.

HTTP. HyperText Transfer Protocol, the language of the Internet.

Hyperlink. Clickable text that allows the viewer to go directly to a Web page or site.

JPEG (Joint Photographic Experts Group). A compressed graphic image format. Many of the photographs and other graphical images that you see online are JPEG files.

Keycode. A unique code assigned to a promotion or a specific link within a promotion in order for a response to be tracked by the advertiser.

Landing (or "Bounce" or "Jump" or "Splash") page. The page on a Web site that is linked to an e-mail promotion. For example, when an e-mail promotion is sent and recipients begin to click through on the links embedded therein, their browsers should open to the landing page of the advertiser's site.

Lead. A prospect that has not yet converted to a paid customer or client.

Lifetime value (LTV). The dollar figure that a company associates with a customer based on his or her past purchases, projected future purchases, and loyalty.

Link. See Hyperlink.

Offer. The incentive or enhancement device used to promote the advertiser's products or services. For example, a business-to-business content site may offer a free newsletter in order to drive its target audience to the site.

Opt-in. When subscribers to a list have chosen to receive promotional messages from designated sites and/or within selected categories. In other words, they've given their permission on the front end, before ever having received a solicitation. This permission enables e-mail marketers to promote to people who are actively, rather than passively, interested and also allows them to target leads based on selected categories of interest.

Opt-out. Recipients are sent a promotion that contains a statement giving them the option to *not* receive such e-mails in the future. In other words, opt-out promotions require a response from recipients if they do not wish to receive future messages.

Paid customer *or* paid campaign. When a customer pays for an offer within an e-mail.

Personalization. An e-mail promotion that uses the recipient's name or address or other unique data in order to increase click-through and conversion rates. The use of personalization within an e-mail can dramatically enhance response.

Pull. This term refers to marketing media that draws a target audience in, such as a Web site or television.

Push. This term refers to marketing media, such as e-mail, that sends messages to the target audience.

Relationship marketing. Using a regular series of personalized and relevant communications to meet the direct marketing goal of building a relationship with customers over a period of time.

ROI (return on investment). Dividing the profit from a campaign by the costs of mounting that campaign. Used as a measurement of a campaign's success.

Rollout. A combination of a campaign's lists, messages, and offers that are sent at the same time and under the same conditions.

Segmentation. Separating your house mailing list prior to e-mailing in order for recipients to get different messages and offers based on what they will most likely respond to. A file can be segmented based on demographics, buying patterns, areas of interest, and more (database marketing) with the different messages based on individual segments (dynamic content marketing).

Spam. Slang term for unsolicited e-mail.

Targeting. Identifying an audience or group that contains likely prospects for a particular set of products and/or services, and then developing the offer and messages for that audience.

Up-selling. When a company develops promotions to its existing customer base designed to sell products that are at a higher price than those customers have paid up until that point. Often new customers are brought into a house with a low-dollar offer, and the next step is to sell them a high-dollar offer.

URL (Universal Resource Locator). A Web site's address or location on the Internet—e.g., what you type into your browser to pull up a desired site destination. For instance, to call up the E-mail Marketing 101 site, you'd enter *http://www.e-mailmarketing101.com* in your browser window.

Viral marketing. Pursuing the goal for recipients to forward the message on to other like-minded individuals. Each successive "pass-along" of the e-mail creates an exponential growth in the number of recipients who receive it because each recipient forwards to more than one person. A viral marketing campaign promotion generally will reward a customer for forwarding with an incentive of a prize or discount.

CHAPTER 3

Opt-In versus Opt-Out— Permission and Privacy

Picture the following scenario to see the industry's quandary on what options to offer customers. At your favorite online music store, you have chosen to opt-in, that is, you signed up to receive special e-mailed coupons and discounts, as they became available. You've already taken advantage of a few of them and have saved quite a bit of money. One day, you receive an e-mail from a competitor of your music store. Although you've never shopped there, nor have you ever registered to receive their promotions, this e-mail offers some significant savings of its own. It also gives you the option at the end to opt-out, that is, to have your e-mail address removed from any further promotions from that store.

Between the two tactics—opt-in or opt-out, which would you prefer? That's the burning question that has been on many a marketer's mind almost since the very first e-mail promotions began. At what level of the customer development cycle should *permission* take place?

One of the theories behind permission marketing is that, presumably, a customer that has given permission to receive promotions is a better, more loyal, and more profitable customer overall. Most marketers will not argue that fact.

However, both opt-in and opt-out policies ask for permission at some stage of the game. To truly understand the philosophy behind each, and to understand why opt-in is the better way to go, let's start at the beginning.

DEFINING OPT-IN AND OPT-OUT

As the previous brief example demonstrated, if a prospect has been added to a company database using opt-in procedures, it essentially means that she has given permission to receive company promotions from the very beginning. In other words, the prospect has looked at a site and then asked to be solicited prior to ever having received one promotion from the advertising company. Any promotions she receives are welcome because they are positioned by the advertiser as containing something that the prospect desires—either in the form of receiving special savings notifications, relevant content within the prospect's area of interest, free registration or trial to something she wants or needs, or some other value-added proposition.

A prospect that is solicited using opt-out procedures, on the other hand, may have never even heard of the promoting company—or the owner of the list where his e-mail address resides—when he receives the first promotion. And when he does, although he is given the option to never receive another such e-mail again, the burden is on him to react if he wants to be removed from the list. He must answer the directive that says, "If you do not wish to receive these messages in the future, please click here." A good opt-in e-mail promotion also gives this or a similar directive, as we'll see later; however the chances of the prospect "unsubscribing" at this point are much less because he has opted-in from the beginning.

THE FOUR-LETTER WORD THAT IS SPAM

It is easy to see why many promotions using opt-out procedures are declared "spam," which is considered the bane of the e-mail marketing industry. *Spam* is the often-used negative slang term that refers to unsolicited e-mail. People who receive spam do not like it for obvious reasons, the main reason being that it typically offers something that is of little or no interest to the recipient. Internet Service Providers (ISPs) also oppose it due to the fact that all e-mail is either sent from an ISP or received by an ISP, and many have been clogged—or even shut down—by spam e-mail. As seen in Figure 3.1, some spams are not only a bother, they're so badly presented that the reader would find the company suspect even if he were interested in the message.

Spam e-mail is considered by many to be illegitimate e-mail and legislation proposals have gone back and forth on whether or not this type of e-mailing should be declared illegal and also what penalties should be assigned for violating the laws associated with it. Unfortunately, the offenders—the "spammers"—only give

FIGURE 3.1 A Typical Spam E-mail

Note the typo, the poor formatting, and the hype-filled message.

```
X-Mailer: Microsoft Outlook 8.5, Build 4.71.2173.5
X-See-Also: 08534CCD0
Sensitivity: Public
X-Other-References: 0AF302B5B
Date: Mon, 28 Feb 15:10:53
To: <recipient@123mail.com>
Subject: E-mail Advertising Special--Ends Friday
Importance: Low


PUT E-MAIL MARKETING TO WORK FOR YOU
Call NOW and receive 50,000
FREE e-mails with your order!
Special Ends Friday March 3
Imagine having a product or idea and selling it
for only $10.
Now imagine sending an ad for your product or idea
to 25 million people!
If you only get 1/10 of 1% response
you have just made $250,000!!
You hear about people getting rich off
the Internet every day on TV,
now is the perfect time for you
to jump in on all the action.
FACT
With the introduction of the Internet, one primary
KEY to conducting your business successfully is
creating massive exposure in a cost effective
manner.
FACT
The experts agree that e-mail marketing is one of
the most cost effective forms of promotion in
existence today.
Electronic mail has overtaken the telephone as the
primary means of business communication.(American
Management Association)
Of online users, 41 percent check their e-mail daily.
```

"A gold mine for those who can take advantage of
bulk e-mail programs"—The New York Times
"E-mail is an incredible lead generation tool"
—Crain's Magazine
"Blows away traditional Mailing"—Advertising Age
"It's truly arrived. E-mail is the killer app so
far in the online world"-Kate Delhagen, Forrester
Research Analyst
Why not let a professional company handle your
direct e-mail marketing efforts for you?
*We will assist you in developing your entire
campaign!
*We can even create your ad or annoucement [sic] for
you!
*No responses? We resend at no cost!
For More Information CALL NOW

For removal see below.
SPECIAL RATES
SPECIAL ENDS Friday March 3
Targeted Rates Upon Request.
BONUS!!!
Call In and receive 50,000 Extra E-mails at No
Cost!
Call NOW

e-mail marketing a bad name. Spammers gather their e-mail addresses from a variety of sources, including bulk e-mail lists, e-mailed discussion groups, online bulletin boards, and Web site contact information pages. The promotions are typically sent in large quantities, with zero personalization. More times than not, the spammers do not have any idea what their audience is interested in, or even if they are an interested audience for the spammers' offers. For these mailers, it's not about targeting at all; they're simply playing the numbers game. Spammers figure the more people they reach, the better their chances that *someone* will respond.

Because even the most useful and targeted *opt-out* e-mail promotion by a legitimate marketer can be perceived as spam, the polices set forth in this book follow *only* opt-in, or permission-based procedures.

GETTING NEW CUSTOMERS WITH OPT-IN LISTS

In order to acquire *new customers*—that is, to get people who have never used, bought, or "tried out" your products or services in the past, you can use opt-in e-mail lists such as the one shown in Figure 3.2, particularly if your goal is to continue marketing through the e-mail channel.

Opt-in list providers own and/or manage a variety of lists ranging across a wide variety of categories. These lists contain e-mail addresses of people who have registered to receive promotions within their selected areas of interest. Once a person has registered, many list providers will send an e-mail to the registered address, asking that person to confirm that he or she did, indeed, sign up. This is typically called *double opt-in* and has been implemented by a number of list providers as extra insurance that any new registrations have, indeed, come from the people who own those e-mail addresses. Once that has been confirmed, those addresses are then "dropped in" the proper categories and sold to advertisers on a one-time-use basis.

FIGURE 3.2 Acquiring Customers on a Site

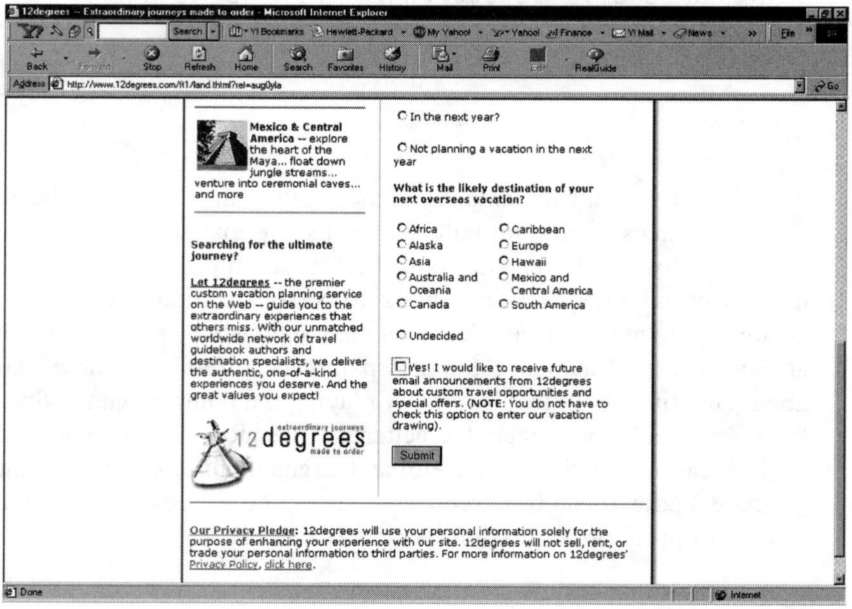

Once an advertiser selects the lists that target its audience, and the e-mail promotion has been created and sent, most opt-in list providers, such as Postmaster Direct and YesMail, include a message somewhere within the e-mail that reiterates *why* the prospect/recipient is getting that particular promotion. It *reminds* the prospect that he "opted in" to receive these types of notifications, promotions, special offers, etc., within his area of interest. The combination of the confirmation e-mail after registration *and* the reminder message at the top of the promotion itself serves to ensure that there is no doubt that the recipient/prospect opted in and there can be no legitimate accusations of spam.

COLLECTING E-MAIL ADDRESSES IN AN OPT-IN MANNER

Once prospects receive the promotion and *find* your site, the goal, of course, is to then get them to do one of these three things:

1. Register as part of a lead-generation program.
2. Make a purchase.
3. Fulfill some other call to action so you can collect their e-mail addresses and other prospect information for future marketing purposes.

We'll delve into the necessary steps to acquire new leads and customers in Part Two; but in order to do so, you will need to collect the necessary information for you to create your own house file of e-mail addresses. Because of the "danger" in gathering personal information, be sure that your collection policies and procedures are above board and beyond reproach. By doing so, your reputation as a permission-based e-mail marketer who is concerned with your customers' and prospects' privacy will be assured.

Privacy Policy

If you are collecting any type of personal, confidential, financial, or transactional data from your prospects and customers, be sure to inform them of what you plan to do with that information. Many companies post a *privacy policy* on their sites such as the one shown in Figure 3.3. In fact, many post links to it directly within their e-mail promotions.

A privacy policy is simply a disclosure of your information collection practices. It tells prospects and visitors exactly what you are going to do with their information, should they decide to register/sign up/purchase. If you plan on renting your e-mail addresses to outside parties, post that fact on your site. If you plan to send prospects promotions of your company's products and services, make that

FIGURE 3.3   Registration Page and Privacy Policy on a Site

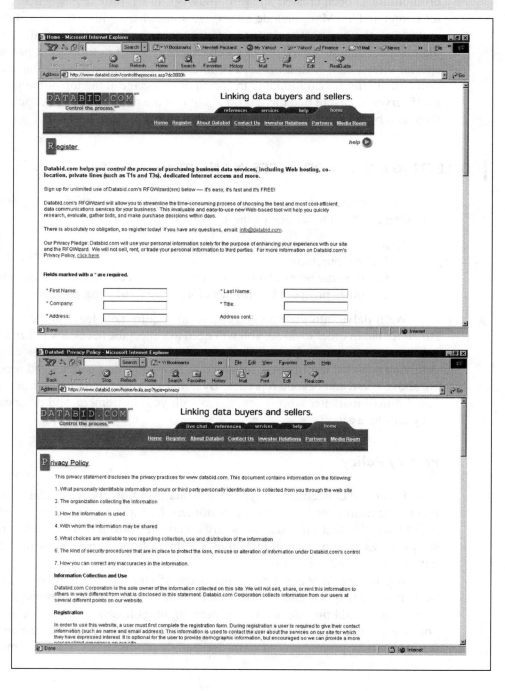

clear. One company that did not do that effectively from the beginning is Amazon. com. There are a number of people who received unsolicited promotions from Amazon, and they were never informed that this would occur: a good example of what *not* to do.

A privacy policy should answer all of the following:

- What type of information are you collecting (e.g., e-mail addresses, postal addresses, cookie/server information, etc.)?
- If there is more than one method of collection, what other methods are employed?
- How will you use that information? Be as specific as possible.
- Who will information be shared with?
- What if a prospect does not wish her information to be included on a database?
- Where do you house or store the information? Is it secure?
- What if a prospect does not want to receive any future communications from you?
- What is your policy if someone wishes to unsubscribe?

Post your company's main contact point—including address, phone, and e-mail—for inquiries related to privacy and collection practices. It is also a good idea to affiliate your company with a privacy seal organization, such as *TrustE*. It is organizations such as *TrustE* that enhance a prospect's or customer's comfort level with your company. Just be sure that you adhere to the standards you've set forth in your privacy policy.

Privacy seal organizations that protect consumers include:

- TrustE <www.truste.org>
- PrivacySecure <www.privacysecure.com>
- BBBOnline Privacy <www.bbbonline.org>
- Privacy Rights Clearinghouse <www.privacyrights.org>

YOUR PROSPECTS HAVE SIGNED ON—NOW WHAT?

Once your hunting and gathering of information is complete, and your opt-in band of prospects is a part of your house file, it is now time to promote to them. The goal here, of course, is to convert them into buyers (if they are leads/ prospects) or to get them to buy more of your products and services (if they have already made a purchase).

Just be sure that all of your permission and privacy-sensitive precautions and policies were not in vain. Maintain those standards in *every* communication you have with these people. Here are a few "best practices" to keep in mind.

Make It Easy for Prospects to Unsubscribe

When you send prospects a communication by e-mail—a newsletter, a special offer, a set of coupons, etc.—be sure to always include an "unsubscribe" tagline somewhere in the body of the e-mail, every single time you send to them. This gives them the opportunity to say, "Thanks, but I really don't want to receive these e-mails anymore. Please stop sending them." Invariably, there always will be a certain number that will want out. If you do not include unsubscribe language of some sort, you will make it difficult for these people and, hence, you risk making them angry. The goal is to keep everyone happy and feeling safe.

Some list vendors are more comfortable with what is commonly known as double opt-in, or confirmed opt-in, where new members who sign up to receive promotions receive an e-mail from the list vendor and must send back an e-mail in reply, essentially stating again that, yes, they have signed up. Single opt-in, or nonconfirmed opt-in, vendors also send a confirmation e-mail, but require a reply from the new members if and only if they wish to *unsubscribe.* As of the writing of this book, there is no hard data on response and profitability about which strategy works best.

Link to Your Privacy Policy

Remember that privacy policy that you so carefully crafted for your site? At the bottom of each and every e-mail, post a link for recipients to view it. This also serves to get them back to your site.

Be Upfront—Always

If you've made a change to your information collection procedures or you've changed privacy seal organizations, be sure to notify the people on your list. If they don't like it, they'll simply unsubscribe. It is not the disclosure, but rather the lack thereof, that can get you into trouble.

PART TWO

Reeling 'Em In (Acquiring New Customers That Stay)

CHAPTER 4

Creating
Your Budget

OBJECTIVES

- Review of the basic essentials.

- Develop an acquisitions/prospecting plan.

- Budget appropriately.

- Determine the essential steps to fulfill the goals and budget of your plan.

Every thorough and effective plan starts with a look at the proverbial "big picture." In other words, what exactly do you hope to accomplish by marketing with e-mail? I'm assuming, of course, you've chosen e-mail as a venue to add to—and not replace—your already existing marketing mix. And, perhaps, you've already allocated a certain percentage of your budget to this dynamic medium you've heard such great things about. Now it's time to take a good, hard look at how you're going to use it.

BACK TO BASICS

Before we begin, however, let's make sure we're all on the same page and redefine a some terms that are *core* to the principles outlined in this chapter.

- *Acquisitions.* The phase in your marketing efforts in which you are actively seeking and acquiring new customers. Prospecting is another term used for this stage of the game.
- *Conversion.* As you read in Part One, this term can have multiple definitions; but for purposes of this chapter (and for most of this book), conversion refers to the number of new prospects (that you may have just acquired in the acquisitions phase) that turn into customers or buyers.

Who are your prospects? Your leads? Your customers? They all make up your target audience and how you refer to them depends on whether you're in acquisitions or retention mode.

Prospects

These are the people that could one day become part of your house file. They have never bought any of your products, nor have they responded to any of your lead generation offers. They are prospects in the purest sense. And in some way, shape, or form they *resemble* your market, such as:

- They may reside in the same physical locations as your target market.
- They may meet the age/income/occupation criteria of your target market.
- They may have similar likes, dislikes, wants, desires, spending patterns, etc., as your target market.
- They may have responded to similar offers or bought products and services such as those that you offer, such as in catalog and publication subscriptions in similar categories.

Leads

These people have responded to one or more of your lead generation offers, but are not yet buyers. The hope is that their interest in your offer makes them a better target than a pure prospect and, hence, a likely future buyer. We'll review various ways to bring in new leads in the next chapter; but for now, suffice it to say that leads are created through the use of a variety of different offers, including free trials, sweepstakes, free registration offers, etc.

Existing Customers

This is, of course, the group of people who are both current and active on your file and have, for lack of a better term, "paid up." They've bought one or more of your products or services and, for the most part, continue to do so. However, no matter what the size of your *overall* group of existing customers, you can count on the fact that not all of them will be top responders. Nonetheless, if analyzed as a whole, your existing customer base should bring you the bulk of your profits. They are typically divided into the following three tiers:

1. *Tier 1.* This is the segment that—based on the fact that their needs mesh well with your offers, products, and services—contains your strongest responders (the "cream-of-the-crop").
2. *Tier 2.* This group responds to your marketing efforts, but less frequently than customers in Tier 1.
3. *Tier 3.* This group can be likened to a bunch of tire-kickers. They're customers, yes—but they stand a good chance of moving into the "Previous Customers/Clients" category soon due to their poor response to most marketing efforts.

Tiers 2 and 3 most likely make up the majority of your customer house file while, Tier 1 makes up the smallest category. You've probably heard this ratio expressed as the 80/20 Rule, or Pareto's Principle, which says that 20 percent of your audience will bring you 80 percent of your business. With the right tools, marketing with e-mail can be a highly effective means to reach that 20 percent. We'll explore more details on that note later in the book. For now, we have to think about how to get from *here* . . . to *there.*

IDENTIFYING YOUR CAMPAIGN'S GOALS

Successful e-mail marketing boils down to a combination of old and new selling techniques. Traditional direct marketing principles make up the "old," while the high-speed immediate access and interactivity of the Internet has created a few "new" rules. Throughout this and subsequent chapters, we'll weave both methods into the mix and explain how these principles apply to the steps we take on the way to developing our campaign.

Start by analyzing your long-term goals. Answer the following:

- Are you marketing to businesspeople or consumers (B2B or B2C)?
- In one year (or two years, or three . . .), how many new *paying* customers do you want to add? How many of those will be through the use of e-mail marketing?
- Through your traditional marketing outlets, how many prospects or leads do you typically need to promote in order to convert a prospect to a paying customer?
- How much revenue—or what average order size—do you want to generate per new paying customer?

- How much revenue do you want each new customer to bring in over the next three years? Five years? Ten years?

Your answers to the above questions will give you the preliminary figures that you need in order to start calculating what numbers you need to produce to meet your e-mail plan goals.

For instance, suppose you're marketing educational software for children (B2C). In a year's time, your goal is to add 1,000 new customers. If your average order is $45 per customer, that's a grand projected total of $45,000 in *new sales* revenue over the course of the next year. But that's just the tip of the iceberg. You've also determined through a lifetime value analysis (LTV) of your current customer base (see Part Four on retention for more information on how to calculate LTV) that those 1,000 new customers will likely purchase, in aggregate, approximately five times that amount ($225,000) over the next three years and eight times that amount ($360,000) over the next five years because of your customer development program, which includes cross-selling and up-selling efforts. Therefore, those 1,000 people are actually more "valuable" than they appear, at first glance. Fine. Now let's take this projection a step further.

The industry standard for marketing venues says that you need to promote to 50 leads to make a sale, so a normal conversion rate is 2 percent. (Here a "lead" is someone who has responded to your offer for a one-month trial download of one of your software products. We'll get into more details on offers in the next chapter.) Assume that your lead-to-sale conversion rate is approximately the same, or to err on the conservative side, assume it will be less.

Therefore, to meet your goal of 1,000 new customers in the next year you need to generate 50,000 new leads during that time:

$$1,000 \div 2\% = 50,000$$

How do you bring in 50,000 new leads with e-mail? Again, look at the bigger numbers and work backwards. Answer the following:

- What is the current industry average click-through rate (CTR) for consumer e-mail offers? (This will, most likely, be a range—e.g., 5 to 15 percent—so for the sake of generating reachable numbers use the middle portion of the range.) And, of course, if yours is a B2B offer and you have current statistics, use those numbers instead.
- What percentage of people who click through are expected to complete your call to action? In other words, how many will complete your form/register/buy . . . or whatever your objective is.

So getting back to the children's software example, you've determined that you are going to use a 10 percent click-through rate (CTR) to estimate the CTR for your e-mail efforts over the next year. However, not every single one of the 10 percent that clicks through will sign up for the free trial—a percentage of them will not complete that final call to action. A good portion will complete the call to action for the trial, however, if it is a lead generation that has been properly executed. Suppose your CTR is 60 percent. Because you need to generate 50,000 leads, that means that 83,000 have to click through, which means that 830,000 people need to be e-mailed initially over your designated period of time.

50,000 leads ÷ 60% (percentage of those who sign up after clicking) =
83,000 (the total number of click-throughs needed).

83,000 ÷ 10% (initial click-through rate) =
830,000 (the total number of people who were e-mailed).

Remember, this is over the course of a year. So to look at it from the very beginning, your prospecting (acquisitions) goal is to reach more than 800,000 most likely responders in enough time for them to buy in the next year. Your customer development (retention) goal is to capture and promote to 1,000 buyers who are likely to buy other similar or higher-priced products and services over a length of time determined when you set your goal.

BUDGET BUILDING FOR E-MAIL MARKETING NEWBIES

Set a time goal for your project. Determine what you need to do to meet those goals within that period of time. Set forth! (Sounds easy, doesn't it?)

In the above example, you have one year. However, that means you have to have 1,000 new customers by that year's *end.* And, going back to the beginning, if 2 percent of your new leads convert, you have to create 90 new customers per month through the *eleventh month.*

1,000 customers ÷ 11 months = 90.9 (monthly paid customers goal)

Rounding things off, and based on conversion numbers above, this means that each month you must convert more than 4,500 leads into paid customers:

90 new customers per month ÷ 2% conversion = 4,500 leads

Based on the numbers and projections above, in order to generate 4,500 leads per month, we need to promote to 75,000 prospects every month.

Because opt-in acquisitions lists can run anywhere from $200 to $400+ *per thousand e-mail addresses,* use an average $300 per thousand to calculate your monthly list costs.

75,000 prospects x $.30 ($300 per thousand) = $22,500 list costs per month

Therefore, your monthly acquisition e-mailings should comprise at least 75,000 prospects (found in targeted opt-in lists) and will cost approximately $22,500. But what about other acquisitions costs? And then what about retention, or existing customer promotions, costs? How do we factor those in to create our overall budget for the year?

On the acquisitions side, other costs may include:

- Creative (copywriting and design) for the promotions
- Consultants to strategize on offer and creative development
- Software or vendors to track and analyze incoming orders and data
- Software or vendors to collect and house incoming orders and data

Many of these additional costs are for services that can be executed by internal staff, if available. Nonetheless, the difference in prices and fees for the services listed runs the gamut. Depending on your projected numbers for deployment—both for acquisitions and retention—you may be able to get by with internal creative personnel for the copywriting and design, and an inexpensive software solution. Our children's software example would fit that category. However, once you start getting into the really big numbers for e-mailing, you're going to find that you'll need the help of outside resources, particularly for tracking, analysis, and processing/database marketing. For those types of activities, figure on adding another $.05 to $.20 for every e-mail address managed in-house. (See Chapter 13 on retention, and the Resources section at the back of the book.)

SHORT-TERM BUDGETING

To plan a short-term e-mail acquisitions plan (less than a year), you can use the same steps outlined in preceding paragraphs but use figures for six months, three months, or even a single campaign. Additionally, if your business sells services rather than products (perhaps you are selling advertising on your site or in your e-mailed newsletters), you still can use these strategies to build subscribers. After all, the more subscribers you have, the more your ad revenue increases, no matter what you're selling.

BUDGETING FOR A PAID CAMPAIGN

For e-mail acquisitions campaigns where the call to action consists of an actual paid sale (as in the case of many online retailers' prospecting campaigns), you may want to create a plan based on your projected breakeven point. This can be a simpler method and can be applied and adjusted from campaign to campaign.

Your breakeven point, as the name suggests, is when your costs and your revenue match. It's one of the best ways to determine what your campaign sales need to be in order not to lose money. For instance, if you sell greeting cards on-line, how do you promote to 10,000 new prospects through opt-in acquisitions lists? First, you determine your costs—including the costs discussed, as well as the total costs to deliver your product (the greeting cards themselves). If they total $7,500, your revenue would need to be $7,500 to hit your breakeven, which means that, if the customer pays $2.00 a card, you'd need to sell 3,750 greeting cards. As you can see from the calculation, you'd need a 37.5 percent final converted response rate:

$$3,750 \text{ orders} \div 10,000 \text{ e-mails} = 37.5\%$$

This, of course, would be a tough goal to achieve. Paid offers can pull double digit response rates—especially with lower dollar offers such as this—but close to 40 percent is not likely. A more likely conversion for this type of offer would be 10 to 20 percent. And the prohibitive costs demonstrate one reason why acquisitions campaigns via e-mail do better with lead generation offers rather than paid offers.

However, every business is different. For those of you lucky enough to offer products with extremely low product and fulfillment costs per order and high revenue per order (as in the case of certain software and high-end publications), "fishing for paid sales" through e-mail may very well pay off.

Action Item: Create Your Budget

Based on the above scenario, you create a budget for your venture as shown in Figure 4.1.

Essential steps to creating a strategy. You started your acquisitions plan and budget by expressing your *overall* goals and objectives. Now it is time to whittle those goals down to the following action items:

- Define your target audience.
- Find sources of *prospects* within that target audience.
- Develop a strong offer to *appeal* to those prospects.
- Create a message to *present* that offer in the best light possible.
- Send!
- Track and read your results.
- Bring in/convert new customers.

FIGURE 4.1 Plan an Ideal Scenario

Month	Number of e-mails sent	Cost	CTR (%)	Click-throughs	Sign-up %	Sign-ups	Conversion to paid percentage	Number of new paying customers	Average order	Total revenue
1	75,000	$300	10	7,500	60	4,500	2	90	$45	$4,050
2	75,000	300	10	7,500	60	4,500	2	90	45	4,050
3	75,000	300	10	7,500	60	4,500	2	90	45	4,050
4	75,000	300	10	7,500	60	4,500	2	90	45	4,050
5	75,000	300	10	7,500	60	4,500	2	90	45	4,050
6	75,000	300	10	7,500	60	4,500	2	90	45	4,050
7	75,000	300	10	7,500	60	4,500	2	90	45	4,050
8	75,000	300	10	7,500	60	4,500	2	90	45	4,050
9	75,000	300	10	7,500	60	4,500	2	90	45	4,050
10	75,000	300	10	7,500	60	4,500	2	90	45	4,050
11	75,000	300	10	7,500	60	4,500	2	90	45	4,050
12	75,000	300	10	7,500	60	4,500	2	90	45	4,050
Total	$900,000			90,000		54,000		1,080		$48,600

- Test a variety of offers, messages, and other variables for both acquisitions and retention efforts.
- Develop campaign strategies to optimize your acquisitions and retention efforts.
- Repeat.

GolfCoachConnection.com Plans Its First Acquisitions Campaign

As you'll recall, we met GolfCoachConnection.com earlier when it was introduced as our hypothetical e-mail marketing "newbie" in the throes of its very first e-mail marketing campaign. Here is how its story begins.

After talking with colleagues and vendors, the GolfCoachConnection.com team has put together some preliminary estimates for its first e-mail promotion. Because this is the team's first campaign, and because it has heard that e-mail is more cost-effective than direct mail, the team is aiming to generate at least as many leads as a traditional mailing, but at less cost per lead.

Its first acquisitions campaign will consist of 90,000 e-mail addresses (more on specific lists used in a future chapter), with a projected click-through rate of 10 percent and a sign-up rate of 60 percent of click-throughs. GolfCoachConnection.com also will outsource the creative for the promotion. Therefore, its preliminary campaign's projected costs are:

Creative (copy and design)	$ 3,000
List cost ($200 per 1,000 names)	$18,000
Total	**$21,000**

It's August 1, and the team roughs out the following schedule:

August

2	Approve copy, goes into design
4	Approve design, goes back to client
5	Set up meeting with information technology department
5	Get approved creative to list vendors
12	Deployment/testing
19	Read results of tests
22	Rollout strategy meeting
23–27	Package "tweaking" in progress

September

7	Rollout

SUMMARY

GolfCoachConnection.com is now ready to begin its first e-mail marketing campaign.

We'll get into the details of creating an offer, testing strategies for prospecting, and finding sources or lists in later chapters in this section. Part Three then delves into the "art" of dynamic and creative e-mail messages. You'll then be ready for Part Four, which explores the ins and outs of retention marketing to your house list.

For now, though, let's take a good, hard look at our customers, as well as those prospects-turned-customers that we aim to reach through e-mail.

CHAPTER REVIEW/EXERCISES

1. What is the difference between acquisitions, conversion, and retention? Think of an example of how your company would acquire new customers.

2. Define a prospect. And a lead. And an existing customer.

3. Which segment of your customer base is strongest? Tier 1, Tier 2 or Tier 3?

4. Analyze your long-term goals.
   a. How many new customers do you want your e-mail marketing promotions to add to your house file in one year?
   b. What is your average order per customer?
   c. What is the value of that customer over three years? Five years? Ten years?
   d. What is your leads-to-sales ratio?

5. Calculate how many new leads you'll have to gather in your target time frame.

6. Calculate how many prospects you'll have to reach to gather your leads goal.

7. If your offer is a paid one, determine your breakeven point.

8. Determine your budget based on the above answers, using the example in this chapter as a guideline.

CHAPTER 5

Brainstorming the Offer

OBJECTIVES

- Define your audience.
- Define your campaign objectives.
- Develop the best offer(s) that meets the criteria of both.

I think it's safe to say that one of the main goals you have as an e-mail marketer contains two steps:

1. Find a highly qualified audience.
2. Develop the most compelling offers to target that audience.

Of course, there are many steps from there and the end result should be a strong response to your promotion and/or campaign. There are different levels of responsiveness, of course. Your business may have a large audience comprising millions of individuals. Therefore, you have a variety of opportunities that will allow you to communicate with those people.

Chances are better, however, that your audience is more finite. So, to find the best opportunities to reach them, you first need to determine who they are. Once that task is done, the fun begins. It is then time to develop an offer that your audience can't refuse . . . an offer that will induce them to *react,* and will pave the way for them to react again and again.

FINDING THE CREAM

E-mail's true strength lies in its ability to communicate with existing customers in such a way that it actually helps forge a "relationship" with them. This is because, after a certain period of time, customers will become accustomed to receiving these regular promotions and, if those messages are executed properly, your customers also will actually look forward to receiving them. As a result, these regular communications can even help build customer loyalty over time. The bulk of those loyal, happy customers that you develop through e-mail becomes stronger . . . and more loyal . . . and more *profitable.*

Therefore, it is critical that you *know* who those customers are, so you can develop the best strategies to both find them and communicate with them—even when they're still at the prospect stage.

For example, I know that I look forward to receiving my e-mail promotions from Levenger when they send them. As a satisfied customer both online and offline, I don't mind being a part of Levenger's house file and the e-mails are always welcome. They're promotional, yet are colorful and well-designed and are whipped together with compelling prose. See Figure 5.1. The marketer in me can't help but love the thought and creativity behind them.

A house file the likes of which Levenger manages is not created overnight, however. So you've got to start somewhere. And if you want to do it all with e-mail, that means you first must hunt for your most likely prospects using opt-in e-mail lists, and then strategically beckon them to become part of your house file. How? Start by defining who exactly makes up your target audience.

YOUR AUDIENCE

Based on your research and what you already know about your target market, imagine a group of your best customers sitting right in front of you. Create a *customer profile* that tells you about the people who will constitute your customer base. Ask questions like "What do they look like?" "Where do they live?" Regardless of whether your audience consists of consumers or businesspeople, the questions to ask also include:

- What is the age range of your customer base?
- What types of occupations, generally speaking, do they work in?

FIGURE 5.1   Good Merchandise with Sparkling Copy Brings Customers Back
Again and Again

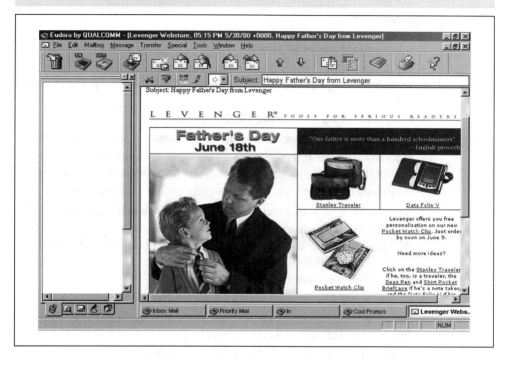

- Are they city dwellers? Do they live in the suburbs? The country?
- What is their income range?
- What types of cars do they drive?
- Do they have children? What ages?
- What are their hobbies?
- Where do they shop . . .
    . . . for food?
    . . . for clothes?
    . . . for household items?
    . . . for office products?

Well, you get the picture.

If you are already in business, you should have this *ideal customer* fairly well-defined, as shown in Figure 5.2. However, the above exercise can help you plant that picture of your customer firmly in mind, which will help you in determining your goals and objectives from here.

FIGURE 5.2   Sample Customer Profile

My customer:

- is between the ages of 35–65.
- resides in major metropolitan markets (e.g., New York, Chicago, San Francisco) with slightly higher concentration of target customers residing in the western U.S.
- has a household income of $150,000 or more.
- is a professional or executive knowledge worker.
- regularly uses the Internet and occasionally or frequently buys online such products as books, groceries, airline tickets, software, health & beauty, etc.
- very likely belongs to a gym, health club, and/or country club.
- is well-educated with a college degree and some graduate work.
- typically reads a major daily newspaper and/or specialty paper such as the *Wall Street Journal,* and subscribes to a variety of upscale magazines such as *Conde Nast Traveler, Bon Appetit, Worth,* etc.
- is not a first-time overseas traveler.
- on average, takes approximately 1.7 leisure overseas trips per year.
- has previously traveled independently and also may have taken a packaged small group active or adventure travel trip.
- is sophisticated, confident, curious, and cultured.
- is demanding—even a bit snobby.
- respects others they see as accomplished and professional; they do not suffer fools easily.
- works hard and plays hard; wants the most out of life and often feels there simply isn't enough time to "do it all"; views time as a precious commodity.
- embraces technology, or is at least comfortable with it as an integral part of her daily life.
- is willing to spend substantial money for travel, but wants great value and service.
- is likely to feel he has the inside track on the latest travel destinations, activities, gear, clothing, etc.
- seeks authentic, unique, experiential kinds of travel.
- likes to be mentally stimulated and physically challenged.
- enjoys good food, drink, and accommodations while traveling (but will camp out if it's an essential part of the overall experience).

THE ALL-IMPORTANT OFFER

The offer is one of the most important components of a successful acquisitions campaign. Beyond any of the products or services involved, it is what ultimately drives response.

A solid e-mail promotion is typically made up of two different offers: (1) the *primary offer* and (2) the *secondary offer.* The primary offer is the offer that has been specifically created to appeal to a certain audience—*your* target audience. It is the platform by which your products and services are shaped.

For example, suppose you run an online content site, geared for salespeople across a variety of industries. You want to drive qualified prospects (i.e. real, live salespeople) to your site to help build your traffic, because the more visitors you get, the more advertising dollars you can charge to those who place ads within your site.

The secondary offer is made up of you, your company, your business model, your credibility, your service, your overall suite of products and services, and other nonspecific components that make up your core business. What types of offers would appeal most to your target audience? Assuming you can find your audience using opt-in acquisitions/prospecting e-mail lists, how do you come up with an offer that truly *resonates* with them—in other words, the proverbial "offer they can't refuse." It's time for you to dig a little deeper.

Build Assumptions

Begin by making a list of a few broad assumptions about your audience and what they like and dislike; what features and benefits are most appealing to them; and what price points and products they most likely will respond to. These assumptions are where real breakthroughs can come from and can be used to further enhance your message and design. It can even help in the list selection process.

When making assumptions, what you really want to come up with is the *appeal* that will hit home the hardest with your audience. Assumptions are built on appeals. In other words, you need to define their hopes and desires, and even where their real pain resides most. Most of these appeals come from basic human needs that have remained consistent through the ages.

Almost 50 years ago, a famous direct marketer by the name of Victor Schwab came up with a list of more than three dozen very strong audience appeals. They are obviously timeless and should be reviewed when making your assumptions:

- *People want to gain* health, popularity, praise from others, pride of accomplishment, self-confidence, time, improved appearance, comfort,

social and business advancement, money, security in old age, leisure, increased enjoyment, and personal prestige.
- *They want to save* time, money, and work.
- *They want to avoid* discomfort, risks, worry, embarrassment, and doubts.
- *They want to* express their personalities, satisfy their curiosities, appreciate beauty, win others' affections, resist domination by others, emulate the admirable, acquire or collect things, and generally improve themselves.
- *They want to be* good parents, creative, efficient, recognized authorities, up-to-date, gregarious, leaders, sociable, hospitable, proud of their possessions, and influential over others.

With those basic desires and needs in mind, let's take a look at a few assumptions as they relate to our previously mentioned content site that targets salespeople. As you can see, we start with a very broad overview of our audience, build our assumptions, and then drill down from there.

- Members of this audience include company personnel ranging from top-level executives, such as Vice Presidents of Sales—who spend their time strategizing—to those in the trenches, meaning the sales representatives who spend their time on regular, face-to-face contacts with their prospects and customers.
- They are busy. They are hardworking. In fact, they're overloaded.
- They look to your site to help them build their selling skills and also to save them time by not having to read a host of various trade publications. Your site acts as a one-stop resource for all of the information they need.
- What they want most is to have more free time, *and* to be able to enjoy it while they have it.
- What they most need is a way to manage their time more efficiently.

The bottom line is that their strongest desire is to have more free time. Their strongest "pain" is their lack of it.

Of course, this is just a hypothetical example; however, you can see how an offer can be developed based on your bottom line assumptions. With the example above, what type of appeal, or offer, would help this audience reach their desires and/or get rid of their pain? Before we answer that question, let's make things a little clearer.

Define Your Objectives

Once again, what is it that you want to accomplish by marketing with e-mail? What is your end goal? And how do you propose to get there? If you market high-dollar products, for example, I wouldn't recommend e-mail to *sell* these products right out of the chute (i.e., the first time a prospect sees your company's name in his or her inbox). Instead, you may want to think about a two-step offer, or a lead generation campaign, of which we'll get into more detail a bit later.

Take a look at the following example objectives:

- Generate sales/orders
- Bring in new leads
- Build subscriber base
- Raise funds

How do you get from Step A, knowing your audience and objectives, to Step B, developing the offer to best meet those objectives? First we need to examine a few different offers.

TYPES OF OFFERS

For acquisitions promotions, all offers boil down to two types: (1) the *lead generation offer,* and (2) the *sales offer.*

Lead Generation

This type of offer is part of a two-step offer because its end goal is only step one in the e-mail marketing process—to *bring in new leads.* Step two, of course, would be to market to those leads in an effort to get them to *buy,* or become paid customers. There are numerous kinds of lead generation offers, many of which begin with the enticement of something that is of value to the prospect, but is being offered for *free.*

The appeal here, of course, is that the prospect will, if he responds, be rewarded with something that costs him absolutely nothing. The thing to keep in mind (and also be wary of) is that there are plenty of *unqualified* prospects who will respond to this type of offer. Prospects that fall in this category will almost certainly never make a purchase—they're "freebie seekers" and are probably not even interested in your end products and services. They typically comb the Web for offers and cannot be counted on to ever become bona fide leads. Using only the most targeted opt-in e-mail lists and relating the gift to what you're actually selling can help deter people in this category.

There are some other more obvious things to keep in mind when developing a free gift offer. First, make sure the gift is truly something you can afford, budget-wise, to give away. In this same vein, if the gift is *too* appealing, it may reduce the need for your new leads to make a future purchase.

Free gift offers can appeal to both business-to-consumer (B2C) and business-to-business (B2B) offers alike. On that note, if new leads are gathered through the use of a B2B offer utilizing a free gift strategy, you should strive to follow up with them immediately with a phone call or an e-mail response. Within an hour is the ideal response; within three days is the maximum—the quicker, the better.

Following are some tried-and-true primary offers in the free gift category, split by business and consumer orientation (according to where your target audience falls).

Business-to-business.

- *Free whitepapers, etc.* This can be a valuable document to a businessperson. It can include a normally expensive research report and/or industry analysis. Or it can be a set of business case studies to help your target audience learn from others. As long as the presentation of the information is presented objectively, this type of offer can have enormous appeal. Another added benefit of this type of offer is it can be delivered to responders through fax or e-mail, so postal mailing costs don't have to come into play.
- *Business tools.* This includes items you may already have on hand that also can be sent via e-mail or fax, such as "to do" lists and worksheets, online and/or software calculators, and industry-specific analysis software that can be downloaded from the Web.
- *Specialized business books.* This is particularly effective if the cost of the book (and its shipping) can be justified, and if the book is specialized enough to appeal to your target audience.
- *Free seminars, online chats, or Webcasts.* The seminar can be in person or online and the Webcast can be produced in advance and loaded onto your Web site for responders to download at their leisure. In either event, the presenter should have credibility within the target market's industry and the content should be as fresh and as timely as possible.
- *CD-ROM giveaway.* This is similar to the downloadable software, only it is sent through regular mail. With this type of offer, you'll collect not only e-mail addresses for future marketing, but "snail mail" addresses as well. Therefore, you may be able to enhance your communications with new leads by reaching to them across mediums.
- *Free registration.* If your site normally requires a fee to use its services, then a limited-time (e.g., one month) free registration offer can be a worthwhile perk.

Consumer.

- *Free lower-priced product.* Also known as a loss leader or "feeder" product, this is one of your products and services that you can afford to give away. In the subscription business, it could be a magazine or newsletter on, say, stock trading for new-to-the-stock-market investors. The idea is to educate those subscribers and, in the process, upsell them to the more advanced publications. In the retail arena, it can be a starter kit of some sort, with or without a purchase. Women have seen many a cosmetic company offer the "free makeup bag" with purchases of $45 or more. This same concept has been brought to the e-mail marketplace as well.

- *Free report.* Remember the emotional desires and appeals from earlier? Think about how you can turn an answer to one of those appeals into a free report that is targeted to your market. For example, if you sell herbal vitamins or some other health-oriented product, you could pull together (or purchase the reprint rights to) a report on how to treat obesity, or diabetes, or aging skin—using the natural way, meaning with your products.

  Again, the free report can be faxed or e-mailed. This can happen all at once, or some marketers offer e-mail reports that have multiple parts that are delivered separately, one by one. This is an excellent method to establish a regular communication with responders.

- *Multiple gifts.* More often than not, these are trinkets and don't cost much; yet these types of offers can be very compelling to the right audience. Often, the idea is for the number of gifts to go up as the dollar amount of the actual purchases goes up. Fingerhut Corporation has used this strategy for years in their direct mail efforts, often giving away between two and four "gifts" for every single purchase.

- *Mystery gift.* The free gift, in this case, is an unknown to the recipients of this type of offer. Again, the proper audience is required, because this won't necessarily cut it with people who absolutely and without doubt need to know what they're getting. An offer such as this might, however, appeal to an entertainment site, or a site that sells *Harry Potter* books and related products.

- *Free complementary products.* These can be small token gifts that can be used with your end products. For example, film if you sell cameras, a nail file if you sell grooming kits, a jar of spice if you sell kitchen products, etc. This offer can enhance the worth of your products and may strengthen your brand in the responders' eyes.

- *"Your choice" of gifts.* This one is a bit of a tougher offer, logistically speaking, to pull off and fulfill. And sometimes giving people too many choices paralyzes them into inaction. It may be worth testing, however.

- *Free catalog.* Large volume, offline catalogers that normally charge consumers for their catalogs can offer to ship a free full color print catalog to e-mail responders. Oftentimes, these catalogs are already printed for other marketing efforts and for in-store use, so the biggest costs for fulfillment would be for shipping.

- *Free shipping.* Everyone likes free shipping because it adds to the convenience of shopping online. Free shipping is offered with purchases of pre-designated orders. For example, Staples offers free shipping on orders of $50 or more. Obviously, the products have to fit the target audience's needs because, after all, what good is free shipping if you don't really care about the products?
- *Sweepstakes.* The thrill of winning a high-dollar prize is the appeal here. Many e-mail marketers have generated tons of leads by using this type of offer. A free trip, a car, and even thousands of dollars in cold hard cash have all been enticements with e-mail. Again, be careful, because a sweepstakes offer without a monetary commitment will draw plenty of people who will never be qualified leads, let alone true paid customers.

Other "free" ideas, for both consumer and business-oriented offers, include free estimates, demonstrations, and lessons or educational material—either online or offline—of some kind. And keep in mind, even the best-planned lead generation offers will only induce your prospects to "open the door" to you, so to speak, *slightly.* Responders here are wary, yet most of the time, they're interested in what you have to ultimately offer, at least to a certain degree.

Of course, it's also possible to generate leads in ways outside of offering something for free. Sales offers are the second type of lead generation offer.

Sales Offers

Trial offers. These can include free trials, of course, as in publication subscriptions and software. Or they can include products and services that are available for a limited time for a reduced price. The responder can, when the trial period is over, either decide not to continue using or receiving the product, or can pay to have it continued. Here are a few examples:

- *A limited-time use of downloadable software,* wherein after the time period is over, the software or the site where the software is housed is no longer accessible. This can be offered for free, or at a nominal charge upfront in order to get the prospect to put in some kind of commitment. (The more she does commit, the more qualified she is and the better chance you have of converting her from a lead into a fully paid customer.)
- *An offer that costs nothing upfront,* but the responder has to enter his credit card number with the understanding that he has a limited time to try out the offer. If he does not cancel within that time, his credit card automatically will be charged when that time period is over.
- *An auto-billed trial offer,* in which the responder can pay in regular monthly installments. You, the promoting company, need to make sure these install-

ments get made by submitting to the appropriate credit card company each month.

Discounts. Many online retailers offer discounts on products when they prospect with e-mail. Often, there is a minimum dollar amount that the responder is required to spend, and typically the "carrot" is the discount offered if that minimum purchase is met. For example, "Click here to take $10 off your next purchase of $50 or more . . ." Yes, this type of offer appeals to bargain hunters, but only if ultimately they're interested in your products.

A discount offer can include any or all of the following:

- *Cash discount,* as above
- *E-mailed coupon,* in which the coupon with an "exclusive" number is on the initial e-mail and responders can redeem the coupon by clicking the designated link
- *New product or introductory order discount,* for first-time customers or new product announcements
- *Early-bird discount,* where recipients are "rewarded" with a price break if they respond early
- *A "sale"* with a reason or a season. The December holidays always see plenty of promotional e-mails, especially on gift and entertaining items.
- *Quantity discount,* e.g., "buy three, get one free" or "take 20 percent off orders of five or more." This offer is good for products that are used (and used up) fairly frequently, such as vitamins and other consumables.

PULLING IT ALL TOGETHER

Getting back to the sale executive/salespeople site we introduced earlier, we've determined the following thus far:

About the audience.

- *Customer profile:* In brief, they are sales executives and representatives across various industries, and are hardworking.
- *Assumptions:* Their severe lack of time is their pain point. They want to streamline the time they spend at work so they can have more free time to do the things they enjoy.

About you and your offer.

- *Promotional objectives:* To bring in more traffic and to drive registrants to the site

- *Secondary offer:* Your site's content, internal offers, credibility, writers, community, and all other benefits that it offers

Now, of course, the question is—what is your primary offer? What will work best to draw this audience that is so hungry for time?

This particular site saw an opportunity to get the word out *and* reinforce their brand at the same time. It pulled together a two-part lead generation offer that made sense, given the circumstances. The main part of the offer was for a free download of its proprietary software, designed to manage scheduling and follow-up in a systematic, easy-to-use (and timesaving) manner. The software could be used both online or offline, but when the user was online, she could link to various pertinent areas of the site right from the software program.

The second part of the offer also appealed to the audience's time issue. In addition to the free software, responders also would be automatically entered to win a sweepstakes prize—the latest in state-of-the-art wireless handheld computers. And not just one, but 100, of these "personal digital assistants" would be given away to make the chances of winning appear that much higher.

So the idea is to create an e-mail promotion wherein the primary offer of the free software and the free sweepstakes entry will induce the target audience, the sales folks, to click through to the Web site. It is here that they are required to register—again, for free—in order to have access to the software and the sweepstakes. Once they opt-in to register (see Part One on appropriate opt-in and privacy language), their e-mail address and whatever other contact information you've chosen to collect is now a part of your house file. They are then yours to promote to—and woo back to your site—in the future. Until, of course, they choose to say "no more."

GOLFCOACHCONNECTION.COM DEVELOPS AN OFFER

In the last "episode" of the GolfCoachConnection.com story, the novice e-mail marketers planned their strategy and their budget.

Now it is time for GolfCoachConnection.com to develop its offer. So the GolfCoachConnection.com marketing team decides to focus its first e-mail promotion on lead generation. It believes that the best way to start long-term, mutually beneficial relationships with golfers (especially the ones who are ready to quit out of frustration!) is to introduce them to the personalized instruction that GCC will provide by e-mail for free. See Figure 5.3.

In order to receive this service, prospects will have to fill out a player profile so that their tips can be customized to fit their games. This also will help the GCC team to develop targeted, benefit-rich offers for future sales and lead generation efforts.

> **FIGURE 5.3** A Sample Offer Development Worksheet for GolfCoachConnection.com
>
> **1. Name the top ten things you know about your customers:**
>
>   1. They are upwardly mobile.
>   2. They have excellent incomes ($75,000–$200,000).
>   3. They are aspiring or are already successful professionals.
>   4. They wish to better their golf game so they can network better.
>   5. They are mostly men (80%).
>   6. They are mostly married.
>   7. They do not want to go to their local golf club to better their game.
>   8. Most belong to a country club of some sort.
>   9. Most travel on extended vacations at least twice a year.
>   10. The majority have children.
>
> **2. What assumptions can you make about their "pain" points?**
>
> Their main pain point is the sense of urgency that they need to improve their golf game. They have little time to do it. They are arrogant, so they do not want to demean themselves by taking lessons where their business clients and associates can see them. They want to be private. They also have little time.
>
> **3. What are your promotional objectives?**
>
> To drive leads to convert to paid customers.
>
> **4. What is your primary offer?**
>
> Free lessons by e-mail for a limited time.
>
> **5. What is your secondary offer?**
>
> Free video.

To give prospects even more incentive to sign up for the golf tip service, and to introduce them to one of GCC's fee-based services, the team sweetens the offer with a chance to win a free "Swing Coaching Video Session" video (valued at $39.95 plus shipping).

As you can see, developing a solid offer is simply a matter of doing your homework—asking and answering questions, making assumptions, and coming up with the necessary ammunition (your offer) to meet the requirements of both

---

FIGURE 5.4 Create Your Own Offer

1. **Name the top ten things you know about your customers.**

2. **What assumptions can you make about their "pain" points?**

3. **What are your promotional objectives?**

4. **What is your primary offer?**

5. **What is your secondary offer?**

---

your audience and your objectives. See Figure 5.4. Next it's time to find that audience, which will be a discussion in Chapter 6.

CHAPTER REVIEW/EXERCISES

1. Define your audience. Be as specific as possible. Come up with a list of not only their demographic profiles, but their psychographic profiles as well, i.e., their most deep-rooted wants and needs.

2. Build assumptions about your audience based on what you discovered above. What are the strongest appeals?

3. Define your objectives. What do you need your e-mail promotion to accomplish? Do you need to drive sales? Or do you need to build more names on your house list to promote to? What are your end goals? Work back from there.

4. Create the offer. Is it a sales offer or a lead generation offer? If a sales offer, what type, and using a discount or two-for-one method? Holiday? If a lead generation offer, what has value to your audience? Or how do you create something of value that will be compelling to them?

CHAPTER 6

All about Lists

OBJECTIVES

- Define opt-in acquisitions lists and their sources.

- Determine how to find lists for your target audience (questions to ask, etc.).

- Review a list datacard and its components (selects, etc.).

- Determine how to choose and test lists and list selects for maximum effectiveness.

Now that we've covered how to define an audience and develop an offer, it's time to learn how to search for top prospects within an audience. In other words, it's time for a little list research.

OPT-IN LISTS FURTHER DEFINED

Before we begin, let me first mention that the back of this book contains a compendium of dozens of opt-in e-mail list sources, including list owners, vendors, and brokers. And let me also mention that, for purposes of this book, we will look only at *opt-in* or *permission-based e-mail lists;* in other words, there are no bulk e-mail lists here.

As we saw in Part One, opt-in lists contain e-mail addresses of people who have signed up at some time to receive promotional offers and announcements within their selected categories of interest. A consumer interested in receiving coupons or sales announcements from online retailers, for instance, might opt-in to shopping categories across a variety of sites that offer it. List vendors such as Postmaster Direct, YesMail, DeliverE, 24/7, and others often collect opted-in e-mail addresses on their own sites; and they also gather them from other smaller sites within their respective networks. In other words, they are either owners of the lists or they are vendors (resellers) of other Web sites' collected opt-in e-mail addresses (some are combinations of both). All e-mail addresses belong to people who have gone somewhere on the Web and essentially exclaimed, "Yes! I'm interested in receiving promotions and product announcements within the following categories." To see an example of how a list is collected, visit <rentals.postmasterdirect.com/homepage/main?page=signup.mhtml>.

For the record, some of the list owners and/or providers use different tactics when opting in new e-mail addresses. Postmaster Direct, for instance, has people sign up on their site and then just to be sure, sends them a follow-up e-mail, requiring them to respond by e-mail from the address they signed up under. YesMail, on the other hand—another opt-in provider—sends a follow-up e-mail, but doesn't require the recipient to respond. It only wants replies from people who have changed their minds about being on YesMail's list, or have received a subscription in error. Two different opt-in policies, two different schools of thought. Those who believe in "double opt-in" also know it as "confirmed opt-in." They believe it is the safest way to prevent forged subscriptions from inundating a nonsubscriber's inbox.

Another category of permission-based list—though many will claim that it's not *completely* opt-in—includes addresses culled from Web sites that offer free e-mailed newsletter subscriptions. IDG, for instance, who manages Industry Standard's e-mailed newsletter list, *used* to collect e-mail addresses with a prechecked box at the end which read, "From time to time, we may allow carefully selected, reputable companies to send you information by e-mail which may be of interest to you." Note that I said that the box was *prechecked,* meaning that new subscribers that didn't uncheck it would receive these promotions.

This seemingly small fact caused a constant commotion with the anti-spammers of the industry. They claimed that the prechecked box often went unnoticed by subscribers and that, in fact, they had not truly opted-in to receiving promotions: they just didn't know any better. (For the record, IDG now collects those e-mail addresses with this box no longer prechecked). See Figure 6.1 for an example of a true opt-in site.

FIGURE 6.1 A Sign-up Box Where It Is up to the Subscriber to Say, "Yes, I Am Interested in Receiving Promotions."

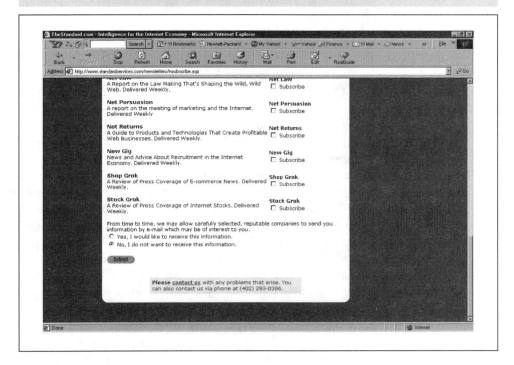

List Owners and Vendors

Now that we've determined that opt-in lists are the way to go, let's begin the search for the right ones for us. First, it should be noted that lists of e-mail addresses are completely proprietary, meaning that unlike the way it is with direct mail list addresses, the only people who actually see and maintain e-mail addresses are the list vendors themselves. Here is how it works: You send the vendors your promotion (your creative, complete with full text and links); they, in turn, will send it out to the lists that you've selected (they will *not* send you the list for you to e-mail directly).

At the time of this writing, there was talk of third-party service bureaus getting involved in the list process to ensure that an e-mail promotion isn't received multiple times by a recipient who may be subscribed on a number of different lists. For the record, service bureaus act as "merge-purge" houses and remove duplicate e-mail addresses from campaigns. This, of course, is a benefit to the e-mail marketer because it will prevent a recipient of a promotion from receiving it more than once. You can well imagine how a duplicate, or even a triplicate promotion could certainly suppress response.

List Brokers

In addition to list owners and vendors, who rent their internal opt-in lists for one-time use, we also can add another source to find opt-in lists—the e-mail list *broker.* A broker is not beholden to one list owner or vendor. Instead, it has access to dozens of vendors and, within them, hundreds of lists. It also can help in the list planning and research process, and can negotiate pricing. A broker earns its keep by charging a commission; yet more times than not, you do *not* pay any more than if you had gone directly to the list vendor because of the pricing method that many list vendors use. Most list vendors charge a gross price, whether they're dealing with an agency, a broker, or directly with the advertiser. The gross price is the cost of the list marked up by a 10 to 20 percent commission. Oftentimes, a broker can negotiate that price down, while still earning its normal commission. Therefore, the benefits to using a broker are twofold: First, you have one-stop access to hundreds of different e-mail lists, and second, you can also, more times than not, get a better deal than if you negotiated directly with list owners.

We'll delve into some nitty-gritty details of opt-in e-mail lists and how to find the ones best targeted for your promotion; but before we do, let's define a few direct marketing terms that have transferred to e-mail and are specific to lists and list research.

Universe. When you first begin the search, your job is to find as many sources as possible for your target audience. If you have a broad audience, you may be able to reach a potential audience of 500,000 or more people across various e-mail lists. Conversely, if you have a small audience, you may only be able to reach 50,000. That number is your *universe,* or your gross potential audience. A universe also can refer to the total quantity of a list.

List test. New lists that have never been used by your company always should be pretested in small quantities. Even if you determine that a new list has 50,000 quantity and your budget can withstand the costs, the general rule of thumb is to test a small quantity of the list first. If it pulls a strong response, you can then go back to it at a later time. A minimum quantity of 5,000 is recommended for a list of 50,000. Generally speaking, the test quantity should be at least 10 percent of the segment or list that you're testing. And to be statistically valid, you should aim for at least 50 responses.

Continuation and balance. After a test mailing has gone out, and certain lists have been deemed worthy by their response to be e-mailed again, a marketer can choose to "continue" on that list if he doesn't want to rollout to its entire universe. Example: If a list has a universe of 50,000 and in the first e-mailing, the marketer tests 5,000 e-mail addresses within that list and it does well, the marketer can e-mail the balance of 45,000 in the next mailing. Or, if the budget is smaller, the marketer can take a *continuation* of that list—a fresh set of 5,000 addresses in which the initial 5,000 is omitted. See Figure 6.2.

Rollout. This comprises all the e-mail addressees within a campaign that are sent at one time, including list tests, message, creative and offer tests, and any other variables.

Statistical significance. In order to get a solid reading on a list, you need to make sure you have enough names so that any response you get can be applied to other promotions. For instance, if you glean a 5 percent click-through rate on a list test of 5,000 (where the total universe of the list is approximately 20,000), you can pretty much count on the fact that new names within that list—i.e., names that have not yet e-mailed—will give you similar results. However, if you get similar

FIGURE 6.2   Test, Continuation, Balance

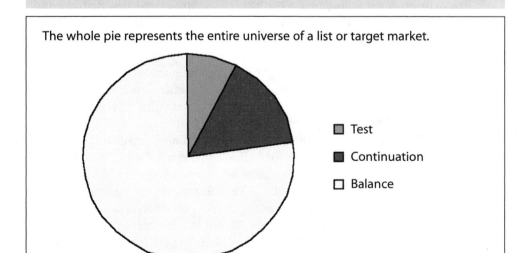

The whole pie represents the entire universe of a list or target market.

☐ Test
■ Continuation
☐ Balance

If the initial test works, you can then use a continuation. If that is still successful, then either continue to use continuations, or use the balance of the file.

results from a list with only 500 names, you won't be able to e-mail that list again with complete confidence that it will yield similar results because the quantity was not high enough to make it statistically significant.

Nth. This term refers to a specific randomly selected quantity, normally used for test quantities of a list. For instance, a list may have more than 50,000 names/e-mail addresses on its file. For testing purposes however, you may choose to pull off an *nth* of 5,000. If done right, it will not be the first 5,000 names on a list and it won't be the last 5,000—it will be names randomly selected across the entire file. This is to ensure that the test quantity represents an accurate sampling of people within the list.

Now that we've determined the basics, let's explore some available categories within lists. Again, the Resource section at the back of the book lists sources of lists, including vendors and brokers, and also includes a brief description of what categories of lists they specialize in, if any.

List Categories

Opt-in e-mail lists are offered by category. If you want to find people who have an interest in cooking, for example, you can rent lists that fall into that and related categories.

Unlike direct mail lists, in which you can select lists based on what people have *subscribed to* (as in magazines, newspapers, and newsletters) and/or what people have *responded to* (such as product catalog mailings), opt-in e-mail lists are made up of people who have simply *said* they're interested in *something*. In other words, they don't necessarily have a history of "paying up" to a similar offer.

Following is a sampling of some of the categories of interest offered by many list vendors: automotive, books, business, careers, computers, cooking, diet and nutrition, education, electronics, entertainment, family, fine arts, games, government, health, home and garden, and Internet.

The wide variety of opt-in lists available is one reason why defining your audience, as noted in the last chapter, is so important. Often, your particular target audience may be found across more than one category. For instance, suppose you sell fitness equipment online and you've determined your audience consists of people who are upscale, upwardly-mobile professionals who are also health-oriented and interested in the latest diet fads. Of course, the obvious lists from those above would be both in the "Health" and the "Diet and Nutrition" categories. But wait. Some list owners can pull e-mail addresses across categories to see which ones are duplicated across lists. So suppose you make the assumption that your audience is interested in careers and, possibly, fine arts. Those people who have *cross-*

pollinated, or signed up to all four categories of interest (health, diet and nutrition, careers, fine arts) may make up your ideal online audience. Just keep in mind that this can only be done with a group of lists owned or managed by the same vendor, and with that vendor's cooperation, of course. Not all vendors offer this "multilist member" select. Also, pinpointing only the people who have signed up to all of your chosen multiple categories can and will reduce the quantity of e-mail addresses *substantially*. If your final count is too small, try selecting people who have signed up to receive offers within three categories . . . or even two.

ENHANCE WITH SELECTS

In every one of your promotions, your goal should be to make sure that not only are you renting the best lists for your audience; but that the portion of those lists that you use are as strong as possible. One way to ensure that is the use of list selections, also known as *selects.*

A select is designed to enhance a list of e-mail addresses by pinpointing even further your true target audience. For instance, getting back to the aforementioned fitness equipment company, one of the lists decided on was a "health" category list of people who also signed up for the "diet and nutrition" category. To enhance that list even further, and depending on the makeup or demographics of your audience, you may want to e-mail only "females." Or you may want to enhance your list with a geographic select, as in e-mailing people who live in certain areas. Additionally, you may also want to e-mail what is commonly referred to as "hotline names"—meaning a group of people who most recently signed onto a file. Hotline names are the best place to start when e-mailing a never-before-used list because they are typically the strongest responders.

Not all vendors offer list selects; but if they do, take advantage of them. They cost more, but can be well worth it in terms of the added response you can get in click throughs and conversions. Selects can get you closer to your target audience and therein lies their power.

What do select lists cost? Generally speaking, you can expect to pay an additional $5 to $20 *per thousand* per select. If you were renting a list of 10,000 e-mail addresses that cost $150 per thousand *base,* your total cost would be $1,500. If you chose to enhance that list with a gender select at a cost of $10 per thousand extra, your cost would be $160 per thousand including the select, for a total cost of $1,600.

Standard selects and enhancements include gender, business or industry, job title, or geographic location. Many acquisitions lists are becoming even more segmented, with offerings of age and income enhancements, and even by number of children in the household.

THE DATACARD

When you begin researching lists, you should ask your broker or vendor for its datacards that fall into your targeted categories. Following is a sample of a list datacard. As you can see in Figure 6.3, in addition to selects, the datacard can tell you quite a bit about a list.

FIGURE 6.3   Sample Datacard

Sample E-MAIL LIST

11,982 Total List $290/M
       Counts Thru 10/99

* Plus $95/M transmission fee

Email list by _____

An excellent source to target information systems (IS) managers looking for a competitive edge in the $211 billion U.S. management of information systems marketplace is with an e-mail list from the publication DATAMATION (last published issue 2/98).

Reach IS managers responsible for specifying and purchasing computers, peripherals, software, and networking/communication systems.

Target IS managers looking to add profit and value to their company through technology.

Additional Selections:
   Acquisition Source @ N/C
   Buying Authority @ N/C
   Computer Systems Installed @ N/C
   Computer Systems On Site:
      Class of System @ N/C
      Specific System @ N/C

------------------ DATE ----------------
11/01/99 UPDATED
11/11/99 CONFIRMED

------------ UNIT OF SALE ----------
N/A

---------------- GENDER ----------------
% N/A
CANNOT SELECT

------------------ MEDIA ----------------
100% INTERNET

------------- ADDRESSING -----------
E-MAIL ONLY

------------- SELECTIONS ------------
N/C NUMBER OF EMPLOYEES
N/C ONE NAME PER SITE
N/C JOB TITLE SELECT
N/C CANADIAN
N/C BUS/INDUSTRY TYPE
N/C PROVINCE
N/C SCF
N/C STATE
N/C ZIP
N/C RECENCY

Database Software @ N/C
Fortune 1000 @ N/C
Network Operating Systems/Protocols @ N/C
Operating Systems @ N/C

---------- MINIMUM ORDER ---------
$5,000

** Business Type: Banking/Finance/Accounting,
Insurance/Real Estate/Legal, Business Services/
Consultant, Communications Carriers, Computer
Manufacturer (hardware, software, and peripherals),
Computer Network Consultant, System Integrators,
VAR/VAD, Data Processing Services, Construction/
Architecture/Engineering, Agriculture/Forestry/
Fisheries, Aerospace, Mining/Oil/Gas, Transpiration/
Utilities, Education, Government—Federal/Military,
State/Local, Manufacturing and Process Industries
(other than computers), Medical/Dental/Health Care,
Research/Development Laboratory, Travel/
Hospitality/Recreation, Nonprofit/Trade Association,
Marketing/ Advertising/Entertainment, and Other
Businesses and Services, Wholesale/Retail Distribution
(computer and noncomputer products)

** Employee Size at Location/in Organization:
```
       1 –     49
      50 –     99
     100 –    499
     500 –    999
   1,000 –  4,999
   5,000 –  9,999
  10,000 – 19,999
  20,000 or More
```

** Title: Executive Information Systems Management—
Chief Information Officer, Vice President of IS/MIS/
Systems/Service/Networks, Information Systems
Management—Communications/Telecommunications,
Database, DP Operations/Security/QC, End User
Computing, Financial Systems, Information Center,
IS/MIS/DP, Networking/Network Computing/LANs,
New Media/Interactive Media, Office Systems/
Automation, PCs/Micros, Programming/Applications/
Software Design, Systems Analysis/Systems
Programming, Systems and Procedures Planning,

(continued)

Systems Integrator, Other IS Management, Corporate Management—Corporate Management with IS Function, Executive Management, Financial Management, Other Corporate Management

*/** Buying Authority: Computers—Intel Network Servers, UNIX Network Servers, Large-Scale Systems/ Mainframes, Midrange/Minicomputers, PCs, Laptops/Notebooks, PDAs, Workstations, Information Technology Services—Consulting/ System Integration/Application Development, Help Desk/Customer Service, Information Technology Maintenance/Outsourcing, Internet Service Provider, Training/Education, Network/Communication Systems—Bridges/Routers/Gateways/Firewalls, Data/Telecommunications, E-mail, Hubs, Intra/ Internet, Local Area Networks, Network Management, Security Systems, Wide Area Networks, Peripherals— Imaging Hardware/Scanners, Multimedia Hardware/ CD-ROM, Printers, Storage Device/Tape Drives/ Controllers, Hard Drives/Optical, Terminals/Monitors, Uninterruptible Power Systems, Software— Accounting/Human Resources/Finance, Client/ Server Development Tools, Enterprise Applications Development Tools, Database Management, Decision Support Systems/Data Warehousing, OLTP/ Middleware, Imaging/Document Management, Languages/Compilers, Manufacturing/Distribution, Networking/Communications, OOPS Tools, PC Applications Software

*/** Computer Systems on Site: Midrange Systems and Servers—ATT GIS/NCR, Apple, AST, Auspex, Compaq, IBM—AS/400, RS/6000, Other, DEC—MICROVAX, VAX/AXP, Other, Bull, Data General, Dell, Hewlett Packard, Intergraph, Netframe, Sequent, Siemens Nixdorf/Pyramid, Stratus, Sun, Tandem, Tricord, Unisys, Other, Mainframe/Host Systems—ATT GIS/NCR, IBM—ES/9000, 3090, 308X, Other, Amdahl, Bull, Convex, DEC (VAX 9000), Hitachi, Siemens, Tandem, Unisys, Other

```
*/** Computer Systems Installed:  Mainframe,
   Minicomputer, PC, Workstation, Other
   Computer System

*/** Operating Systems:  AIX, DOS, Lotus
   Notes, MVS, Macintosh, OS/2, OS/400, Sun
   OS/Solaris, UNIX, VAX/VMS, Windows NT
   Workstation, Windows 3.x, Windows 95

*/** Network Operating Systems/Protocols:
   LAN Server/OS2 Warp, LAN Manager, Lantastic,
   Netware/SNA, TCP/IP, Windows NT, Other

*/** Database Software:  CA, Cincom, Computer
   Associates, Gupta, IBM-DB2, Informix,
   Microsoft, Oracle, Software AG, SQL, Sybase,
   Other

 * Multiple response
**Contact a list owner account executive for
up-to-the-minute counts

Prepayment check if you are a first-time
renter.

Updated daily.

Last Update:  11/01
```

The datacard is only the first part of your task, however. In order to make good decisions on which lists to e-mail or test, you need to ask your broker or vendor plenty of questions. Those questions should be based on the following basic guidelines for new lists:

- *Test lists that have the best potential first.* We'll take a look at how to determine this shortly. If one of these top lists works, success is then simply a matter of going deeper and deeper into the list.
- *Test a variety of lists from varying vendors.* This strategy will allow you to leverage any potentially poor lists against your stronger ones.

- *Send in test quantities only.* Despite what some list vendors might say, you can get a statistically significant read on a test quantity of 5,000 e-mail addresses. In lieu of testing 50,000 or 100,000 of just one list, spread out your money across a variety of lists, as noted above.
- *Tests of large universes.* Be sure to test a significant quantity of each list (1/10 of 1 percent is a solid quantity to strive for). You could test lists that have a total of 5,000, 10,000, or 15,000 on their file, in which case you could simply test the entire file. For much larger lists, however, your best bet is to test solid portions of those lists.

DATACARD COMPONENTS

You'll want to review the datacards of your broker or vendor carefully. Following is information that should be found on just about any opt-in e-mail list datacard:

- *Number of subscribers/members/registrants/buyers.* This will tell you the total universe for a particular file. You'll then know your potential for future test and rollout quantities.
- *Description.* This section will tell you things such as the description of the site or offer, and potential target markets.
- *Source/Media.* This section will tell you how the e-mail addresses were collected.
- *Minimum orders.* Many e-mail list providers require a minimum order. Sometimes it's a dollar figure; but often it's a quantity of names e-mailed for a particular campaign. As discussed earlier, test quantities of 5,000 per list are recommended; 3,000 should be the minimum.
- *Selections.* The most effective lists will offer a potpourri of list selections for you to choose from; as we saw from examples earlier in this chapter. However, even if no selects are offered on the datacard, it doesn't mean they are not available. Especially for someone (like you, perhaps!) who can make a good case for the fact that if you can enhance a file enough with selects to make the campaign profitable, you'll gladly take those same names again and again.
- *Cancellation policies.* Most list vendors charge penalties if you place an order and then cancel it before fulfillment. Usually, it amounts to a base cancellation charge and, often, a cost per thousand charge on top of that. This is all spelled out on the datacard.
- *Sample requests.* Oftentimes, list vendors and owners require a sample of the copy (the creative) that will be sent to their list. This is to ensure them

that your message fits their audience. It is all part of the opt-in gathering process. Reputable and credible vendors want to make sure that they are delivering relevant promotions to their members.

TOP THREE QUESTIONS TO ASK YOUR BROKER OR VENDOR

Based on the above best practices, and to make sure that you're dealing with credible lists, it is highly recommended that you ask the following three questions of your broker or vendor prior to placing any orders:

1. *How did you (or the list vendor) gather this list?* This question clarifies two points. First, the answer tells you whether or not the names/addresses were gathered in an opt-in manner. Second, it helps you determine whether or not list members truly are a part of your audience. For example, say you're targeting corporate executives who themselves need to find vendors in the telecommunications arena. You want to target these decision makers by e-mail, and your broker gives you a list datacard titled *Telecommunications Magazine.* The description on the datacard tells you that this list reaches "key decision makers in the fast-paced telecommunications industry." Sounds good, but do yourself a favor and dig a little deeper. If your vendor or broker tells you that this is all the information known about the list, then search until you find out how to contact the powers-that-be at the magazine itself. It could be that, yes, you'd reach decision makers when using this list; however, those decision makers may just be on the *selling* end (like you are), instead of the buying end (the people you really need to reach). Speaking with the owner of the list directly can yield some pretty specific information such as this. Do it. It could make the difference between a poor and a phenomenal response.

2. *Who else has used this list?* This one question can tell you volumes about the list. Often, this information can be found on the datacard under "list usage." If not, then ask your broker or vendor what other companies have *tested* the list. When they tell you, then ask this telling question: "Of those that have tested it, which have continued or rolled out with it?" If none of the test advertisers used the list again, that may just tell you all you need to know. But don't let it stop there. Pick up the phone and contact a key person at one of the companies mentioned. It may be that either the list didn't fit that advertiser's particular market, or it could be something much more serious, such as the list is old. This brings me to your next "must-ask" question.

3. *How often is this list updated, and when was the last time it was updated?* If a datacard doesn't list the date of the last update, *ask*. E-mail addresses change frequently—business e-mail users change companies and, hence, their work e-mail addresses. And home users switch e-mail accounts (e.g., switching between AOL, Hotmail, Yahoo, etc.). Therefore, e-mail lists require regular updates. This simply means that old addresses that don't work anymore must be pulled off and/or replaced with correct ones. This is something I cannot emphasize enough: Some lists do not work because the list owners or vendors don't take care of them. They leave bad or old e-mail addresses on the file for months without updating and then the advertiser wonders why its promotion didn't even pull a half percent click-through rate. So the question of "How often do you update or clean your list?" is a vital, yet often unasked, question because if a list is *not* updated at least once every couple of months, you risk e-mailing addresses that are no longer valid.

WRAP UP

The following represents a recap of what we've learned in this chapter, as well as a few added list testing "best practices":

- Make assumptions of the best segments to test in a list first. For instance, hotline names versus nonhotline names; or males versus females; or CEOs versus sales staff, etc.
- Based on results of prior mailings, go back to your best, most responsive segments first. If there are any segments of a particular list that are hugely successful, test small quantities of other compatible segments.
- Test in quantities of 5,000 each. For those lists that bring in a solid response, delve deeper into those files. Depending on the strength of those lists, as well as how aggressive you want to be, take an additional 20,000, 50,000, or the balance of the list. Do not go deeper into weaker files; however you may want to retest a poorly performing list, particularly if the response goes against your original assumptions.

GOLFCOACHCONNECTION.COM PICKS A LIST

As you'll recall, the GolfCoachConnection.com team decided to create a lead acquisitions campaign for its first e-mail marketing effort.

The team decided to target golfers within the following key target markets because they account for most of the spending on golf-related products and services:

- Avid adult golfers (golfers who are at least 18 years of age who play 20+ rounds a year)
- Beginning golfers (have played for two years or less)
- Golfers with a household income in excess of $50,000

The GCC team works with an excellent list brokerage company who specializes in prospecting e-mail lists. They are able to find 90,000 names corresponding to GCC's targets at a price that meets its budget ($200/1,000): 30,000 avid golfers and 30,000 beginning golfers (excluding "avid" beginners) from one vendor and 30,000 golfers of all participation levels from another vendor.

Now the team is ready to target these groups with relevant creative, which will be discussed in Chapter 9.

CHAPTER REVIEW/EXERCISES

1. Using the opt-in list resource section at the back of this book, do a little research and contact a few appropriate vendors and brokers. For your business, determine your:
   a. total universe of your opt-in list audience.
   b. categories of interest fitting your target audience.
   c. list selects that have the most potential to enhance your lists.

2. Based on your budget, determine which lists to test first. How many names should you choose from each?

3. Suppose you tested a quantity of 5,000 from a brand-new list with a total universe of 45,000. Your results are fantastic—15 percent click-through rate, with a 75 percent conversion. These numbers mean your goals are well on their way to being met. Do you (choose one):
   a. E-mail those 5,000 people again?
   b. E-mail a continuation of another 5,000?
   c. E-mail a balance of 40,000?
   d. E-mail a balance of 40,000 *and* e-mail the original 5,000 separately?
   e. None of the above.

   (Answer: d. Because your original 5,000—a statistically significant number—pulled such a great response, the balance order will most likely do well. And it's also an excellent idea to e-mail the original 5,000 again at the same time, just so you can see what your reduction in response (falloff) will be as compared to e-mailing the file fresh.)

CHAPTER 7

Acquisitions Testing Strategies

OBJECTIVES

- Determine different types of tests.
- Create a keycode system.
- Set up tests.
- Review testing basics.

We'll delve into numerous ways to test your house list in Part Four. However, there are plenty of things you can learn through testing while acquiring new customers as well: These include strength of different lists, for example, plus message, offer, and subject line strengths and weaknesses.

We've already covered offer development in the last chapter, and message creation is covered in the next section. However because the message/creative is an integral component of your prospecting campaign, we will review some acquisitions "best testing practices," which naturally include information about message testing. Possible tests include:

- *List tests across one vendor versus list tests across various vendors.* Suppose you wanted to learn as much as possible about the strength of the opt-in e-mail lists that are out there—or as much as your budget allows, anyway. Sure, you could test a good portion of the lists owned and/or managed by PostmasterDirect—and only those lists, for instance, because it offers a multitude of categories and selects to choose from. But chances are you wouldn't learn enough of what you *need* to learn—namely, that different vendors and different lists are bound to have different response (or click-through) rates. To get a good reading on the huge number of lists out there, test a good variety of them—meaning variety from a source standpoint, but also from a vendor standpoint as well.
- *List tests by selects.* Within each list, you also may want to test available selects, such as males versus females. And, if it's relevant to your business model and offering, you also may choose to test different geographic selects, such as West Coast residents against East Coast residents, or state to state. See Figure 7.1 for a sample list.
- *Subject line tests.* Because this is your first communication with your prospective customers (the very first message that they will see), make it a good one. To determine your most rewarding subject lines, come up with a variety of them and test them against each other (more on this in Chapter 9).
- *Offer tests.* We saw how many offers are possible in an e-mail promotion in the last chapter. Test side-by-side offers against each other—offer tests such as free reports versus free newsletters, $20 off versus 20 percent off, and a sweepstakes for a trip versus a sweepstakes for cold, hard cash. The list can go on and on.
- *Core message tests.* Do you hard sell? Soft sell? Sell with conversational prose or hard-hitting news and urgency-creating information? Your copy (and design, if you deploy in HTML) will play a huge part in your results. Make sure you're putting your best foot forward and test several different messages and designs.
- *Link tests.* What are people clicking on? Are they clicking on your catchy subheading? Are they clicking on the gorgeous photo in your HTML-designed message? Are they clicking on the call-to-action text within your close? Your logo? You can "flag" each link individually in order to test where the majority of your click-throughs originate.
- *Deployment date tests.* Do all consumer offers really pull better results at the end of the week? Do business-to-business offers fare better towards the beginning of the week? Test your winning offers and messages at different key days within the week. Every business model and audience is different, so you may very well be surprised with your results.

FIGURE 7.1 Sample Select Test Breakdown

	Test	Quantity	Date	CTR (%)	Total CT
I	List A, no gender	5,000	1 Aug	8	410
II	List B, no gender	5,000	1 Aug	4.1	205
III	List C, no gender	5,000	1 Aug	6	300
IV	List A, MALE	5,000	1 Aug	9.20	460
V	List B, MALE	5,000	1 Aug	5.70	285
VI	List C, MALE	5,000	1 Aug	6.30	315
VII	List A, FEMALE	5,000	1 Aug	4.80	240
VIII	List B, FEMALE	5,000	1 Aug	3.20	160
IX	List C, FEMALE	5,000	1 Aug	4.20	210

SETTING UP YOUR TESTS

Many opt-in list vendors and owners can track and report on click-through numbers and percentages for their lists. For instance, if you send out your promotion to a vendor's A, B, and C lists, at the conclusion of (or even during) the campaign, you can request a report such as this:

List	Total E-mails Sent	# of People Who Clicked Through	CTR (%)
A	5,556	189	3.4
B	8,342	345	4.1
C	6,500	421	6.47

(Notice that lists A and B contain odd quantities of e-mails sent. This may be due to the fact that those particular segments had small enough *total* quantities that the marketer decided to roll out to the entire file, instead of taking an *nth* as in List C.)

How does the list vendor offer tracking and reporting within a given promotion or campaign? Normally, it inserts what is called a *redirect link* into the link (or links) within your e-mail. We'll get into specifics of your links in a moment, but the redirect link simply directs any click-throughs from your promotion back to the vendor's site or reporting area. This process is invisible to the people who have clicked through, yet allows the vendors to track the promotions' results. (Not all vendors have this ability.) You should implement your own tracking to see if your results match up to your vendors'. To do this, you must first assign keycodes and/or unique URLs (links) for every promotion with a unique variable. That unique variable can mean a new list segment, a different offer, a new subject line, etc.

CREATING KEYCODES

The easiest way to separately "flag" each promotion with a unique variable is to assign keycodes and then add them to the end of your URL. The keycode should make it easy for you to "read" the results of those unique variables at the conclusion of the campaign. To do this, you may want to create keycodes that will have the following information *embedded* into that code:

- List used
- Segment of list
- Date of promotion

This would be the simplest of keycodes, of course. They can certainly get a lot more complicated as your tests become more complicated. To demonstrate how to create keycodes that show this type of information, let's go back to our A, B, and C lists scenario.

As noted, all three lists are from the same vendor. You, the marketer, wish to test all three. The lists all fall under the "online shopping" category—meaning that members of each list are interested in shopping. The difference between each list is the specific area of shopping that the member is interested in: List A is for shoppers of books, List B is for shoppers of gifts, List C is for shoppers of music CDs.

Suppose you've set your promotion date for June 5. You'll want to make sure to retain that information in your keycode so months or even years from now you can look back at your historical results and *know immediately* when this particular campaign occurred.

So we have two pieces of information to plug into those codes—the segment of the list and the date of the e-mailing. You can start by creating a key, which should be kept with your records and keycodes. In this case, the key tells you what each unique section of the code means:

Key:

1. Lists:
   V1 = Vendor 1
   A = Vendor 1 list, Shopping with Books interest
   B = Vendor 1 list, Shopping with Gifts interest
   C = Vendor 1 list, Shopping with Music CDs interest
2. Date:
   0605 = Date of deployment (June 5)

So now that we have our "key," we can create those codes. It is simply a matter of putting all the pieces together:

V1A0605 = Vendor 1 Shopping list with Books interest, mail date of June 5
V1B0605 = Vendor 1 Shopping list with Gifts interest, mail date of June 5
V1C0605 = Vendor 1 Shopping list with Music CDs interest, mail date of June 5

Now what do we do with this information? We drop that information—via the assigned codes—into the links/URLs within the promotion. For example, suppose our promotion ends with the following call to action: Click here to download your free trial version:

http://www.ClickHereNowDoNotWait.com

If all of our promotions contained the same link, we wouldn't know anything when all was said and done. In this particular example, we wouldn't know which list worked. Without a unique flag, or signifier, the only information we'd have on file is the total number of click-throughs. Therefore, we need to create three copies of the message, and add our different keycodes to each link. How? Let's look at our link again.

http://www.ClickHereNowDoNotWait.com

Obviously, our goal here is to drive people to this particular page or site. As we'll see in Chapter 15, it will help our promotion immensely if we can drive them to a specific "landing page" on our site that is customized. To simplify this example, however, let's just direct people who click through to the main home page of the ClickHereNowDoNotWait.com site.

To retain this link, and still be able to read which list pulled better, we must add our keycode in such a way that it will not affect the link itself in any way whatsoever. To do this, we simply add a question mark ("?") and our unique keycode to our link. From your browser's perspective, the question mark symbol nullifies *itself* and *any symbols and/or alphanumeric characters that follow it*. Therefore, the browsers of the people who click through won't get "confused" as far as which site address the link should lead to. It allows you to add your keycode so you can track results but it will not mess up your URL.

For purposes of this example, we've created a special offer page on the site—appropriately titled <specialofferpage.htm>. (More information on developing a specific landing page is in Chapter 15.) Because this page is part of the site, it becomes a part of the URL:

http://www.ClickHereNowDoNotWait.com/specialofferpage.htm

Once we've implemented the codes and symbols as noted, let's take a look at the three different versions and their individualized calls to action:

List A
"Click here to download your free trial version:
  http://www.ClickHereNowDoNotWait.com/specialofferpage.htm?V1A0605"

List B

"Click here to download your free trial version:
   http://www.ClickHereNowDoNotWait.com/specialofferpage.htm?V1B0605"

List C

"Click here to download your free trial version:
   http://www.ClickHereNowDoNotWait.com/specialofferpage.htm?V1C0605"

You can see how simple a system this is. Some marketers take it a small step further and actually note within the link that the area following the "?" is a key-code. For example, they may insert a "?key=V1A0605" or "?ref=V1A0605"—it all depends on what makes the most sense for your particular business and what will make it easier for you to read those results.

TRACKING AND REPORTING SOFTWARE

So how do you take these beautiful keycodes you've just created and actually read from them? If you do not have any kind of internal tracking or reporting system or software in place, you can simply view your Web site's server log files. Keep in mind, however, that it is a laborious and time-consuming process to wade through the amount of information that is provided therein. However, you'll be able to see how many of each unique URL's keycodes were clicked, because they will show up as locations where your site visitors came from. You can then manually count the number of each, take the total number as a percentage or number of e-mails sent, and determine your click-through rate. However, that's after sifting through pages and pages of other "hits" and visitor information contained in those server logs—a painstaking process, to be sure.

You'd be better off implementing a tracking system, such as the software provided by WebTrends or similar vendors. These easy-to-use solutions are simple to install and can track not only your CTR but also your total conversion rates—or the number of people that not only clicked through, but signed up/registered/bought as well. Also, rather than reading volumes of server log materials, most solutions of this kind provide an easily generated full report. The Resources section at the back of this book lists a number of these providers.

MORE VARIABLES, MORE TESTS, MORE CODES

We've just reviewed how to set up a tracking system. The only unique variable was the lists used for each test. What if you want to test more than just lists, however? How do you set up promotions and campaigns with things like different offers, subject lines, message, and whether or not the promotion is plain-text or HTML? Let's go back to our key system and assign new codes for each variable:

Key:
Note: We can add the following to 1. Lists, and 2. Date:

3. Offer:
   LG = Lead Generation
   P = Paid
   1 = Free trial software
   2 = Free report
   3 = $20 Off
   4 = 20% off
4. Subject Line:
   S = Subject Line
   1 = Subject Line #1 (Question: "How Can You Compete . . .")
   2 = Subject Line #2 (Trial Call to Action: "Get Your Complementary . . .")
   3 = Subject Line #3 (Savings: "Save $20 on . . .")
5. Message (Note: You can showcase each unique message in your key, or reference its file location, or simply drop in the "heart of the message," or theme, as shown here:
   M = Message
   1 = Theme: Appeal to People with a Fear of Losing
   2 = Theme: Appeal to Opportunity Seekers
   3 = Theme: Appeal to Money-Conscious Individuals
6. Format:
   T = Text
   H = HTML
   R = Rich media (Note: We'll explore rich media e-mails in Chapter 10.)

Using the key above, you can see how easy it would be to apply the above codes and read the results from them. Here are some examples:

Test 1
1. http://www.ClickHereNowDoNotWait.com/specialofferpage.htm?V1C0605LG1S2M1T
2. http://www.ClickHereNowDoNotWait.com/specialofferpage.htm?V1C0605LG1S2M1H

The test, as you can see, is simply to determine whether the plain-text or the HTML promotion is stronger. The same list has simply been split into two, and all other variables—deployment date, offer, subject line, and message—are the same. Another thing to keep in mind is that if you split a list to test a variable, keep the quantities in each segment the same.

Test 2

1. http://www.ClickHereNowDoNotWait.com/specialofferpage.
   htm?V1C0605LG1S2M1T
2. http://www.ClickHereNowDoNotWait.com/specialofferpage.
   htm?V1C0605P3S2M1T
3. http://www.ClickHereNowDoNotWait.com/specialofferpage.
   htm?V1C0605LG2S2M1T
4. http://www.ClickHereNowDoNotWait.com/specialofferpage.
   htm?V1C0605P4S2M1T

Now the same list has been split into four equal groups. And this time, we can determine a few different things, based on the final results: The first two segments (listed in 1 and 2) pit one lead generation offer against one paid offer. The third and fourth segments (3 and 4) do the same. Additionally, this test will also tell us which lead generation offer—LG1 or LG2 (listed in 1 and 3) is stronger, and will also tell us which paid offer—P3 or P4 (2 and 4) is stronger. This is provided, of course, that we are using one list, and that list has been split into four equal *nths* of like-minded people, and that all other variables are the same within each segment.

TESTING RULES 101

Based on the previous examples, you've probably already figured out that there are indeed a few rules to keep in mind when testing. No matter what your business or offering, you'd be well advised to heed the following:

- *Test "apples to apples."* Test only one variable at a time. In the previous example, we saw how four different segments could yield four different pieces of information. However, notice that each segment contained only one determining factor that was different from the rest. Had we tried to test one segment of the list that had a different subject, message, and format against another segment of the list that had a different offer and format, we wouldn't have been able to learn anything. In other words, when one segment pulled a better response over another, we wouldn't have known whether that lift was due to the message or the format, because there were too many differences in variables. Keep in mind that the deployment date and time is also a variable, so if you've got four different segments/variables that you're testing, make sure that each goes out at the same date and time.
- *Assign keycodes for accurate and easy-to-read testing.* Depending on your business, make sure that the keycodes you assign to each test will give you the information you need to make good future decisions, as well as will make it easy for you to determine your best offers, messages, formats, etc.

The method that we just went over is just one way to assign keycodes. You may decide that there are other, simpler ways for you to get the same amount of information.

- *Retest, if necessary.* If your test results between two variables, for instance, are very close (as in within 5 to 10 percent of each other), you may want to think about retesting those same variables. It could be that they *do* yield similar results time and time again. However, it could also mean that an error occurred.
- *Test in statistically significant quantities.* We reviewed this earlier, but it is worth repeating for this section. As stated earlier, the test quantity for each list or segment should be a significant percentage (1/10 of a percent). Sometimes that means 3,000 is enough (if you were testing a total universe of 30,000) and sometimes that means that 15,000 is required to be statistically valid. Just remember that the quantity needs to give you a solid representation of the list or segment.
- *Apply your "lessons learned" to future campaigns and promotions.* This may sound like a no-brainer; but many marketers build their whole work lives around testing and, due to things like poor response record management, they never get around to rolling out with those winning results. If you find one subject line that pulls 50 percent better than your others, don't mess with success and continue to test this variable. Roll out with it until it invariably loses its power. That's the purpose of testing!

You can create, track, and report on tests of all different kinds of variables. It's a matter of staying organized, being diligent, and implementing solid processes and systems (manual or otherwise). Following are two sample reports. The first demonstrates a few testing results from a single campaign. The second shows the kinds of things you can learn across several campaigns.

As you can see, there's a lot to be learned. And a lot to be gained.

GOLFCOACHCONNECTION.COM TESTS AND READS RESULTS

GolfCoachConnection.com's first e-mail marketing campaign is finally under way!

Because opt-in lists are relatively expensive, the GolfCoachConnection.com team decided that it wanted to test the strengths of different lists before it rolled out the full promotion. See Figure 7.2. The team also decided to test two different subject lines to see which stimulated the most click-throughs:

Subject 1: Save strokes! FREE Golf Tips from Your Coach
Subject 2: Win a FREE Golf Swing Coaching Video Session!

FIGURE 7.2 Test Breakdown for GolfCoachConnection.com

Panel 1—Subject line 1	Panel 2—Subject line 2	Panel 3—Subject line 1	Panel 4—Subject line 2	Panel 5—Subject line 1	Panel 6—Subject line 2
Avid golfers	Avid golfers	Beginning golfers	Beginning golfers	Golfers with HHI $50K+	Golfers with HHI $50K+

Panel/Keycode	Click-throughs	Click-through rate (CTR)	Conversions (registrations or leads)	Conversion rate (as % of click-throughs)
Panel 1	345	11.5%	246	71%
Panel 2	636	21.2%	492	77%
Panel 3	729	24.3%	546	75%
Panel 4	366	12.2%	303	83%
Panel 5	147	4.9%	90	61%
Panel 6	216	7.2%	141	65%
Total test	2,439	13.6%	1,818	75%

To make sure that the results would be statistically significant (and because the total universe sizes were relatively small), the team included 3,000 names in each panel, for a total test quantity of 18,000.

Keycodes were set up as follows:

Panel 1: http://www.golfcoachconnection.com?ags1
Panel 2: http://www.golfcoachconnection.com?ags2
Panel 3: http://www.golfcoachconnection.com?bgs1
Panel 4: http://www.golfcoachconnection.com?bgs2
Panel 5: http://www.golfcoachconnection.com?50s1
Panel 6: http://www.golfcoachconnection.com?50s2

Panels 2 and 3 emerged as the clear winners among the lists, so the GCC team decided to roll out using expanded quantities of these lists only. The team was surprised by the relative weakness of Panels 5 and 6, given the strength of golf spending among this group. It speculated that this group's relative price insensitivity might require a different kind of offer to generate more response.

The team added this proposition to its growing list of ideas to test in future promotions.

FIGURE 7.3 GolfCoachConnection.com's Acquisitions Test Results

	Click-throughs	Click-through rate (CTR)	Conversions (registrations or leads)	Conversion rate
List 1 (Avid golfers, quantity = 36,000)	8,028	22.3%	5,904	16.4%
List 2 (Beginners, quantity = 36,000)	8,568	23.8%	6,192	17.2%
Total rollout	16,596	23.1%	12,096	16.8%
Test	1,365	22.8%	1,818	30.3%
Promotion totals (out of 90,000 e-mailed)	17,961	20.0%	13,914	15.5%

Rollout Results

Thanks to testing that showed the GolfCoachConnection.com team the strongest lists and subject lines to use, its first e-mail campaign was a success. See Figure 7.3. The team generated almost 2,000 more leads for the same amount of money that it spent on its recent direct mail campaign.

Of course, the quality of the leads remained to be tested. So the team started planning its first e-mail retention promotion.

GolfCoachConnection.com's Acquisition Campaign Rollout Results:

$20,000 advertising cost/13,914 leads = $1.52/lead

CHAPTER REVIEW/EXERCISES

1. Create a key for your upcoming test mailing. Assign unique codes for each variable you plan to test.

2. Set up your tests. Assign keycodes to your URLs.

3. If you e-mailed the following breakdowns/segment tests against each other, what would you learn? Would your results be accurate?
   a. Segment 1: Message 1, Subject Line 2, List A
   b. Segment 2: Message 2, Subject Line 2, List B
   c. Segment 3: Message 2, Subject Line 1, List C
   (Answer: You wouldn't learn anything concrete with such a test because there is more than one variable in every segment.)

PART THREE

Creative Pointers and Tricks of the Trade

The Dialogue: How to Speak to Your Prospects and Customers

OBJECTIVES

- Discover why the relationship with your customers is integral to your success.

- Look at dialogue and relationship-building strategies for introducing your company, products, and services.

Think about how you develop a friendship: You meet. You "click." You get to know each other.

That friendship—if properly cared for, and if all common values and viewpoints between the two parties are in place—will presumably blossom into a closer and deeper bond as time goes on. Your closest friends will make you laugh, make you cry, entertain you, listen to your complaints, and make you feel good about yourself. This is as it should be.

When you really think about it, building a "relationship" with our prospects and customers is really not that different. We introduce ourselves and get to know them just as they get to know us. And if we handle ourselves right, we will delight those folks who mean so much to us. We'll make them smile, listen to their woes, and make them feel valued and worthy of our "care."

As I have already suggested, e-mail is a fantastic place to build this kind of relationship, for several reasons. Because of the high quality presentations it can display—full color and graphics, even animation and video and audio—e-mail has the branding strength and the impact of television and radio. Because of the easy-to-read space it encompasses, as well as its frequency of use (*millions* use it regularly), it holds the "in-your-face" power and up-to-the-minute "newsworthiness" of print-based advertising, at a fraction of the cost.

Best of all, because of its method of delivery—that is, direct to the prospect/customer's eyeballs—the "bond" that can be created has exceptional possibilities. An e-mail promotion can be created in such a way as to sound like it is truly *one person* "speaking" to *one person*, rather than *one company* dictating or announcing to the *masses*.

For instance, you could get an opt-in e-mail from the president of Company X, where she describes why and how she started her company and what benefits the company offers to *you*. This "dialogue" can continue over time, as long as you accept her e-mails. As she promotes her products and services, she divulges more and more of her own personality and philosophies. As she does so, she is strengthening that bond, that relationship, with you. She's not just a businessperson spewing ads. She's the president of Company X and, gosh darn it, you've kind of grown to like her. Think about how you'd feel if you received a friendly e-mail from Michael Dell of Dell Computers, after you've opted in to receive Dell's e-mailed special offer announcements. It's not just about a sales pitch; his tone is warm and he appears to want to help you benefit from his products. If you do not ask to be unsubscribed from such communications, these e-mails from Mr. Dell continue. With every single one, the relationship evolves even further. And one day, you may even purchase something from one of these e-mails. That is the hope, anyway. Therein lies the beauty of a continuous e-mail dialogue.

Building a one-to-one relationship with a prospect or customer is one way to successfully promote with e-mail. Of course, not *all* winning e-mail promotions employ this tactic. But it is one of the basic strategies and—I cannot emphasize this enough—one of the true powers of e-mail marketing. We'll keep this in mind as we go through this and future sections.

To take those first steps towards developing that bond, you need to get into your typical customer's skin. Your goal is to create a friend, an advocate, a lifelong member of your business "family." You want the relationship with your customers to be tight as a drum. So tight, in fact, that if you sell birthday cakes and they need a birthday cake, they *immediately* think of you and your company and, more importantly, they *act*. The same goes for whatever product or service you're selling.

That kind of "loyalty in action" doesn't happen by accident, or even by luck. A good portion of the strategy behind it comes from building an effective dialogue, which boils down to *presentation*. In other words, how well do your e-mails represent you, your "spokesperson," and/or your company? How clear are you in who you are, what you do, what you offer? What is the tone of your message? Who are you talking to? Does your "voice" fit your audience? If your e-mail has been sent in HTML, does your design appeal to your target market, as far as color and layout and form?

We'll get into details of good copy, design, and formatting later in this section, but for now, let's focus on the backbone of every good e-mail presentation: *prospecting* and *retaining* customers.

THE INTRODUCTION

In the last section, we went over a few components and strategies for acquiring new customers through e-mail—including the offer, the lists, and the tests to set you up for success. Just as important, however, is the message itself and, perhaps more importantly, the manner in which you convey, or communicate, that message.

Think again of what happens when you first meet someone. Introductions are made. Pleasantries are exchanged. Maybe you develop rapport, maybe you don't. You need to keep this in mind when "introducing" yourself directly to a prospect for the first time as well, no matter if it be on a sales floor, by a telephone call, or, of course, via an e-mail. With that in mind, following is a list of *best practices* for "speaking" to your target audience for the very first time:

- *Tell them who you are right away.* Your introductory e-mail can have an incredibly compelling subject line and an offer that is out of this world, but the good stuff will get quickly diluted if recipients don't know who the sender is. Make that great offer a part of your company or business that is offering it. Instead of the generic, "Announcing 50% off our normally low, low prices . . . ," come up with a way to make the offer—and the introduction—at the same time. A better approach would be, "HaveWeGotADealForYou. com is proud to present an unheard-of offer—50% off . . ." Yes, this has been simplified for example purposes, but you get the picture. Make it clear at the onset who you are.
- *Address who they are.* It doesn't mean that you need to address them by name. Some list vendors don't offer this personalization option. However, even though you are using 100 percent opt-in lists, you should still expect them to want to know, "Why me?" So acknowledge who they are. Often, this can be accomplished in the salutation at the beginning, as in "Dear Business Builder," or "Dear Fitness Fanatic," or "Dear Savvy Investor." Or it can be in the subject line or introductory paragraph, as in "Breakthrough Alternative Therapy for Arthritis Sufferers . . ."

- *Tell them why you're e-mailing them.* Make your purpose (meaning your offer) crystal-clear from the very beginning. Don't even attempt to camouflage the fact that you're trying to sell them *something*. Bring your offer to the top of your e-mail and make it stand out.
- *Speak in their terms.* In other words, you already know—at the list level—that if you're targeting teenagers, you're most likely not going to find them on a list of hardcore investors. And vice versa. From a targeting perspective, you know who your audience is made up of, at a demographic, geographic, and possibly even a psychographic level. Carry that same knowledge through to your message. Your teens will most likely not respond to language geared towards an older audience. One of the best methods I've found to prevent this miscommunication is to pretend that one of your best customers is sitting right in front of you. Sit back for a moment and imagine him or her. What does he (or she) look like? What is he wearing? Is he friendly or sullen? Comical or serious? What is his income? What kind of car does he drive? Imagine having a conversation with this customer as he's sitting right in front of you. *Now* imagine that you're telling him about your offer. Your interaction—your dialogue—is based, in large part, on your prospect's personality and style. Your own personality and style—the tone and theme of your message—will follow suit.

AS THE RELATIONSHIP EVOLVES

The more communications you have with your prospects and customers, and the more value you can provide within those communications, the more comfortable they will feel with you and the more they will look forward to receiving your messages. So you can see how vital the dialogue is to your core communications . . . to your success in these efforts.

Another key component to your dialogue-relationship development is the degree to which you make yourself (your customer service people, etc.) accessible. Many times, a transaction is not completed simply due to the fact that a question has been left unanswered. Sometimes the e-mail message isn't clear. Or sometimes, even if people *do* have enough interest to click through, the "landing" page on the advertiser's site doesn't provide enough information. Or it doesn't provide the *right* kind of information—the all-important (to some prospects) contact information.

The lesson? Even if you are beyond the introduction, or even further along than that, with those prospects and customers, *always* provide an immediate means to contact you or your service personnel. Or, at the very least, between the e-mail message itself *and* the landing page where the e-mail message "points," always provide enough information for those people to make a decision.

As this dialogue continues, your e-mail message's role is to play the part of a trusted and loyal friend. We'll explore plenty of actual copywriting details and best practices in the next chapter. And Part Four will go over customer relationship building strategies. *This* chapter is only meant to lay the groundwork, to give you some things to keep in mind as you create your messages, as you build your customer dialogues. Much more with regards to the relationship-building process—including personalization, segmentation, and more—is coming up.

CHAPTER REVIEW

1. A good portion of customer loyalty comes from the relationship you have created with your customers.

2. When prospecting through e-mail, be sure to do the following as soon as possible: introduce your company, your products and services, and your offer.

3. Know your audience and speak to them in their unique language and terms.

4. Make sure you've answered all of their questions.

5. Give recipients the opportunity and the method to respond or find out more.

CHAPTER 9

Copywriting for E-mail: Best Practices

OBJECTIVES

- Define how copy sells.
- Discover your prospects and customers.
- Examine how sales copy is constructed.
- Learn the hidden rules to solid copy.
- Outline the components to winning e-mail copywriting.

The joy of *words*. They can instigate. And excite. They can bring out the rawest of emotions—from the highest of the highs to the lowest of the lows. Yes, if crafted properly, words can even *sell*.

Of course, that's not news to anyone who's ever been involved in direct marketing or advertising of any kind. It's a fact: words have power. It doesn't matter if they're written on paper, served up in cyberspace, or spoken.

HOW GOOD COPY SELLS

Before we get into the specifics of copywriting for e-mail, let's take a look at how properly crafted copy works.

Essentially, the art of selling—and of being sold—boils down to the human psyche. What truly motivates us to buy something, or to even respond to an offer where a sale isn't involved? In a word, it all comes down to our emotions. Although we may often buy on impulse because something stirred our emotions or gripped our hearts—in actuality, we do not want to be "sold." We want to be the ones making the decisions about what we will or will not respond to.

I used to sell new homes. One thing I was always taught is that most people buy a home because something about it "hit" them emotionally. That is one reason why, in just about every community where I sold, we would have two or three "model" homes that were completely furnished and beautifully decorated. And the decorators would do their best to make sure the models had that "lived in" look. They'd fill it with fake televisions and computers, plastic plates with plastic eggs and bacon sitting on the breakfast table, glasses of plastic wine on the mini-bar, etc. The goal, of course, was to have people mentally "move in" to the home. Our jobs, as the salespeople, were to showcase the benefits of each home, get the prospects to pick out their favorite, and then we'd move in for (an attempt at) the final close. It was actually a lot more complicated than it sounds, but you get the idea.

What I learned is that the buying decision is an emotional one—nine times out of ten. However, what I also learned is that prospects/potential buyers needed to have their emotional decisions substantiated by real live (and beneficial) facts to back them up. If buyers had objections, we had to come up with ways to get around them. So, for instance, for every lot or homesite that we showed, we had to uncover and come up with the features—as well as true benefits of those features—for every single site, despite how poor the location. If the homesite backed up to a street—hey, at least it had that great southern exposure (a feature). The benefit to southern exposure, of course, was that the home would have wonderful light all day long. If it backed up to another home—well, at least it had a huge lot (a feature) where you could plant plenty of trees (the benefit).

It was a logical set of steps that took a prospect from Point A (just a "looker" in the early stages) to Point B (a bona fide "buyer" who signed on the dotted line). It was a process that had a momentum to it. See Figure 9.1. Here's how it typically worked. Prospects came into the sales office cold, that is, their attitude was, "I'm not buying anything today." We'd then walk them through the model homes and the available lot locations, all the while pointing out features and benefits. As their excitement grew, so did their list of objections. We would, of course, have an answer

FIGURE 9.1 From Prospect to Close

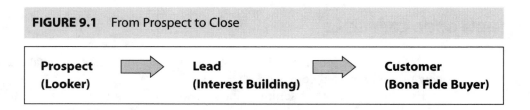

to every single one of those objections. In fact, more times than not, we'd turn those objections into true benefits.

The process really isn't that different when you're selling with the printed word. If you've ever bought from a newspaper, magazine print ad, or direct mail piece, I'm sure that when you first started reading it, you didn't expect to buy anything. However, as the copy drew you in further and further, your excitement about the product grew. But wait, you would think, you can't do this. You can't buy this product or service because of this and this and this. As you read further, you discover that, yes—you *can* buy this. Because this is the answer you've been waiting for!

Do you see how that works? What I have just described is the underpinning, or the foundation, of what makes good copy sell. You have to propel your prospects—your readers—into a self-generating process of their own sales momentum. That momentum starts slowly and with each passing objection, quickly grows until eventually it reaches the point where—if the product is right for them—they will respond. Best of all, when they finally do respond, it is because of their own impetus, and not because some salesperson sold them. The reasons why are based on emotion—emotion built with logic, benefits, and momentum.

KNOW THY PROSPECT

Before you can begin to develop those emotional ties with your prospect, however, you must first get to know her. And I mean really know her. This is a must to establish the necessary "rapport." In any type of selling environment, whether real or virtual, you need to have rapport. And a good portion of it comes from *knowledge*.

What's the best way to do this when you're essentially dealing with nameless, faceless people? That's easy (and then again, it's *not*): Research and discover. Here are five ways to do this:

1. *Customer profile.* Take a look at your company's customer profile, or at least review segments of your database. Study it in terms of where your

customers live, as well as any demographic information you can pull. Begin to form a picture in your mind of your typical customer.

2. *Successful promotions.* If your company has promoted with direct mail, or any other measurable direct response venue, review the most successful promotions. Look for any references to the target audience—the customer. Note the language and the tone, as well as any descriptions therein. Hunt for the word "you" as it refers to the customer, and begin to piece together just who that promotion was speaking to.

3. *Your competition.* Speaking of promotions, review your competitors' direct response mailings or print ads (or even recall their radio or television ads that have a direct call to action). There may be subtle differences between their best customers and yours; but there may be some crossover. At the very least, you'll learn more about the differences between the two.

4. *Seed yourself.* An excellent way to get to know more about your potential customers, and to keep on top of your what your competitors are doing with e-mail is to seed yourself—or subscribe—to their e-mailed newsletters or offers. You can do this across media and also see what they're sending in the postal mail, etc. This also will allow you to learn plenty of things about timing of offers, types of creative, strategies, etc.

5. *Practice and pretend.* This may sound silly, but it helped me enormously when I was in sales. It also helps me when I write copy. Now that you've determined who your best customers are and have a "picture" of them in your head, the practice comes in *pretending* that you're interacting with them. Have a conversation with them. Chat. Mingle. Sit around the living room coffee table with them. Enjoy their company and let them enjoy yours, as well as your own natural personality. Take the dialogue that you've developed with them and remember: therein lies the tone and the rhythm that you need to use with them.

HOW GOOD COPY IS CONSTRUCTED

As I mentioned a moment ago, the venue where your copy is "showcased"—whether it's a postal mailing, a print ad, or an e-mail—is much the same as a physical sales floor. In other words, the way in which you build sales momentum with your reader is similarly structured. See Figure 9.2. The copy embedded within your own sales arena should strive to follow some version of the following format. It should at least include most, if not all, of the components therein.

- *The "greeting" and the interest begins.* Also known as your headline (or subject line, as in the case of an e-mail), this is where you need to tanta-

FIGURE 9.2 Turning a Prospect into a Customer

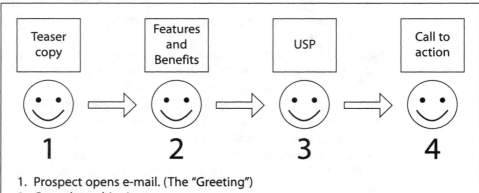

1. Prospect opens e-mail. (The "Greeting")
2. Copy draws him in.
3. Excitement (momentum) builds.
4. He has to have what you're selling.

lize. I've literally spent hours upon hours in developing solid headlines because they are so incredibly important to response. Why? If the headline doesn't cut it—if it doesn't pique the interest of your reader—they will read no further. And that's a death knell as far as response goes. We'll explore tactics for developing winning subject lines shortly.

• *The interest grows.* Now that you have your reader's attention, it's time to take that attention and interest and build upon it. This is where your promise is made. Perhaps the promise is your no-can-lose offer. Or in your special savings package. This is the area where you spill your guts, so to speak, but delicately, and in a succinct and compelling manner. You need to alert the reader what she's about to undertake if she reads any further. But you need to position that undertaking as a pleasant experience, and one with great benefits if she chooses to accept.

• *The tease.* You want to tell the reader enough to hold and develop her interest, but you also need to hold back a few things. This will pique her curiosity even more, with the end result being that she will read further and may even respond.

• *Features and benefits duly noted.* Of course, what sales floor would be complete without a sales staff extolling the virtues of your products and services? Somewhere in the text of a successful promotion lies plenty of mention of features and benefits. And when I say benefits, I mean direct benefits to the reader—the target potential customer.

- *The laying out of your unique selling proposition (USP)*. This is what sets a company apart from its competition. Is it pricing? Customer philosophy? Attention to service? To give a more detailed example, perhaps a company offers an outstanding product that is built to last, yet its prices are way above its competitors. The fact that the products are so far superior, and price is not even an issue with buyers, is part of the company's USP.
- *The answer to the promise*. Presumably, if the reader has read a majority of your sales letter, she wants to find out how you can live up to her expectations. When you're selling with words, and because you can't give her a live demonstration of what your offer is, you need to form a picture in her mind. *Show* her, in her own mind, how your product can work for her. If you can, provide her with other customer testimonials to back up what you are saying. Give her proof.
- *The final close*. Although in reality, a solid example of copy "closes" in bits and pieces from beginning to end, there is always a definite conclusion when that final close must take place. Wrap up your offer, your benefits, your USP, and why your product is the best solution . . . and *ask* for the order. You want to do it in such a way to make it as easy as possible for the reader to respond (e.g., a toll-free number to call, or provide an easy click of an e-mail). Just remember to *ask for that response*. To entice them further, sometimes it's a good idea to hit the reader with another "carrot," or perk. In other words—offer an added incentive if she responds *now*. This is something to keep in mind for all your promotions, and not just e-mail.

In a few moments, we'll take a look at the specific how-to's of each component above, especially as each relates to e-mail. We will also see how this type of format fits into an e-mail promotion. Before we get into all that, however, we must define some of the nitty-gritty details—the "must-knows" of solid copy.

COPY DETAILS AND TRICKS OF THE TRADE

There are a few not-so-obvious "rules" to good copywriting. Apply them and you're sure to increase the reception of your sales copy. Not to mention you'll probably increase your response rate in the process.

Rule 1. Avoid Repetitive Statements and Redundancies (Was *that* Redundant?)

One mistake that I see constantly in lengthy e-mail promotions is a thought that is repeated more than once. In an e-mail, particularly, you don't have time to be verbose, but you must give your reader every reason why he should accept your offer. It used to be that "short and sweet" was the way to go in an e-mail, but that's not necessarily the standard anymore. And my guess is it probably won't be ever again. Testing long versus short will help *you* determine what's best for your business.

Take one last good look at your final copy. Check for areas that can be chopped because you've said the same thing, using different words, in other areas. The goal is to have as your final product an attention-grabbing, yet tight, piece of sales prose.

Rule 2. Write Like You Talk

Yes, I've said this before (now who's being redundant?), but it bears repeating. You want to give the reader—the prospect, *your* potential customer—the feeling that someone really is speaking directly to her. Keep the conversation flowing. Even though your reader can't respond or talk back as she's reading, you still can address this one-way flow of information by anticipating her every objection, then answering each—one by one. It's all part of the building, or the construction, of your copy. Lay out the features and benefits; demonstrate your offer and/or products; showcase your USP. The trick is to do it all in a conversational manner.

Rule 3. Don't Be Concerned with Rules

Grammatical rules, that is. I've seen sales copy come across my desk or arrive in my home mail or e-mail box that was picture-perfect as far as grammar, punctuation, etc. But it did nothing for me. It didn't thrill me. It didn't entice me to read on. Sure, it was perfect, but it was *boring*.

A key part of being able to write conversationally is to be able to create a rhythm and a flow in your writing. If you were to take a live conversation, transcribe it to print, then dissect it into adjectives, adverbs, complete sentences, and phrases, you'd find that the spoken dialogue is not always grammatically correct. That is because we, as humans, do not talk like robots. We have thoughts and feelings and experiences all bubbling to the surface as we speak. We do not think in terms of, "Did I say that correctly?" or "Was that grammatically correct?" *That* is precisely why we need to write in that same manner—the manner in which we speak. Beware, however, that a verbal message contains vocal nuances and body language that written copy cannot express.

Rule 4. Punctuate for Emphasis

Every seasoned copywriter knows that punctuation has a lot to do with how the reader "drinks in" the words. In and of itself, punctuation can determine a good portion of that just mentioned ebb and flow and rhythm in the copy.

With print and direct mail, *italics* and underlining and **bold** can work wonders to help create a special rhythm and emphasis on certain key words and phrases. With e-mail, on the other hand, because of the readability of the online medium (or the lack thereof), italics and underlining do not emphasize because they are difficult to read. We will get into more details shortly.

Rule 5. Get Excited about Your Product(s)

This may very well be one of *the* most important things you need to know. Because you are selling with emotion, and writing with emotion, it stands to reason that *you* must get emotional about what you're selling! When I truly *love* a product or company, I can come up with tons of benefits, and can pour out my passion for them in my prose. So *love* what you sell—and if you can't truly love it, then *pretend* that you do. That excitement, that energy, that emotion will come through.

COPYWRITING FOR THE E-MAIL LANDSCAPE

Now for the good stuff. Keeping in mind everything you have read in this chapter thus far, we can now delve into specific copy points as they are used in an e-mail promotion. First, let's quickly examine, from a writer's perspective, the five main parts of an e-mail:

1. Subject line—read first on your list of new mail
2. From line (a.k.a., the sender)—read second either on your list of new mail or after you've opened an e-mail
3. Introduction
4. Body copy
5. Call to action

See Figure 9.3 to understand where each part appears.

FIGURE 9.3 The Five Parts of an E-mail Offer

```
From: Sample E-mailer [mailto: you@yourdotcom.com]◄──[ 2. From line ]
Sent: Tuesday, August 08, 2001 3:21 PM
Subject: Here's YOUR Chance to Win a ◄───────[ 1. Subject line ]
One-of-a-Kind Dream Vacation
-------------------------------------------------------------

Here's YOUR Chance to Win a One-of-a-Kind ◄───[ 3. Introduction ]
Dream Vacation*

http://www.URL.com

Ever sail the azure waters of the West Indies?      [ 4. Body Copy ]
Explore fairy-tale castles of the Bavarian Alps?
Discover the cliffs and tiny villages of seaside
Greece? Now you can . . . thanks to the travel
guidebook writers and experts at 12Degrees who
specialize in creating customized vacations of a
lifetime! To find out how you can enjoy the
custom trip of your dreams, visit today:

http://www.URL.com

Our Privacy Pledge: 12Degrees will use your
personal information solely for the purpose of
enhancing your experience with our site. We
will not sell, rent, or trade your personal
information to third parties. For more
information on 12Degrees' Privacy Policy,
click here:

http://www.URL.com

*Your unforgettable getaway can be valued as
high as $15,000! And there is absolutely
no obligation, so visit today! ◄────────[ 5. Call to action ]
```

THE SUBJECT LINE

The subject line is the first opportunity you have to make an impression on your prospect/reader. Make it a good one. The trick is to be able to write a subject line that is enticing, yet at the same time not so enticing that the offer sounds completely out of reach—as in the case of most spam e-mail. (Typical spam subject line: "Earn $40,000 a month in your spare time!" You can almost always spot the unsolicited e-mails—even before you actually open them—just based on subject lines such as these.)

Think of it this way: You have mere seconds—probably less than *three* total—to impress the recipient so much that she is persuaded to open the e-mail. In fact, many people have compared the subject line to the catchy headline or teaser on an envelope. Actually, that's not a bad analogy because both the subject line and the headline have the same purpose—to persuade people to read further.

So the idea is to grab the reader's attention without coming across as a spammer. Therein lies the challenge. Your best bet? Stay clean, write tight, do not be too provocative, and demonstrate a benefit that is realistic. And remember—you only have about 30 to 40 characters, including spaces (about five to eight words), to show your stuff. Most e-mail programs will only display a limited amount of space in their preview window, which is the area that the reader sees before she opens her e-mail. So make it good. Pack your best wallop—your biggest benefit, your most interesting statement, your most enticing teaser—into those first few words. You also may want to follow one or more of the approaches below.

The direct approach. Unless a "cutesy" tone truly fits your offering, as well as your audience, do not try to be cute or funny. State the facts. If it's an acquisitions promotion, who are you and what, exactly, is your outstanding offer? A subject line need not be overtly clever to be effective. Take a look at two very successful and long-lasting headlines from the direct mail world, both written in a matter-of-fact (yet compelling) style:

- *We're looking for people to write children's books* (Institute of Children's Literature)
- *A Perfect Cup of Coffee.* (Gevalia Kaffe)

The two above are brilliant in their simplicity. The first works (and has continued to work for decades) because it appeals to writers of all kinds. The headline contains a need, and any author or author-in-waiting would love to find out more about an organization that could potentially need *him*. What author wouldn't? If this were a subject line, in all likelihood, only the "We're looking for people to write . . ." would be visible in most e-mail programs' previewing windows. But that is all right—that is the most inviting piece of the sentence.

The Gevalia example immediately tells the reader if he reads on, he can expect to find out either how to make or how to get a perfect cup of coffee. Coffee lovers around the world are bound to want to learn more. The key to this approach is to entice in a no-nonsense manner.

The benefits approach. No matter what approach you use (whether it's one or a combination of several), you should always strive to weave a benefit into your subject line. Entice people to read further by the possible benefits the subject line promises. In other words, if they have a problem or a desire that you can provide a solution for, then they will yearn to hear more. Take a look at two solid headlines—one was the envelope headline in a very well-known Literary Guild direct mail package. The second was used as a subject line in Quicken.com's e-mailed newsletter:

- *We're going to spoil you!* (Literary Guild)
- *More Ways to Make the Most of Your Money* (Quicken.com)

Each is effective in its own way. Both offer a promise of rich rewards. It is *that* promise that is the draw for the readers.

The question approach. Questions work because they *involve* the reader. As they read the question, they inadvertently try to answer it in their own heads.

- *Do* you *have what it takes to be a millionaire?* (Hume Publishing)
- *Want to be financially independent?* (Hume again!)

The strength of the question approach, of course, boils down to the answer. Again, benefits are *alluded* to with the use of this approach.

The teaser approach. When you're promoting content, as in the case of online or offline publishers, teaser subject lines are easy to incorporate because you can use your most interesting tidbits of information as part of what is not yet disclosed. Here are a few good teasers from a couple of well-known publishers:

- *What never to eat on an airplane.* (Boardroom Reports)
- *What credit card companies don't tell you.* (Boardroom Reports)
- *Trigger your body's own natural immunities.* (Rodale Press)
- *Live the (intellectual) adventure!* (Levenger.com)

But teasers can also come across as campy and downright silly, if used improperly. The key here is to make sure you can address what's promised in the teaser.

The cultural tie-in approach. If you can write a subject line that fits your offering, and can tie it in to a newsworthy or popular piece of information from the outside world, you can grab attention. For instance, Stamps.com came up with a timely subject line right around the time when the television show *Who Wants to Be a Millionaire?* reached its height of popularity. The subject line read, "Is that your final answer?"—host Regis Philbin's famous one-liner in the show.

The personalized approach. This approach could, of course, be used with any of the other approaches above. With the right software or solutions provider (which we will learn about in future chapters), you can add a name or some other customized piece of information to your house e-mail promotions. It can certainly go a long way in drawing attention, but may lose its staying power as more and more marketers take advantage of this approach.

As you think of new and creative one-liners for your subject line, think in terms of what would most entice your prospects—your target audience—to open and read on. Depending on your market, you may want to use a customized version of one of the ideas below:

- *Your Gift Certificate Is in This E-mail.* This contains a benefit (the gift certificate) and it also arouses curiosity (what is the gift certificate for?).
- *Reply Within 5 Days And . . .* As long as it's clear who the sender is, this approach can be used quite effectively. The use of ellipses in a subject line provokes the recipient to read further to see how the sentence ends.
- *How to Have ____ [fill in the blank] Forever.* This is definitely a teaser, yet it holds the promise of some (hopefully) terrific benefit. The reader is moved to read on to find out how to get that benefit.
- *Is Your [Wife, Mother-in-Law, Boss, etc.] Driving You Nuts? Here's Help . . .* This one presents a problem, and the offer is the solution. It also can hit the right buttons, emotionally speaking, with certain people. And, as we saw earlier, emotional buttons can be hot buttons.

Of course, if all else fails and you're promoting an e-commerce offering, you can always go back to the tried-and-true—that is, the discount/special/coupon/$$ off approach. But think about this: When 90 percent of the commercial e-mail that you receive touts "$20 off . . ." and "Save 10% on your next . . .", doesn't that somehow lessen the value of these types of offers? Be creative. Think in terms of true benefits, aside from any cost savings.

Here are two more (and remember these because we'll take a look at the remainder of the copy later in this chapter):

- "YOUR CHILD can STAR in an amazing sports highlights video—FREE"
- "Welcome Artisans . . . Your First Sale Is On Us"

THE *FROM* LINE (A.K.A., THE SENDER)

This is the second information a recipient will read—the first being the subject line. Some people will want to know who the sender is before they double-click and open up the e-mail fully. Look at this space as an opportunity to be creative and stand out among the crowd of e-mail marketers out there. There are some things to be mindful of, however, depending on whether you're in acquisitions or retention mode.

Acquisitions. If you're prospecting with opt-in lists, always be sure to find out how much customization the list vendor can provide. For instance, many of them either cannot or will not change the sender from the list owner or vendor's name, simply because they do not want their list members to become confused by the unknown name and think they are being spammed. Some list vendors will allow a full name change, where you can use either the name of your company or the name of your CEO, VP of marketing, customer service director, etc., to fill in the "from" line.

Use a real person's name whenever possible to enhance the one-to-one aspect of your communication. Keep in mind that if recipients hit "reply," they won't, in all likelihood, be able to send an e-mail to the person in the "from" line because it will either be sent directly back to the list vendor, or it will go to a non-working address. When in doubt, provide a working e-mail address in one or several locations within your copy.

Retention. When you're dealing with your house list, of course, you have more leeway . . . *and* more room to be creative. Many e-mail marketers simply use their company name and if it's well-branded, that is often enough to generate interest. Others, such as Send.com, use the name of their CEO. I'm a regular user and a fan of Send.com, and every once in a while, I'll receive a quick e-mail "from" Mike Lannon, its CEO and founder. I look forward to these e-mails because they are not sent too often, and they always include something of timely value to me. By the way, the subject lines are often personalized.

Determine how you want to be positioned in the marketplace, then create a captivating "sender" to use in your "from" line. If you sell flowers online, have your house promotions come from "Your Flower Shop." If you sell investing advice, your offering can be from "Your Investing Guru." If you're marketing business services for the decision makers at small companies, your e-mail might be from "Your Favorite Business Resource." Of course, your sender doesn't always have to start with "Your" and then follow with a synopsis of what your company does. That is just one idea. Use it. Expand on it. Or think of some other creative way to position your company for maximum response.

THE INTRODUCTION

Also called the opening statement, it is the first thing your reader sees if and when he decides to open up the e-mail. This is where your promise is made. And it is also where the reader's hope begins—his hope that you can deliver on that promise. From here on out, you have to grab, and maintain, his attention. If you don't, you will lose him.

In an e-mail promotion, the length of the introduction is typically quite brief—no more than one short paragraph. Sometimes it is woven directly into the body of a promotion. Sometimes it mimics the subject line verbatim.

This promise is posed at the beginning so that by the time the reader finishes reading it, he is completely aware of who you are, why you're sending the e-mail, and what your special offer is. Presumably, if you can hold his interest up to this point, you have someone who is at least fairly interested in what you have to offer.

And here's an important note: Because you still have the attention of your prospect/reader at this point, it would behoove you to catch him while you can. In other words, add a live link to the text that holds this promise. It doesn't have to be the only link within your promotion. As you'll see in a few moments, it is recommended that you include more than one link within each promo. If the reader is interested, he'll click. Once he's on your site, he'll then be one step closer to fulfilling your final call to action.

Tavolo promotes with very colorful and well-designed HTML e-mails that almost look like online minicatalogs. See Figure 9.4 for a sample page. One of Tavolo's promotions heralded the subject line, "Take a Southern Picnic!" The sender was Tavolo, of course. And the introductory statement, which was more of another headline, read, "Here's a Picnic That Packs a Punch!" You can "hear" the promise there. In fact, this headline linked directly to the Tavolo site if people clicked on it. The rest of the e-mail showcased all of Tavolo's products that fulfilled this promise—picnic baskets and cheese biscuit mixes and chicken barbeque spice rub. We'll get into more details on the body of the e-mail in the next section. For now, though, let's go back to those two promotions that were introduced in the subject line section:

1. The following introduction presents the offer and the sender at the same time. The benefits are made clear: (1) YOUR child can become a star and (2) It's FREE.

   ```
   "FREE trial offer--Your child can star in an amazing
   sports highlights video . . . FREE when you sign up at
   [URL]"
   ```

   The rest of the copy goes on to explain how the product, a Web-based video editing tool, works. It presents the information in a lively, engaging format. Again, the promise is fulfilled.

FIGURE 9.4 Some Pages Look Like Minicatalogs

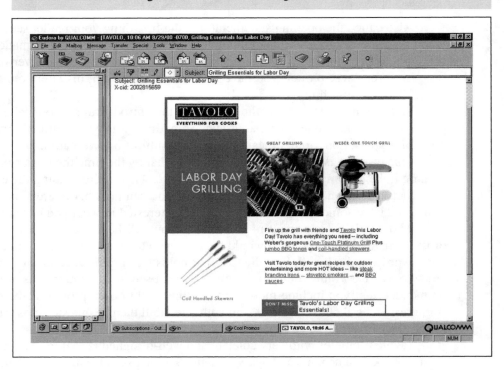

2. This next introduction is longer. The idea here is for the reader to develop
a sense for the site's unique selling proposition, as well as to begin the desire for the benefits—the site's promise:

> "Welcome to OneMADE, a thriving online community of
> talented artisans and passionate buyers. Now YOU can
> have a highly visible "storefront" to showcase your
> handcrafted items. Best of all, register now and you
> won't pay ANY commission on your first sale. (And trust
> us--you WILL have a first sale. And a second. And a
> third . . .)"

In this intro, two promises are made: First, that the artists and craftspeople that receive this message will save money on their first sale. And
second, that there will be more sales to follow. Again, the rest of the message contained in the body goes on to explain how and why the site
works.

The one thing to remember about this very visible, very important area of your promotion is to make the benefits and the offer completely clear for the reader. They may have opened the message due to curiosity or the catchy subject line. But the introduction is where you can make your offer, products, and company truly shine. However, you have to be careful not to leave room for any doubt or questions up until this point.

THE BODY

You can probably already tell that the body of your message is where you "bring it home." It's where you explain how you're going to provide the benefits, as outlined in your subject line or intro. It's also where you're going to prove why your solution is the only solution for your readers at that time. Just remember that this is an e-mail and that most people do not want to read through a lengthy tome. Make it snappy, and wow your readers with every sentence and phrase. Load it with benefit-rich copy, show them what you've got, and they're bound to be yours.

Body Copy

Figure 9.5 shows the body copy for the sports video site, introduced earlier. As far as the content goes, this copy works for several reasons. We'll go through them one by one.

- *Benefits.* As far as content goes, notice that the very first question, "Are you one of those proud parents . . . ," leads to one benefit after another. Literally. Read the copy again. Just about every sentence contains a true advantage to the target audience—the parents. The first benefit answers the appeal to pride. The message then goes on to describe the benefits of the tool itself. It then casually mentions the fact that there is no special equipment or software to buy. And it is easy to use. The benefits do not let up. That is what you should strive for in your body copy—nonstop benefits. As soon as the benefits are not clear, your momentum comes to a screeching halt.
- *The USP.* The unique selling proposition also is made clear. The ease of use, the free starter kit, and the star power of sportscaster Chris Berman all serve to make this a completely unique product—a must for every sports loving family.
- *The offer.* To drive home the offer, it is clearly stated and punctuated in both the introduction, as well as in the body copy.

FIGURE 9.5 Sports Video Body Copy

Are you one of those proud parents who likes to videotape your young athlete in action?

Well now you can turn your game footage into a thrilling sports highlights video starring YOUR child! Complete with upbeat music, graphics, and action calls from acclaimed sportscaster, Chris Berman! FREE!

Sportscapsule.com lets you turn ordinary game footage into EXTRAordinary sports highlights of your child that you can enjoy forever. And you don't need to buy any special software or equipment.

Just sign up at http://www.sportscapsule.com by [DATE] and we'll send you a FREE Starter Kit right away! At no obligation to you.

Here's how it works.

* STEP 1--Send us your favorite video footage using the postage-paid mailer in your FREE Starter Kit.

* STEP 2--We'll transfer it to CD-ROM and send it back to you, along with your original videotape.

* STEP 3--Go to Sportscapsule.com and create the most amazing sports highlights video . . . starring your child! It's easy. With Sportscapsule.com's point-and-click editing tools, adding sports-themed music . . . colorful graphics . . . and sportscaster's live calls to your child's best plays is as simple as pressing "Start" and "Stop."

And there you have it. It's FREE. It's easy. It's something to cheer about! So sign up today at http://www.sportscapsule.com!

- *Prove it.* Proof can be demonstrated in a number of ways. In this case, due to the fact that the product was an introductory offer and was so new that there were not yet any users, the proof was shown in the three easy-to-follow steps of how to use the product. What could be any easier?

Details and that extra "Oomph." The format of your copy plays an integral part in its success. This is because the online landscape creates a different kind of a place to read text. Long blocks of copy can be tiring on the eyes. Also, many people are impatient when they get an e-mail. Even if they're interested in the offer, they may not be interested to read the entire e-mail. It is for reasons such as these that you should follow these well-heeled "rules":

- *Break up the copy into small paragraphs.* The idea is to hold the interest of the readers with the use of bite-sized and easy-to-read chunks of compelling copy.
- *"Sprinkle" links (located with your calls to action) throughout the message.* You'll remember that, in this particular example, there was a link in the introduction. And, as you can see, there are two more in the body copy. Some people like to click at the beginning of a message, simply because they do not want to sift through the entire offer. Others need as much detail as possible before they decide whether to respond or not, so they need to read through until the end. For these reasons, some of the most successful promotions have included call to action links at the top, middle, and end.
- *Create a sense of urgency.* This message clearly tells the reader that he or she must sign up for the free starter kit by a certain date or lose the advantage of that offer. People don't like to miss out on things. Create a strong desire, as well as a strong sense of value for the offer, and they will *not* want to lose it.
- *Use capitalization for emphasis.* With plain text in the online space, you have to be careful about certain types of punctuation. Unlike the world of direct mail, italics don't always cut it because many e-mail servers convert them back to nonitalicized formats. The same problem affects underlining.
    Notice how the writer capitalized words that she wanted to punch up. Not only does it make the reader highlight those words and phrases in his own mind, it also makes him pause for just a moment. That pause can help him reflect and rereflect upon the offer that is presented to him. The more time he has to think, the more time he has to make his decision.

If you remember nothing else, remember this: Effective body copy for e-mail promotions boils down to these six things:

1. Your claim or promise appears to be sound.
2. The benefits are made crystal-clear.
3. Your USP is highlighted effectively.
4. A sense of urgency is created with a limited time or similar offer.
5. You've made it easy to read.
6. You've made it easy to respond.

THE CLOSE

We've already seen one way to close the deal—that is, by embedding more than one call to action link within your copy. But what is necessary to say at those critical points? How do you ask for the order?

First, you need to sum it all up for the reader. As you can see in Figure 9.5, the writer ended it with a blanket statement that encapsulated all of her main points: "And there you have it. It's FREE. It's easy. It's something to cheer about! So sign up today at http://www.URL.com!" How could it have been made even more special? You could have given the reader another "carrot."

Where's the Carrot?

What is this carrot that I keep talking about? In promotional terms, it's an additional incentive for a prospect to respond to an offer. Many marketers show their carrot early on, in an attempt to enhance their promotions from the get-go. Don't make that mistake. If your offer is sound and there is already a strong series of benefits attached therein, the carrot can be saved for the end.

In the case of the sports video site above, the carrot could have been a free pack of VHS videos. But the trick with this type of incentive is that, because it is mentioned once—and only at the end—the offer must be if they act now. That is the strength of the carrot—it can get people to respond immediately, but the necessary directive must be there. In other words, it can't just be, "We'll also throw in this three-pack of VHS videos." It has to be, "Click here NOW and we'll . . ." Again, you're creating a benefit, while at the same time creating a strong sense of urgency. So find that premium, that carrot, that your prospects won't want to resist.

GOLFCOACHCONNECTION.COM CREATES SOME COPY

Up until this point, the marketing team at GolfCoachConnection.com has created a strategy, developed an offer, selected a group of lists, and come up with some solid tests. Now it is time to get down to the nitty-gritty—the copywriting of the e-mail piece itself, which is an integral part to the entire campaign.

The team hired a freelance copywriter, who had experience writing for e-mail, to write their first promotion. Here is how they outlined the promotion for the copywriter:

- *Promotion goals*—Generate leads. Persuade prospects to start an ongoing relationship with GCC by introducing them to free and fee-based instructional services.
- *Promotional offer and call to action*—Receive game improvement tips by e-mail and the chance to win golf swing video analysis by registering on the GCC Web site.
- *Key offer benefits*—Free game improvement tips from certified golf teaching professionals that are tailored to the prospects' games.
- *Target audience characteristics*—Desperately want to improve their games and place a lot of faith in the abilities of golf teaching professionals to help them do so; favor private over group lessons so that lessons can focus on their individual games.

After the team briefed the copywriter on the promotion, she outlined some of the techniques that she would use to help them generate the desired response:

- *Start with an attention-getting subject line.* It has to promise a benefit that appeals to golfers or many will delete it unopened.
- *Lead with the offer and a click-through opportunity.* E-mail users tend to scan messages. If you don't tell your target audiences right away how the offer is going to help their golf games, many will delete the e-mail without reading the whole message. By including clickable text in the offer, you give golfers a chance to fulfill your call to action as soon as they see it—and many will!
- *Keep the overall promotion fairly short and easy to scan.* What's short? About 250 words or fewer—possibly much fewer. The powers-that-be at GolfCoachConnection.com felt that a short, compelling message would hit their market most effectively. They also figured they would need plenty of click-through opportunities (three is a good guideline).
- *Emphasize benefits.* This is particularly crucial in the short-attention-span world of e-mail. Emphasize how GCC is going to help golfers accomplish what they want most—to improve their games. And if it's free help, even better!

Happy with this approach, the GCC team asked the copywriter to submit text as soon as possible so they would have time for revisions, if necessary, before sending it on to the designer. Used to the fast-paced world of e-mail marketing, the copywriter delivered text shown in Figure 9.6 within a few business days.

FIGURE 9.6 Acquisition E-mail Promotion

Client: GolfCoachConnection.com

Subject1: Save strokes! FREE Golf Tips from Your Coach
Subject2: Win a FREE Golf Swing Coaching Video Session!

Does your golf game need an overhaul? Just some fine-tuning?

Whatever condition it's in, you can get help from a professionally certified golf coach . . . just like the touring pros. (But you don't have to win big tournament purses to afford one!)

Get FREE **Golf Tips from Your Coach** . . . delivered by e-mail and customized to *your game* . . . from GolfCoachConnection.com, a countrywide network of certified golf teaching professionals.

Sign up at http://www.golfcoachconnection.com/coach by Aug. XX, and you could also win a FREE **Swing Coaching Video Session** with a GolfCoachConnection.com teaching professional (a $39.95 value)!

Golf Tips from Your Coach cover all aspects of the game: full-swing, short-game, putting, strategy . . . and more! And Tips can be customized to meet any player profile.

Are you a beginner who tends to slice? A long-hitter who lacks consistency? A straight-hitter looking for more power?

Whatever your skill level or tendencies, Golf Tips from Your Coach will be tailored to improve *your game.* And colorful, clear illustrations make Golf Tips from Your Coach very easy to understand and apply.

Professional help for your golf game is just a click away! Save strokes with personalized Golf Tips from Your Coach . . . FREE!

Sign up today at http://www.golfcoachconnection.com/coach, and you could also win a FREE **Swing Coaching Video Session** (a $39.95 value)!

CHAPTER REVIEW/EXERCISES

Read the body copy in Figure 9.7. Then answer the questions that follow.

FIGURE 9.7 Copy Exercise

It's like having your very own Web site backed by a friendly
and knowledgeable support team! Plus you'll benefit directly
from the thousands of new visitors we bring aboard every
month through our multimillion dollar promotional campaign.
You don't spend a penny on advertising.

ZERO COMMISSION on your first sale

Isn't it time for you to tap into the power of the Web to
connect with millions of potential buyers?

OneMADE makes it easy to get started. You'll pay ZERO
COMMISSION on your first sale, regardless of the item's
value. Register now--at no cost or commitment--and take
immediate advantage of all these great benefits:

1. Your shop will be open 24 hours a day, 365 days a year.
2. You get a FREE SHOWCASE--Tell viewers who you are, why
   you do what you do, and what you have for sale.
3. Auction or Fixed Price Sale--You decide how you want to sell.
4. You sell as many or as few items as you want.
5. Direct to buyer--You deal directly with buyers and receive
   feedback along the way.
6. Overall low commissions--Even beyond your first sale, your
   commissions are only a fraction of what you would pay
   elsewhere.
7. You get to focus on MAKING great artworks--Leave the
   selling to us!

Register today and start selling immediately!

http://www.onemade.com

1. Count the number of benefits to the prospect. How many did you come up with?

2. Are there a sufficient number of call to action links within this message? What other location within the text could have been a good place to fit another link?

3. Circle the blocks of text that make the copy easier to read.

4. What is this particular site's USP?

CHAPTER 10

The Power of Design

OBJECTIVES

- Define effective design.
- Outline the "must-haves" of HTML design for e-mail.
- Learn how to format a text promotion.
- Define rich media and review its strengths and weaknesses for e-mail.

If you plan on promoting with HTML-enhanced e-mails, you must first and foremost think of your promotion as an interactive print ad. That is, an interactive direct response print ad—meaning that the ad is not just for branding and awareness. In other words, there is a clear call to action within it as well. It is asking for sign-ups or sales *now*.

Many of the principles between a direct response print ad and a direct response e-mail promotion are the same when it comes to layout and design. Both have to be designed for easy reading. Both have to be clean and neat, with plenty of white space (but not too much) surrounding the text and images. Both must design headlines that "pop" off the page and screen. And both must include calls to action that are noticeable.

Before we explore the necessary design components behind HTML e-mail promotions, let's take a look at a few of the core design basics.

DESIGN 101

Essentially, a good design comes down to four main guiding principles for how the elements of a design should work together. They are:

1. Proximity
2. Layout and alignment
3. Balance and contrast
4. Repetition

1. Proximity

This principle states that items that are related should be grouped close together. This helps a design look organized and tight. Take a look at the announcement in Figure 10.1 and you'll get an idea of how proximity could have helped this particular piece.

FIGURE 10.1   Example of Design that Doesn't Know the Importance of Proximity. Notice how your eye doesn't know where to go and that the "visit" is not connected to where it should be.

Your Place for Golf   **1-800-555-1212**
     VISIT . . .

GOLF COACH
CONNECTION

www.golfcoachconnection.com

Now see what happens in Figure 10.2 when we group together the chunks of text that go together—they now have a relationship with one another, either by complementing or enhancing what each is conveying.

Grouping together like-minded objects or text helps make it easier for the reader to follow the message. There is a clear beginning, as well as a clear ending. The copy "flows" better, and the surrounding white space has meaning as well because it leads the eye to the next message.

If you have a huge laundry list of items you want to display, instead of laying it out, one item at a time, the principle of proximity says to group "sublists" into their proper categories, with their own titles. For instance, instead of . . .

- Eggs
- Butter
- Cheese
- Beef
- Lamb
- Chicken
- Rolls
- Potatoes
- Rice

FIGURE 10.2 Example of Reworked Design with Proximity in Mind.
The eye naturally scans the information in the way it was intended.

Visit . . .
GOLF COACH CONNECTION

Your Place for Golf
www.golfcoachconnection.com
1-800-555-1212

- Green Beans
- Okra
- Carrots

. . . you could group the items as follows:

Dairy
- Eggs
- Butter
- Cheese

Meat
- Beef
- Lamb
- Chicken

And so on. You get the idea.

To begin incorporating this principle in its most simplified form, follow these three steps:

1. Take your text and graphics and separate them into pieces of information that belong together.
2. Play around with each group to see how you can fit them together. Add titles to text, and subtitles to graphics, if necessary.
3. Once each group is formatted, put them all together on the page. You'll need to keep in mind the other three principles, outlined shortly.

In a nutshell, the principle of proximity simply makes a design easier to read and follow. It also makes it more interesting to look at. And wouldn't you agree that a nicely laid out design will hold your attention better than one that has been haphazardly thrown together?

2. Layout and Alignment

This principle includes the rule of "connection." In other words, no single element should be placed on a page at random. There should be a visual connection between all elements of your design.

Think of each element—or each group of elements—as being connected with an invisible line.

Beginner designers tend to put their graphics in any available space that their text has not taken as shown in Figure 10.3. This type of placement truly makes a design look amateurish and even boring. There should be a relationship between text and graphics. Always. See Figure 10.4.

FIGURE 10.3   An Example of a Poor Layout and Alignment

John Smith   1-800-555-1212
Marketing Director

GOLF COACH CONNECTION

123 Main Street   Phoenix, AZ

FIGURE 10.4   A Better Layout.
Notice how the design looks more organized.

GOLF COACH CONNECTION
John Smith
Marketing Director

123 Main Street
Phoenix, AZ
1-800-555-1212

If you are completely new to design, then simply align all elements of your design either left, right, or center. Take a look at the following very simple elements in Figure 10.5 to see how disjointed a design can appear when alignment is not used properly.

FIGURE 10.5   A Disjointed Design

E-mail Marketing 101

The Book

by Kim MacPherson

There is no visible relationship between the three elements, although there should be. A better use of these elements is shown in Figure 10.6 where everything is aligned left. Or see Figure 10.7, where the top group is aligned left and the bottom "sentence" is aligned right, *but* the last letter of that bottom section is aligned with the last letter of the top section. So there are two lines in this design.

FIGURE 10.6   A Design Unified by Left Margin

E-mail Marketing 101
The Book

by Kim MacPherson

FIGURE 10.7   A Design with Two Elements

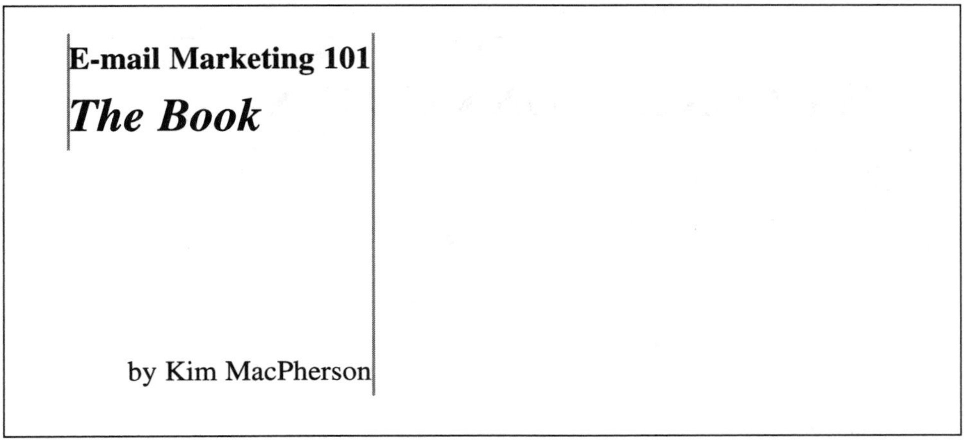

E-mail Marketing 101

The Book

by Kim MacPherson

Granted, this is an oversimplified example, yet it demonstrates how layout and alignment can make a tremendous difference between a design that is visually stulti-fying, and one that is visually stunning. It gets trickier with more elements, of course, so this is a good principle to review and keep in mind as your design is in progress.

Things to keep in mind, as far as alignment goes:

- Think about how all of the elements of your design "fit" together. Make sure that each of them is aligned with something else. Remember that straight line.
- Don't use more than one text alignment on a page, unless you can merge them together.
- Try to make your main alignment either left or right aligned because these have more visual strength than a center alignment.

3. Repetition

This principle applies to the repetition of some component or element in your design. This can include a color, a line, a headline, a font, a bold or italicized word, etc. Repetition, if used properly within a design, creates a look of consistency. See Figure 10.8 for an example of how two bold lines draw the eye. And consistency will make a design appear well planned and easy to follow. Repetition also helps to unify various pieces of a design, making them appear as one. See how the bold line in the lower part of Figure 10.9 unifies the design, even with the white space in the middle.

FIGURE 10.8   A similar layout to the last example, but notice how the bold company name draws the eye to the first two lines.

GOLF COACH CONNECTION
John Smith
Marketing Director
123 Main Street
Phoenix, AZ

123 Main Street
Phoenix, AZ
1-800-555-1212

FIGURE 10.9   Can you see how the eyes are now "pulled down" because of the repeated bold in the company name and the phone number?

GOLF COACH CONNECTION
John Smith
Marketing Director
123 Main Street
Phoenix, AZ

123 Main Street
Phoenix, AZ
1-800-555-1212

Repetition can definitely make a design more compelling; but here are a few rules to keep in mind when using it:

1. Use it sparingly. Too much repetition can detract from the entire design.
2. Repetition should be used as an accent—not as the main element of your design.
3. Think about where you can use it. As long as you don't use it in too many areas around your design, you're safe in making each repetitive component strong. So if you are repeating a distinctive font on all of your subtitles on your page, you can bold those subtitles to make them stand out even more. By the same token, if you are repeating an extra graphical element (a shape, or a letter or a number, for instance), as long as you don't overwhelm the design with it, you can make it stand out as well.

4. Balance and Contrast

Balance is the symbiotic relationship between two elements of a design. Figure 10.10 shows how moving the smaller address type next to the larger, bolder sans-serif telephone number creates a whole new balance. Contrast is created when these two elements are completely different. There must still be a relationship between the two, however—this is where the trick comes in.

FIGURE 10.10 The same business card is getting better, but it's still rather boring.

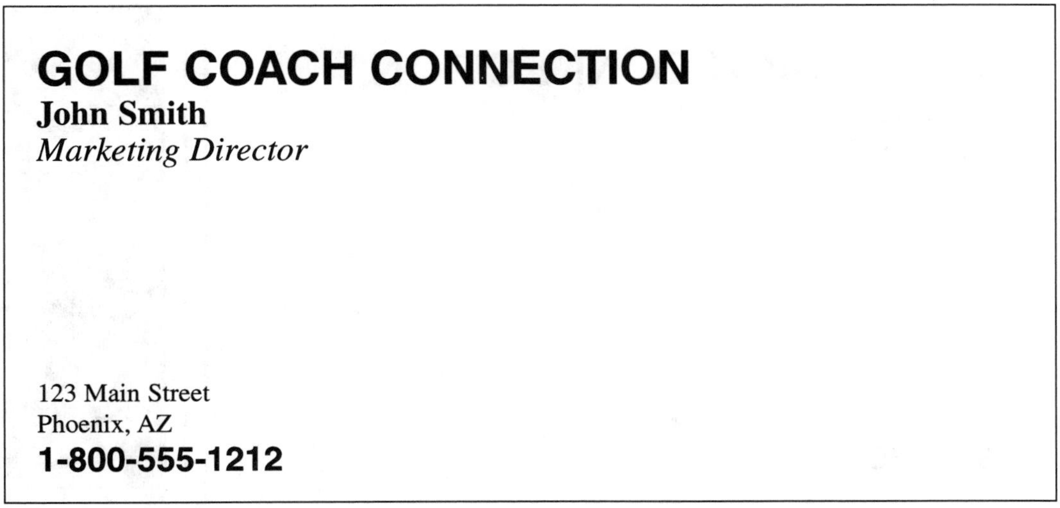

GOLF COACH CONNECTION
John Smith
Marketing Director

123 Main Street
Phoenix, AZ
1-800-555-1212

You can contrast (and thereby balance) light against dark, bold against fine, a strong sans-serif font against a thin serif font . . . the list of items to balance and contrast can go on and on.

You can make headlines stand out with the use of contrast. Although too much reverse text (light text against a dark background) is not recommended, sometimes it is a great technique for focusing the eyes on certain items intentionally. In Figure 10.11, the dark design elements tie the type together and keep the eye's focus on the card instead of letting it wander off the right side. If you think about how you skim through a page, you'll begin to notice that your eyes jump from the elements that stand out most to other elements that stand out most. This is why headlines are typically bold in advertisements. The headline typically encompasses a theme or thought that helps sell the product that is advertised. For impatient readers, headlines are sometimes the only tools you have to draw them into your message.

Balance and contrast is effectively used when:

- Text and graphics flow together and are easily viewed by the reader. In other words, they are balanced and none of the contrasting elements therein are overpowering.

FIGURE 10.11 Notice how the addition of one contrasting visual element makes the entire piece more interesting and easy to read. This is a very simple example, and although the design element is not necessarily related to golf, you can see the point.

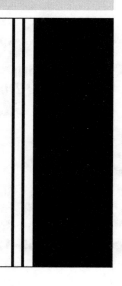

GOLF COACH CONNECTION
John Smith
Marketing Director

123 Main Street
Phoenix, AZ
1-800-555-1212

FIGURE 10.12   The contrast between headline and body provide an eye-catching design.

GOLF COACH CONNECTION NEWS

This is a serif font. Notice the contrast between the bold, sans-serif headline above against this text below it. This kind of contrast is good for newsletters, print and e-mail promotions, and advertisements.

- The contrast must be strong. Don't think that you are using contrast effectively just because you are using two different fonts. If both fonts are semi-bold, for instance, there is little contrast and, in fact, the end result will probably be muddled. One example of effective contrasted fonts would be a strong, bolded sans-serif font alongside an easy-to-read (and unbolded) serif font for the text beneath. See Figure 10.12.

MORE DESIGN BITS AND BYTES

In addition to the four core principles outlined, take note of the following rules when designing your piece:

- *Do not overuse capitalization.* Lowercase words, phrases, sentences, and headlines are easier to read. Occasionally, a capitalized heading can add more impact; but if you use too much of it, it can drown a design's other strengths.
- *Avoid too much spacing between lines.* This is another common beginner's mistake. Don't separate groups by using several lines of spacing in between. Sometimes this makes it hard to differentiate the groups as well. White space is important, but too much of it can make a design visually boring and disjointed.
- *Negative space is important.* Just as your positive space (your text and graphics that make up your design) is important, so is the negative space surrounding it. Often, this is the white space, but sometimes it may be a color or a background.
- *Avoid too much of any one element.* Too much repetition, too much contrast, etc., can make a design look busy and/or overcrowded. The result? A visually unappealing finished product—and one that no one will want to take the time to read.

DESIGNING AN E-MAIL

How is an e-mail designed? Most designed e-mails take advantage of HTML—HyperText Markup Language, the same language that most Web sites use. It allows the recipient of the e-mail to view it in all its full graphics glory, along with a variety of fonts, images, and colors. For the right markets, it can make an e-mail more interesting, and can even enhance response.

The design principles that we reviewed earlier in this chapter should be incorporated into any designed e-mail. In addition, there are a number of other e-mail–specific "rules" to keep in mind as you design in HTML. They have to do with how an online audience views your messages.

Essentially, think of your HTML e-mail promotion as an "interactive" print ad. You want the design to be sleek, well thought out, and easy (even delightful) on the eyes. However, you also want to make it both inviting and easy for people to respond.

E-mail Design Dos and Don'ts

Design for quick downloading. Because there is still a large contingent of people out there (particularly those on the consumer end) who connect online via a dial-up modem, time is of the essence when it comes to e-mail download time. An HTML e-mail that is graphically rich can be beautiful; however, it can cost a click-through and even a sale if it takes too long to open.

Many online viewers and e-mail readers are too impatient to wait for too many heavy graphics to open up. If they still have modem access, this process can seem like an interminably long time. In the meantime, what happens is that some of the text within the HTML promotion is showing . . . and, yes, they can read that while the rest loads. But often they've finished reading before the graphics are visible.

The lesson? Keep your overall file size—including the HTML file and any associated graphics therein—to less than 20 kilobytes, if possible. As time goes on and "bandwidth" goes up, we can begin to increase that size limit little by little. To be on the safe side for now, however, stick with the lower end of the spectrum—especially on the acquisitions side. A stranger will be even less tolerant of a slow e-mail ad than will a member of your house e-mail database. You still can create some dynamite HTML designs for repeat customers.

Avoid large blocks of text. While a print ad can often get by with showcasing a long block of text copy, an e-mail cannot. Text can be cumbersome to read online, so too much of it can quickly signal a prospect to cease and desist. If your promotion copy is large, break it up into manageable "chunks." One way to accomplish this is to separate pieces of copy with catchy headlines (yes, as in direct mail) or bits of color or repetitive shapes. Make sure there is enough white space between each grouping. Organize each group according to theme or subtheme. For instance, one sports enthusiast site we worked with had us create a separate subheading for each of the top five benefits of its offering. As long as your copy is broken up into these quick "bites" of copy, your message will have a better chance of being read. Remember—plenty of white space is *mandatory* for easy online reading. See Figure 10.13 for an example.

Don't overcrowd the promotion with too many graphics and text.
The best rule of thumb is to make good use of your white space and/or your negative (i.e., not used) space surrounding your text and graphics. You need enough negative space to give your message room to breathe; but you don't want so much that it overpowers the message.

Figure 10.14 is an example of how white space was used to enhance the design; in fact, it truly becomes a part of the design.

FIGURE 10.13 Break Up Copy and Graphics for Easy Reading

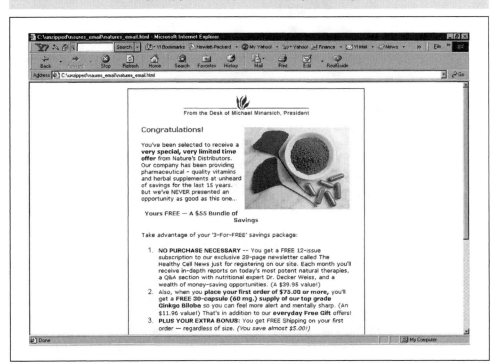

FIGURE 10.14 White Space Makes the Message Appealing and Easy to Read

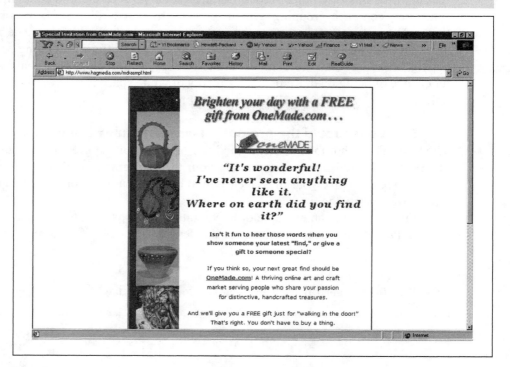

Include clear banners and headers. Many marketers end up putting their sites' navigational bar (or some version thereof) at the top or at the side of their designed promotions. This often works well, particularly if one of your goals is to encourage visitors to go to various areas of your site.

Another type of introduction can be created through the use of customized banners or headlines. For example, one consumer newsletter publication uses the same masthead that's printed on their print newsletter for the top of their promotions.

Don't overdo the use of reverse text. Reverse text, light text on a darker background, can be an excellent method to make text "pop" off the page. The problem is when it is used too much, particularly online. The electronic landscape can make this type of layout difficult to read, so use it sparingly.

Make your links clear. The call to action—where you ask for the order— within your message is critically important. As mentioned previously, your outgoing message should include more than one call to action. For example, "Click here to download your free trial software . . ." or "Register today for . . ." or such calls to action.

Remember those lengthy tracking links we created in the last section? The information that they end up providing us, in terms of measuring our response rates, is invaluable so that length is necessary at times. The good news with an HTML promotion is that you can embed those links directly in these calls to action, meaning that you do not necessarily have to show a long or ugly URL in your HTML message. So "Click here to order E-mail Marketing 101: http://www. e-mailmarketing101.com/?book0801" becomes "Click here to order E-mail Marketing 101" where the full URL shown above is embedded in the words "Click here." Even if your URL is simple, the ability to "hide" it is certainly a great advantage of HTML. You cannot accomplish that with a text-only promo.

Link everything. As noted above, embed a link into every call to action. Additionally, you should also consider embedding a link within text that offers certain products. If you sell baby products, for example, instead of the routine: "Click here to view our bassinets, changing tables, rattles, and receiving blankets," position at least part of your copy in a less formal way, such as "We have all the necessities that every new mom needs—from bassinets and changing tables to rattles and receiving blankets."

With this particular method, each product would link to a page that showcases only that product. So if a recipient of your e-mail message were to click on "bassinets," for instance, she would go directly to a page on your site that sells bassinets. The method is repeated for the other products. Nonetheless, even if you use this particular methodology for embedding links, you should still make sure you have at least *two* clear-cut calls to action within your promotion—meaning a "Click here to . . ." or a "Visit . . ." or a "Register here . . ." and so forth. Many people respond to these clear directives, rather than the more subtle text and product links as noted above.

We'll get into more specifics of how to create custom destinations for your promotions in Part Five. Just keep this in mind as you develop your HTML promotions that showcase multiple products because it can be a very effective means to draw people into a site, particularly if they are only interested in one or two specific products.

Another tip about links is to make even your graphics clickable (and "linkable"). That includes any product shots, and your logo. Therefore, if you have a photo of one or two of your products, be sure to embed a link in there as well. Be sure the link goes to the page on your site that showcases that particular product. For logos, link directly to your home page or another customized page on your site.

This brings up another point regarding the links themselves. As we saw in Chapter 7 about testing strategies and setting up your test links, you can "read" the results of a number of different variables, just based on the links that visitors use. List strengths, message, offer, subject line, etc., are all core variables that can and should be tested on a regular basis. The beauty of an HTML promotion is that you can even take it a step further and test where people are responding, or "clicking," on your message.

Suppose you want to *only* test message location strengths—i.e., where in the message people are clicking. And suppose you are promoting (and mentioning) two products within your text, and are showing two photos and a logo. Your message may look something like Figure 10.15.

You need to somehow note the difference between your logo, your two product shots, and your two text product references. That is a judgement call that is solely up to you and how comfortable you feel reading your results. It may simply be a matter of ending your unique URL with an "L" for logo; "G1" and "G2" for the graphics or photographs of products one and two (or you can specifically reference the products themselves); and "T1," "T2," and "T3" for the text references to the two products. So the links you would embed in each may be something like the following:

Logo:	http://www.xxxx.com/?L
Product 1:	http://www.xxxx.com/?G1
Product 2:	http://www.xxxx.com/?G2
Text Link 1:	http://www.xxxx.com/?T1
Text Link 2:	http://www.xxxx.com/?T2

The end result? If a recipient of this promotion clicked on the logo to go to your site, that URL would be visible in your server logfiles (or in your own internal tracking report, depending on what type you use and whether or not you set up these particular URLs prior to your promotion going out).

Text Promotion "Design"

Because we are in the design section, it seems relevant to go over the key components to "designing" a plain text e-mail. After all, there are some important formatting issues that we must implement when setting up these types of messages.

Many of the same design rules as for HTML apply here. Maintain plenty of white space, include multiple links (to give people variety and choice); and—particularly with a text promotion—keep it simple.

FIGURE 10.15 Where do visitors click? Tracking your results reveals what messages get results.

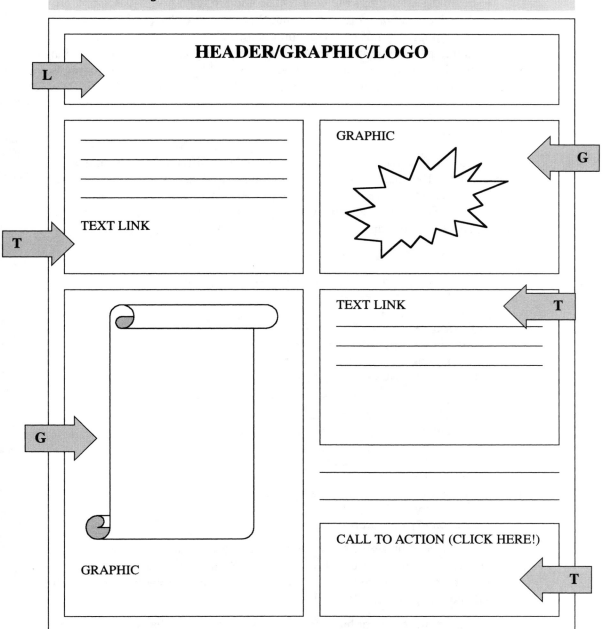

Creating a Text E-Mail

To be on the safe side, write your text promotion in an ASCII-based text program such as NotePad or WordPad, but not Word or Word Perfect. This way, you will create a completely unformatted, "unprocessed" text document that is free of message-tainting add-ons, such as "Smart Quotes." (If you have ever received an e-mail wherein apostrophes and quotes were replaced by funky-looking symbols, then you have been a recipient of an e-mail that did not use straight ASCII.)

Formatting

Due to the fact that e-mail programs "wrap" text differently—meaning some end each line at 100 characters across (including spaces), and others end at 80 characters, you are sure to have more universal success if you put in a hard carriage return (in your ASCII editor) at somewhere between 45 and 65 characters, including spaces, across. If you didn't, your message may look something like this:

```
For the dad who likes the finer things
in life,
visit the Men's Club, Mondera's "private"
section filled to the brim
with elegant gifts
for all tastes.
Excellent craftsmanship is the name of the
game for items found here. http://www
.xxxx.com/?productsA

You also can find great Father's Day gift ideas
at our Holiday Celebrations section . . .
like the internationally renowned Edwin
Jagger shaving
kit--a beautifully designed
accessory, with
high-polished chrome in traditional
Chatsworth style http://
www.xxxx.com/?productsB
```

Not a pretty sight, right? Not only that, the skewed formatting also makes the message extremely difficult to follow and read. Remember: first impressions *do* make a difference, so strive to make even your plain text promotions look well-designed and thought out.

- Add a hard return, or hit "enter" after every 45 to 65 characters (again, including spaces).

- Split up your paragraphs to leave more white space between each of them. One-liners are very common in e-mail promotions and make for easy viewing.
- Format so that each URL link is showcased on its own line. This very small change will make your call to action much easier to follow. See the difference:

```
For the dad who likes the finer things in
life, visit the Men's Club, Mondera's "private"
section filled to the brim with elegant gifts
for all tastes:

http://www.xxxx.com/?productsA

Excellent craftsmanship is the name of the
game for items found here.

You can also find great Father's Day gift
ideas at our Holiday Celebrations section . . .

Like the internationally renowned Edwin
Jagger shaving kit--a beautifully
designed accessory, with high-polished
chrome in traditional Chatsworth style:

http://www.xxxx.com/?productsB
```

For those of you who come from traditional direct marketing and you like to use titles or headlines to make certain points stand out, you still can accomplish this with a text e-mail message. There are quite a few ASCII characters that can help in this regard. The ">" symbol can make an introductory offer stand out:

```
>>Introductory Special: Get a FREE Trial Download at:

http://www.xxxx.com/?offer

The rest of your text would follow here. The rest of
your text would follow here. The rest of your text
would follow here. The rest of your text would follow
here.
```

See how that headline pops? Another character is the asterisk (*), which is especially good for showcasing multiple headlines:

```
**Get Your FREE Trial Software for 30 Days**

The rest of your text would follow here. The rest of
your text would follow here. The rest of your text
would follow here. The rest of your text would follow
here.

** Enjoy the Benefits of Your Free Trial**

The rest of your text would follow here. The rest of
your text would follow here. The rest of your text
would follow here. The rest of your text would follow
here.
```

Asterisks also are good for creating bulleted items. When using bullets in a plain text promotion, the use of tabs may end up formatting your message improperly with certain e-mail programs. If you create bullets with asterisks, however, simply hit your space bar instead of your tab key before writing the text that goes along with that bullet:

```
There are SO MANY benefits to this offer. Take a look:
* Here is one benefit. How about that?
* Benefit #2. You just can't beat it.
* Here is a third. What do you think?
* We can go on like this forever. Here's number 4.
```

A FEW WORDS ON PUNCTUATION AND SPECIAL EFFECTS

Due to the limitations of ASCII, the use of italics, underlining, and bold are not recommended in a plain text e-mail. Capitalization is strong when used effectively to emphasize specific words and phrases that you want to stand out. From a design standpoint, as we saw earlier, and from an online readability standpoint, however, the overuse of capitalization can produce the effect of shouting. So use it sparingly.

In addition to avoiding the use of tabs, centering, with plain text promotions, can cause problems. Centering a headline has long been known in the direct mail world as a way to make headlines shine. With certain e-mail programs, however, it may make your message appear cockeyed.

With an HTML promotion, **bolded** text—especially colored and **bolded** text—can make words leap off the page. However, the use of underlining, because it can create the appearance of a live link, can be a detriment to your message. Italics can be very difficult to read online, so do not use them, even though you *can* with HTML.

ONE MORE THING . . .

When creating your message, use a courier font as shown at left. Because of its fixed width (each and every character and space is the same size), you can better determine your character count so you can be sure not to exceed a certain width of your message.

GOLFCOACHCONNECTION.COM COMES UP WITH A WINNING HTML DESIGN!

Figure 10.16 shows GolfCoachConnection.com's appealing and effective Web page. Notice how the small blocks of type are easy to read, there are plenty of opportunities for click-throughs, and the graphics are clear, relevant, and appealing.

FIGURE 10.16   GolfCoachConnection.com's HTML E-mail Promotion

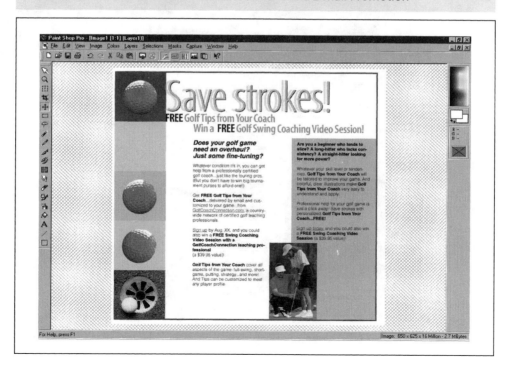

RICH MEDIA E-MAIL

First there were plain-text e-mail advertisements. Then came HTML. Finally, rich media exploded onto the e-mail marketing landscape and things will probably never be the same. Why? Picture this: You turn on your computer and check your e-mail. As you open one of your messages, suddenly you hear a voice, see a video clip, and are "served" with an easy-to-follow order form where you can purchase the advertised product—all without ever leaving your e-mail program! See Figure 10.17.

Here is how it works. With most rich media providers' solutions, a recipient of a rich media e-mail message need not download a program, nor does he need to click on an attachment to view it. He simply checks his messages and when the message is highlighted, the audio and/or video (depending on what the advertiser uses) will stream into his e-mail program and begin automatically.

FIGURE 10.17 A Rich Media Example Embedded into a Newsletter

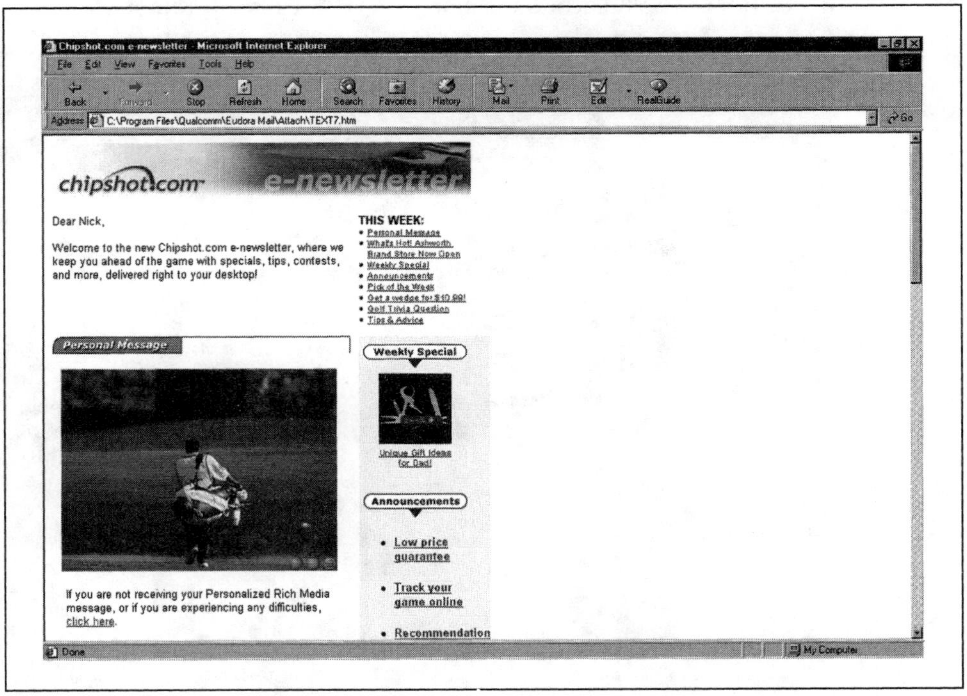

As more and more people connect to the Internet with DSL, cable, and T1s, rich media will most likely become even more mainstream. One of the objections in the past has been that it takes a faster connection to view a rich media e-mail properly. Another objection has been that a recipient of a rich media e-mail who reads his or her e-mail offline will not see or hear the ad because the content is "streamed in" live from the rich media provider. Because of these bandwidth and connectivity issues, and because it is quite a bit costlier than creating a plain-text or an HTML promotion, rich media has been used by a select few.

But times, they are a-changing. Now many rich media promotions can be viewed quickly and easily, even for people who are still on dial-up modems. And it is getting less expensive for marketers to use. In fact, the advantages are beginning to outweigh the cost and connectivity issues.

One of the greatest advantages is that the call to action—meaning the signup, the purchase, etc.—can take place within the e-mail. The recipient doesn't have to click through to a Web site to complete the transaction.

Another advantage to rich media is its tracking ability. Marketers can track how many recipients opened the message and whether or not the ad was streamed in. They can also determine how many original recipients forwarded the promotion, so a viral component can be easily implemented and tracked.

Executable versus Nonexecutable

Some rich media providers create their campaigns in executable files, meaning that they must be sent via attachment to a person's e-mail inbox. The quality of the video and sound is better, according to these deployers. The other rich media providers send out their promotions so that the video and sound are streamed in from their serving site. In other words, no executable file needs to be attached. The ad starts serving the prospect when she checks her e-mail. These deployers claim that using this method will alleviate any worries about transferring computer viruses within attachments. Again, two different schools of thought.

Rich Media Conclusions

You needn't have a fancy site or a high-tech offering to take advantage of the power of rich media. Nonprofit organization, UNICEF, for example, used rich media for a house e-mail promotion. UNICEF is an organization mandated by the United Nations General Assembly to advocate for the protection of children's rights, to help meet their basic needs, and to expand their opportunities so they can reach their full potential. Much of UNICEF's work involves gathering and sharing information, resources, and education to promote the well-being of children around the world.

According to inChorus <www.inchorus.com>, the rich media company that developed UNICEF's campaign, the objective was to build awareness for the release of the Seventh Annual Progress of Nations Report and press conference to UNICEF's in-house e-mail list.

The e-mail offer was a free copy of the report, and it was sent out two days prior to the official press release as a strategic measure to build awareness of the press conference and release. The rich media platform allowed for full graphics, animation, and sound throughout the 30-plus second promotion. A link to UNICEF's home page was offered for those who wished to make donations.

The e-mail was sent to approximately 36,000 addresses on UNICEF's house database. It was even sent to remote places around the world where one would wonder if the technical infrastructure was available to support it. The percentage of undeliverables—that is, the e-mails that did not "connect" to a working e-mail address—was low, however. Only 18 out of 35,819 fell into this category.

One of the powers of rich media is that marketers can track not only how many e-mails were opened and, in fact, "played" (due to the streaming of audio and video), they also can track how many e-mails were forwarded to other people. According to inChorus, the UNICEF promotion had a 36.77 percent "view rate"—meaning that 13,170 people saw the promo. Not only that—709 e-mails were forwarded on to other e-mail addresses. The final click-through rate of people that responded and went to the UNICEF site was 43.76 percent of total views, which is 16 percent of the total e-mails sent.

CHAPTER REVIEW/EXERCISES

1. What are the four main principles to good design?

2. What is your maximum file size when designing an HTML promotion?

3. What should you link in an HTML promotion?
   a. Products
   b. Calls to action
   d. Graphics/photos
   d. Logos
   e. All of the above

4. Suppose you are an e-mail marketer for an online marketing site called MarketingForTheNewMillennium.com. See Figure 10.18 to see an HTML e-mail promotion for it. Create mock unique URLs for the following areas of the piece:

FIGURE 10.18 Use This to Answer Chapter Review Exercise 4

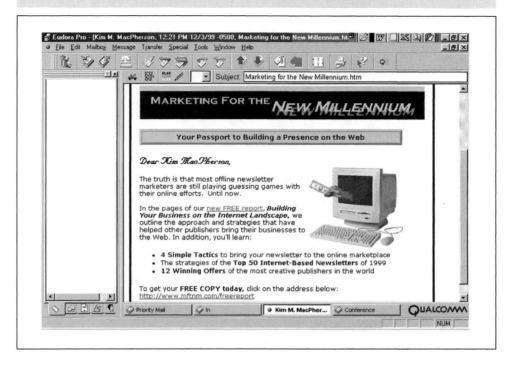

a. The header graphic/logo
b. The computer graphic
c. The first text link ("new FREE report")
d. The second link (URL)

5. When writing a plain text e-mail, what is the maximum number of characters plus spaces that should appear before a hard return needs to be inserted?
   a. 20
   b. 80
   c. 100
   d. 65

6. What is/are the most effective methods of punctuation for a plain text promotion? An HTML promotion?

PART FOUR

Best E-mail Retention Practices

Promoting to Your House List: The Other Side of E-mail Marketing

OBJECTIVES

- Define top retention strategies.
- Review a few components of retention strategies to enhance a customer file.
- Determine how to calculate lifetime value of a customer.
- Review a few house list testing ideas.

E-mail marketing is not all about acquiring new customers through the e-mail channel. Yes, that is an important part, as we've seen in previous chapters. Especially if you are running an online business, it makes sense to prospect in the same medium where you are selling.

However, as we'll see in this section, one of the most profitable ways to utilize e-mail is in your communications with an existing e-mail database—in other words, your own house list. Acquiring *new* customers can be expensive—some estimates gauge the costs at roughly five to twelve times higher than they are for *keeping* existing customers. And this definitely applies to the world of e-mail. With acquisitions opt-in lists now averaging $150 to $350 per thousand and above (which equals $.20 to $.40 per name and higher), it is easy to see how prospecting—particularly through the e-mail channel—is so much costlier than retention e-mail efforts. Therefore, the goal should be that once you have those precious customers in your site, you must constantly find ways to keep them. You must demonstrate that your products and services have true value for them: so much value, in fact, that your customers will buy from you again and again over time.

CREATING AN OPT-IN HOUSE LIST

In order to be able to communicate with your house list and market to it using retention efforts that we'll see here, you need to make sure that all members have opted in. As we saw in Part One, the main way to do this is to be crystal clear in all your offers and e-mail address collection areas. Suppose you run a prospecting promotion, for instance, and you drive people to sign up for a free something-or-other, or you offer a sweepstakes entry of some kind. If you plan on promoting to those new registrants/subscribers/trial members, etc., through e-mail, you must make it clear from the very beginning that this is indeed what you're going to do. If you are collecting those new leads and customer information on site, be sure to post a disclosure that states your intentions. And don't try to hide it: make it stand out.

RETENTION MARKETING 101

A retention marketer's job includes using e-mail to accomplish the following:

- *Conversion.* When a prospect becomes a registered lead or a customer—meaning said prospect has either registered for a free offer of some kind or purchased her first product from you—she becomes a member of your house file. Chances are good that if she purchased something the first time out, the purchase was based on a loss leader, or "feeder product," type of offer. This is an offer designed to convert new customers through a truly outstanding offer, however unprofitable it may be to the advertising company. While it is nice to have a database of leads and customers, you're not going to make any money with this group of people unless you convert them into true full-price paid customers. Customer specials, discounts, and newsletters can help accomplish this.

    Converting leads into customers takes time. It doesn't happen immediately; however with patience and care, the efforts make the wait worthwhile. A typical scenario is as follows: New leads are brought in the door (added to the house file) using opt-in acquisitions methods. A free offer of some kind is usually inducement enough to get people to sign up, thereby opting into the promoter's database. Subsequent e-mail efforts are sent to this list of leads at regularly planned intervals. Over time, a certain percentage of these recipients *will* "pay up."

- *Cross-selling.* Once a new customer or registered lead is added to the file, and especially when she has converted, the time is ripe to get her to purchase other products or services. For example, an online bookseller can promote to the paid-up customer database through regular communications. Whether those communications include a regularly scheduled newsletter or special offer announcements, the bookseller can promote its other books within them.

- *Up-Selling.* Many businesses offer products and services across a wide range of categories, fees, and prices. Those who do may include up-selling efforts as part of their retention programs. For example, a cruise line may start off by promoting a feeder or entry-level product such as a three-day cruise. Once those customers have purchased and opted in, the cruise line may promote a more expensive five-day cruise. From there, each successive promoted product gets more expensive . . . more luxurious . . . more valuable. Each also becomes more profitable to the seller as price goes up and marketing costs go down. Therein lies one of the beauties of up-selling.

THE STRATEGIES

The online marketing world has started to embrace such traditional offline strategies as calculating customer profitability by lifetime (or long-term) value and customer lifespan. These are definitely worthwhile things to know. Lifetime value, in particular, can determine exactly how much you can spend on both acquisitions and retention. Suffice it to say that the following tools and components play critical roles in developing your overall budget and goals—particularly those relating to retention.

Database Marketing and Segmentation

As we saw in the chapter on acquisitions offer development, your customer is most likely worth *more* than his first order. In other words, if you treat him right, chances are he will come back to you again when he needs the type of products or services that you offer. And if he really feels devoted to you, he'll also become your biggest advocate and will recommend your "solution" to like-minded people with similar wants and needs.

For example, suppose you market a site that sells fishing gear. Your site, FishermenRUs.com, markets in a number of different ways, including e-mail. As a result of offline and online direct marketing strategies over the years, it has managed to build a house e-mail database of more than 10,000 buyers who have paid up.

You, as the site's primary e-mail marketer, have determined that the average first time buyer's purchase at your site is about $45. If each buyer only bought the first time and then went away, never to be seen again, your total existing sales to date would be only $450,000. However, based on your marketing efforts, in which you attempt to get those customers to "trade up" to more deluxe equipment, or you try to get them to purchase other complementary products, your total sales derived solely from your house list promotions actually far exceed that figure.

This is what database marketers continually strive for—a house list that is profitable and continues to be so. They accomplish this by segmenting the file based on historical information. Previous response rates, past buying behavior, and even demographic and geographic information can all come into play. Database marketers also play a critical role in determining a business's best, most profitable customers while at the same time setting them apart from those customers who take little action. We'll take a more detailed look at this very critical application later in this section.

Lifetime Value Analysis

Let's go back to our fishing gear site. You've already determined that $45 is the average first time order. However, you've also figured out that if you can keep just one customer loyal and can get him to continue to buy from you, that customer becomes worth much more than $45. Over five years, he may be worth $300 or more. Over ten years, that figure could jump to more than $1,000. And those revenues come from pure retention efforts. If they're through e-mail, the costs can be relatively low, compared to acquisitions e-mail marketing. In order to do it right, a professional e-mail solutions provider is recommended. This type of company's main job is to help companies test, deploy, segment, and communicate with their customers in a variety of *optimized* ways. Now I say "optimized" because that is the key to building lifelong relationships with your customers through e-mail. You need to market to them individually, rather than en masse. They have to feel as if what you are sending them has value. A lot of it has to do with your offers, but a lot of it has to do with frequency of communication as well as content.

To calculate lifetime value, you need to know how much your best customers spend with your business. You also need to know or make assumptions about your customer retention rate.

Suppose your new customer retention rate is 50 percent—meaning that for every two new customers that buy from you, one of them will continue to buy, or will buy again, and one of them will go away. Now suppose that during one e-mail promotion, you bring in 100 new paying customers. At a $50 average order, you've got $5,000 in revenue. However, between opt-in acquisitions lists and creative costs, it cost you $7,500 to bring in those 100 new customers. If you can retain half of them, and they continue to spend $50 per year with you *at no marketing cost to you,* it would take one year for you to make your money back. Obviously, you'll have to spend money in order to get them to continue to buy from you. But keep in mind that your costs will go down after that first hefty acquisitions cost of $7,500. In-house e-mail programs are much less expensive, even if you use an outside solutions provider. Instead of $.15 to $.35 per e-mail address, and depending on whether you use a professional provider or a software solution, costs can range from a penny to a dime. (See solutions providers and software solutions in the Resources section at the back of the book.)

Given the acquisitions lists costs that you do *not* have to pay, you figure you are cutting out the majority of your costs when marketing to that list of 100. Suppose—worst case scenario—you spend $10 per customer each time you send out a promotion. This includes deployment costs and any creative costs you might have. And you send out five promotions per year. That is $50 per customer for that year. During the first year, half of these customers were those that were going to spend $50 per year, anyway. Because of your marketing efforts, half of your house file members' yearly expenditure with you jumps to $150 per year. That's $7,500 in revenue. The other 50 members of the list of buyers, remember, were not going to spend a dime. However, based on your first year's marketing efforts, suppose you've managed to retain another 10 percent who will continue to spend $50 per year with you as long as you market to them. That is an additional $500 per year. Your revenue from your first year's efforts is now $8,000 at a cost of $5,000. You are now in the positive—you've managed to increase revenues, while at the same time marketing to your house list *and* defraying your upfront acquisitions costs. Figure 11.1 charts your costs and revenues for one year.

Now let us take it a step further to see how we can calculate lifetime value of these customers. In a nutshell, your lifetime value is your customers' average revenue over the term of their relationships with you. And although not every customer on your file will spend the same amount with you (and many, as we've seen, will only buy from you the first time), the average lifetime value of your *actual buyers* is spread out across all of your customers.

So, getting back to the last example, we saw that after the first year we were profitable. Every year thereafter, although we will continue to see customers fall off the file, our retention rate will increase. By the following year, we may have

FIGURE 11.1   Marketing Costs and Returns. (Numbers in parentheses are negative)

Acquisitions Revenue/Customer	$ 50	
Acquisitions Cost/Customer	$ (75)	
	$ (25)	Revenue/Customer after acquisitions
Year 1 Revenue/Customer	$ 133	
Year 1 Cost/Customer	$ (50)	Revenue/Customer after one year
	$ 83	Revenue/Customer because of customer buying after acquisition

60 percent who spend $150 and 10 percent who spend $50. Now keep in mind those percentages are based on the new quantity of the list. In other words, of that 60 percent from the last example of that original 100, or 60 people, a total of 70 percent will spend *something*. So 36 people will bring in $5,400 and six people will bring in $300. Grand total: $5,700 in revenue ($95 per customer, based on 60 customers) and $3,000 in costs ($50 per customer, based on 60 customers). So your profit per customer is now $45 per customer. And it goes on from there. You can continue this exercise for five, ten, or fifteen years . . . or however long you have customers. Once you've determined your profitability from these customers over a certain time, you then add up the profits over the years and divide by your original number of customers. See Figure 11.2 to see how these costs and revenues look over a five-year period.

FIGURE 11.2   A Five-Year Picture of Costs and Revenues

Year	Total # of Customers	Retention Rate	Total Revenue	Total Cost	Profit
Acquisitions	100	60%	$ 5,000	$7,500	$ (2,500)
Year 1	60	70%	$ 8,000	$3,000	$ 5,000
Year 2	42	80%	$ 5,586	$2,100	$ 3,486
Year 3	34	85%	$ 4,469	$1,700	$ 2,769
Year 4	29	90%	$ 3,857	$1,450	$ 2,407
Year 5	26	95%	$ 3,458	$1,300	$ 2,158
	291		$30,370	$17,500	$13,320
					133.20 LTV

This is a simplified example and does not take into account things such as fulfillment costs, nor any other fixed or variable costs, such as:

- *Cost of goods.* This usually is a fixed cost.
- *Fulfillment costs.* Includes order entry, shipping, and handling. It also is usually a fixed cost.
- *Overhead.* This is typically calculated as a percentage of sales.

This example is based only on the marketing costs, and is used only to demonstrate the lifetime value calculation, or in this case—*long-term* value. Once you've determined whether or not to include your other costs, as noted above, and you have that total costs number set, you can then determine how much you can spend on your retention marketing efforts.

Loyalty Programs

Loyalty programs are often the backbone of any good retention program. To get a customer to completely "buy in" to you as sole proprietor of something that he wants or needs, again and again, is the key to decreased marketing costs and increased profits.

To develop that level of buy-in through e-mail takes time, money, and dedication to make it pay off. Some loyalty programs are built on incentives and rewards. Others are based on good, old-fashioned customer relationship building. Following are a few ideas for some loyalty-building offers. Before implementing any of them, you may want to consider testing to a select segment of your house file before rolling out.

- *Step-up limited time offer.* If you have a retail site, you can implement a special offer program with an expiration date. It can be something like, "For Our Best Customers Only: Take 5% off every single new book purchase from now until September 30." Obviously, the technology must be in place for this type of promotion to work. Most likely, recipients would be instructed to add a coupon code (attached to the offer, and with an expiration date) at checkout. Or, in the case of specific products offered, each e-mail would simply take recipients to a specific offer page for that week. The offer page would have the discount already built in.
- *Learn from the airlines.* Frequent flyer programs work because they reward customers for their loyalty. It is the same principle that we see with those punch-out cards at the video store or dry cleaners. The more we buy, the more we get. We are rewarded with free gifts, free or discounted product, or even cash.

- *Regular communications from an executive of the company.* This can be an effective way to "keep in touch" with your customer while also instilling brand loyalty. It is a practice that has been used offline in traditional direct mail for years. Just be sure to make the e-mail newsworthy and valuable.
- *Reminders.* If you collect items of information about your customers, such as birth dates, use that information to your advantage and send out e-mailed birthday and anniversary cards. Even if it is sent online, it still can have that personal touch that many people respond to.
- *Exclusive club.* As part of your overall marketing efforts, you can ask customers to opt in to a members-only club, wherein they are e-mailed each week/month/quarter on special offers and/or discounts. The e-mail can be in the form of a regularly scheduled e-mail newsletter.

There are other ways of increasing customer loyalty, of course. Think in terms of your business model and what will have true value for your customers. The main thing to remember with any kind of customer loyalty and relationship-building program is to strive for excellence in everything you do. That means outstanding products, service, follow-up, attention, and value—whether it's by e-mail or not.

GOLFCOACHCONNECTION.COM STARTS TO DEVELOP A RETENTION STRATEGY

Because avid golfers account for 60 percent of golf spending, the Golf-CoachConnection.com team decided to target a sales offer for the avid golfers in its leads database that had not yet purchased anything from the GCC Pro Shop. The team's research showed that avid golfers, in general, ranked "latest technology" very highly among purchasing criteria.

So the team developed an offer that showcased a "hot" new driver. It decided to offer free shipping, a popular incentive in their direct mail campaigns, to make the driver even more attractive to the "gotta have the latest and greatest" golfer crowd.

CHAPTER REVIEW/EXERCISES

Take a look at the specifications for our hypothetical company:
  a. Customers are seen over a five-year period
  b. Acquisitions cost: $15,000
  c. Retention cost per customer after acquisitions: $85

    d. 250 new customers brought in initially

    e. $200 revenue per customer during acquisitions

    f.   First year retention rate: 50 percent and $200 revenue per

    g. Second and third year retention rate: 65 percent and $300 per

    h. Fourth and fifth year retention rate: 75 percent and $450 per

Now answer the following questions, using the above data:

1. What are the revenue and the cost totals after five years?

2. Calculate the long-term value of these customers.

3. Is this a profitable scenario?

CHAPTER 12

Communications to Retain

OBJECTIVES

- Determine quantity and types of house e-mail communications.
- Review various retention offers.
- Create a strategy for welcoming and exiting subscribers.
- Define retention best practices.

In the last chapter, we reviewed a compendium of strategies to help build and develop customer relationships to enhance profitability. Now we get into the nitty-gritty and take a look at some of the more finely tuned offers and methods of communication in order for us to accomplish this difficult, yet potentially rewarding, feat.

HOW MUCH IS ENOUGH? HOW MUCH IS TOO MUCH?

First, we need to explore a few details on timing issues—how often should you communicate with members of your house database? This is certainly something that needs to be tested because every business model will yield different re-sults, depending upon frequency, or how often a message is sent. Not to mention the fact that a good bit of your results depends on whether you are e-mailing cus-tomers or registered leads . . . *and* at what stage of the game they are.

Also, you need to make sure that if you start a weekly newsletter, you fulfill weekly. If it's a monthly communication, send it off every single month, like clockwork. In other words, stick to your promise and you will maintain that all-important credibility with your customers, subscribers, and leads. That is the first step to building and maintaining a successful house retention program.

As far as timing goes, it's important to distinguish how often you need to send out an e-mail communication. The decision depends on whether you are pro-moting to paid customers, registered users, or registered leads. Following is a def-inition of each.

Paid customers. These are, of course, the people who are the true cus-tomers of your site, if you are offering products and services for sale. They have bought something from you at least once and are considered your best subscribers. If revenue is the core of your business model, then this particular segment repre-sents the cream of the crop. They will be your most responsive subscribers. Not to mention that they have the potential to become your biggest advocates as well.

Therefore, you should aim to send out a regular communication—whether that is *once every two weeks*, or once a month. However, if you have the technical database capabilities of segmenting these customers even further—e.g., by how often they purchase, the size of each purchase, etc.—then the timing factor is something that you would need to test. We'll have more details on that in the next chapter on segmentation and personalization.

Registered subscribers or users. Yours may be the type of business model wherein revenue comes from advertising on your site or by paid sponsor-ships to your subscriber newsletter. For instance, suppose you have an online mag-azine geared toward new mothers. The content includes online articles of helpful information geared toward this particular audience. And it is all free. So your revenue stream comes from advertising placed on the site and in your regularly e-mailed *free* newsletter. Obviously, it is mandatory that you get your newsletter out as planned. Additionally, when subscribers opted in to receive this newsletter, they also may have opted in to receive special offers by you, as well as those of your "special advertisers and partners" (depending on the language used at the point of collecting e-mail addresses). These are also internal mailings, of course, but they should be treated with kid gloves. In other words, although you may want to advertise a new product for your own income, or you want to sell an opt-in data-base of your own for another advertiser's prospecting efforts, you need to be mindful of how much your subscribers do *not* want to be promoted. They will unsubscribe if they receive too many advertisements from you and your advertisers, so beware. Because it takes some work and money to develop an internal list of registered users and subscribers, you, of course, want to make sure that you *keep* a good portion of them.

Another type of nonpaid registered subscriber is the *registered user,* where the site owner's revenue stream comes from a commission or a fee of some sort from a third party that wants eyeballs. For instance, Databid.com is a business-to-business company that doesn't sell anything directly. Its business model is based on registering users, who are made up of IT decision makers, in order for Databid's affiliate vendors and suppliers to sell their products and services to the list. Therefore, it benefits Databid to grow its number of registered users and to promote its own various services and vendors to them internally because third-party sales is how it makes its money.

Registered leads. These are the people who have not yet fulfilled whatever your ultimate goal is. However, they have become a part of your e-mail database because of a lead generation offer of some kind. Maybe they signed up when they downloaded your free trial software . . . or when they requested to receive your free report . . . or when they registered on your site for your free demo, or online tool, or online seminar. No matter what the method that you're using to generate registered leads, your ultimate goal is to convert them to either paid customers or clients. So the next step is to get them to buy. There are a number of ways to convert these leads to full-fledged customers, which we will discuss next.

WHAT TO E-MAIL?

First, you need to plan your "shell" strategy—or your overall house communications plan—which includes your subscriber messages at the beginning (the welcome), the ongoing ones (newsletter, updates, etc.), and the final ones (the goodbye). This strategy can be used, no matter if you are "speaking to" paid customers or nonpaid registered users and/or leads. A welcome strategy consists of the following elements.

Welcome Message

This is the e-mail that your new subscribers—whether they are paid customers, leads, or users—receive directly after they opt in to your offer, whatever that offer is. A welcome letter should:

- *Remind recipients who you are.* Remind them why they joined—the outstanding benefits of your offer.
- *Detail your products and services.* This is not mandatory to include in the welcome message, though this type of information certainly can't hurt, unless the text is too long. Many welcome messages introduce various "departments" of a site, each with its own link to the exact page on the site that showcases it.
- *Be personal.* A welcome message shouldn't sound like it is coming from a large organization that is sent to the masses. Instead, position it as a sincere welcome from the head of your company, or at least someone in senior management *who cares.* His or her job is to make the recipients feel comfortable and happy with their decision to visit the site. They also should look forward to receiving future communications.
- *Include an unsubscribe option.* This should be the standard for all of your outbound communications with your customers and/or subscribers. It needs to be easy for them to unsubscribe if they no longer wish to receive your messages. Technically speaking, it can be as simple as inserting a *mailto:unsubscribe@yoursite.com* or it can be a bit more complex (but actually easy on the subscriber) if you have a solutions provider who can handle that for you automatically. This unsubscribe option can be placed on the bottom of each of your messages, but remember to keep it highly visible. The last thing you want to do is anger your subscribers, even if they do want to leave the fold.

Regular Content

What do you send after the welcome has been made and your company has been reintroduced? Again, it depends on who you're talking to. Generally speaking, though, the following communications can work across the board:

Newsletters. This, of course, is one of the most popular means to keep in regular contact with your customers, registered users, and registered leads. The newsletter can be brief and to the point. See Figure 12.1 for a sample newsletter.

Or your communication can be of the more lengthy but information-packed variety, such as the one offered by ChipShot.com that we saw earlier. You can review the case studies from both of these companies at the back of the book.

Most e-mailed newsletters include a header or an "In this issue" at the top so that recipients can quickly scan the contents. There are then two or more brief "stories" or links to stories on the advertising site. In the case of a site with an advertising model, text or banner sponsorships can be subtly "woven" into the content.

FIGURE 12.1   Mondera Newsletter

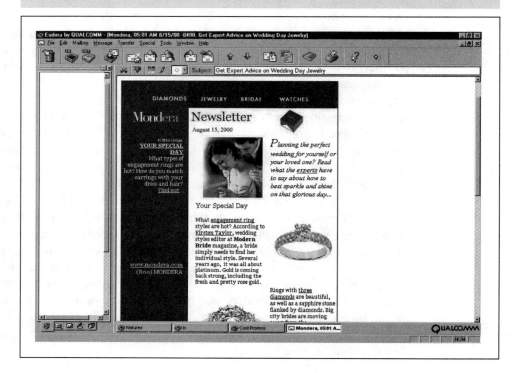

The main thing to keep in mind with a newsletter is that if you are going to call it a newsletter, you'd better make it newsworthy! Mondera offers quick bites such as interesting facts on select gemstones of the month—where they're found and how they're mined. It also provides advice on wedding jewelry, selecting a diamond, and other helpful tidbits, all in a brief weekly newsletter that encapsulates the best that Mondera has to offer.

Chipshot.com also provides content along with a pitch. Its newsletter—geared for golf lovers—provides tips on swings, lessons, equipment, and more. And there is always an embedded promotion or two.

Special offers. If you've ever bought anything online, you know what these are. Some online retailers send out a regular "special offer" promotion once a week, while others save these communications until they can offer something truly special.

See Figure 12.2 for a look at another one of Tavolo's house promotions. Similar to a snail-mailed bulletin or small catalog, this type of offer can showcase a

FIGURE 12.2 The Lure of Special Offers Has Customers Returning to This Site Again and Again

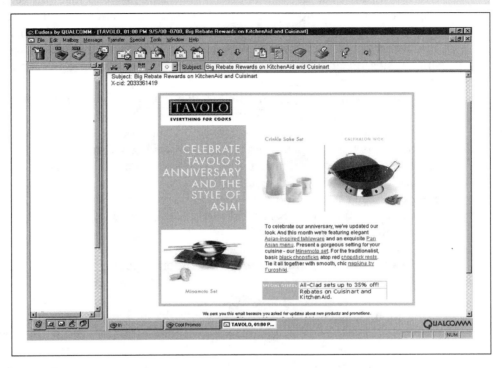

big sale, or can highlight specific products and services that have just been introduced, or can announce a special discount of some kind. There are plenty of examples of these at the back of the book in the Case Studies section.

Holiday/timely updates and promotions. Because a direct e-mail is about as close to direct postal mail as you can get—as far as space, type of offer, and measurable response—*and* because it is so closely connected to merchandising Web sites across a variety of categories, an e-mail has become a favorite of on-line retailers everywhere. It's especially a favorite in the gift-giving seasons, such as the two to three months before the December holidays, not to mention Valentine's Day, Mother's Day and Father's Day, and even Easter.

There is one caveat to holiday promotions, however, and that is that you have to *be prepared* to get lower response rates than at other times of the year. Why? Because just about everyone with an e-mail marketing budget will be promoting during those key times. And it stands to reason that the more e-mailed advertisements that consumers receive in their inboxes, the more likely they are to hit the "delete" key. However, this does not mean that *your* particular e-mail marketing efforts will do worse during such times. You may just find that you get a lift in response during the holiday season. The recommendation would be to e-mail lightly during that time. If you achieve success, you can become increasingly aggressive. If you see a falloff in response, you will then know to cut back on any similar subsequent efforts, unless a higher per-customer buying average makes up for the lower response rate.

The main thing to keep in mind so that your promotions stand out from the crowd is to be creative. Create a unique offer and present it in a timely and/or compelling manner. Yes, it is easier said than done, but you *can* do it. Follow the steps laid out in previous chapters with regards to planning and creating promotions and you'll be more successful than a good portion of your compatriots.

Additionally, because we are talking about retention promotions here, your odds are greater (that you'll get a higher response) than another marketer who is simply prospecting. Just be sure that you have maintained your credibility and that you are offering content that truly is of value.

Members-only club offers. In addition to getting hard core results (such as click-throughs and conversions), this can also be a dynamite way to create loyalty, which is also a part of the retention process. Posed as a "for your eyes only" proposition, recipients can be made to feel welcomed and special: not to mention that they believe they are getting the best discounts, deals, or special offers possible.

Chipshot.com occasionally offers a "Secret Sale" to its subscriber customers and has found this a worthwhile tactic to get them to buy. Think about what strategies you can use in this category for your unique business model.

Coupon offers. Typically these types of offers are sent to people who have signed up to receive them. There are sites with business models built on driving people to their affiliate sites, so coupons are what they send. There also are online retailers who offer coupons as part of their "special offers" e-mails.

Announcements of updates to or specials on site. This can sometimes be beneficial, from a sales standpoint, but more often than not this strategy is used to maintain customers' top-of-mind awareness. Amazon's Jeff Bezos, for instance, will occasionally send an update to Amazon's customer database, informing them of *this* change or *that* improvement to the Amazon Web site. It also can be a worthwhile method to drive folks back to the site where they can (guess what?) make a purchase.

There are plenty of other methods for you to communicate with your subscriber base of customers, leads, and users, including gift certificate announcements, special alerts, and more. Any of the above methods can be set up in either "full-blown" or "teaser" formats. A full-blown format is where *all* or most of the content is laid out in the e-mail. The links either go to specific pages related to that particular story or showcased product. A teaser e-mail contains quick bits of information and the completion of a thought or story can only be found on the site by clicking on a "continue" button or link. Either can be effective: results depend on the content of your e-mail and how much space you need to present it. Brevity often can be the key to success here.

The Exit

How do you say goodbye? First keep in mind that no matter what type of house retention offer you are sending, there always will be a certain percentage of people who opt to unsubscribe. Plain and simple, it is a fact of life. However, if your unsubscribe rate goes higher than 2 or 3 percent per mailing, you'd better do some serious analysis of your method, your content, and your frequency of communications.

If you have a normal unsubscribe rate, however, be sure to let those subscribers go easily. Don't make it difficult for them. Once you get the unsubscribe notice, be sure to send them back a personalized autoresponded message that says you are sorry to see them go. Remind them why they subscribed to begin with by highlighting your benefits. Make one last-ditch effort to get them to resubscribe if you must. Then just let them go.

CHAPTER REVIEW/EXERCISES

1. Suppose you are running an online retail site: what type of subscriber will most likely be the most responsive to your internal offers?

2. Suppose you are running a retail site that sells educational, but fun, computer software for kids. Your subscribers are made up of adults who buy this software for their children, grandchildren, etc. Answer the following questions and create a brief plan:
   a. What would you send: a newsletter, special offers, or other (specify)?
   b. Would you send it sporadically? Regularly? How often?
   c. How would you sell products?
   d. What kind of content would you include?
   e. Write a brief welcome message for new subscriber customers to this site.

CHAPTER 13

Segmentation and Splits for Top Retention

OBJECTIVES

- Define an optimized database.
- Review top three segmentation strategies for retention.
- Define RFM.
- Learn what main components make a customer respond.
- View top segmentation tests.

Having a house e-mail list that you can communicate with on a regular basis gets you one step closer to improving the results of your e-mailed promotions, as compared to those used in acquisitions mode. This is simply due to the fact that your house file is made up of people who know your name. They are not strangers to you, nor are you to them. Therefore, response rates from internal e-mailings can far exceed those gleaned from prospecting. Based on that fact, costs per person e-mailed go down, and profits go up. Therein lies the beauty of retention.

To enhance your retention efforts even further, aside from what we've learned in the last two chapters, you can increase response rates by segmenting your database and communicating to them based on things such as interest, products purchased, timing of purchases, etc. In other words, you can optimize your campaigns by individualizing and customizing messages, instead of sending en masse.

OPTIMIZING A DATABASE

According to consistent reports by research firms such as Forrester Research and others, segmenting a database in order to provide personalized, custom-driven e-mail communications to your house file can make a huge difference in response. Often referred to as "data mining," this method of splitting a house file and sending unique messages can increase click-through percentages 3 to 4 percent so your final rate is 8, 10, 14 percent or higher.

The process can be as seemingly simple as either of the two scenarios.

Scenario 1

1. You collect information on your site when you opt people into your house file. That information can consist of the obvious and necessary, such as e-mail address and even name. It also can include city and state, categories of interest, age, birth date, and other personal tidbits.
2. You make assumptions about which segments of your database audience will give your internal promotions a lift in response. (For example, your house file may be split into various cells, based on when members last made a purchase, as in Figure 13.1.)
3. Based on these assumptions, you have your internal database personnel or your outside solutions provider split up your house file.
4. You create unique messages for each segment. (More on this later in this chapter.)

FIGURE 13.1   Scenario 1

Which members of house file?	Quantity	CTR	Conversion as % of CTR	Average Sale
Control—*Nth* across entire house file	5,000	5.4%	10%	$46
Cell A—Last month buyers	5,000	8.8%	12.5%	$42
Cell B—Last three month buyers	5,000	7.2%	11.2%	$35
Cell C—Last six month buyers	5,000	5.8%	9%	$34

5. You also create a control, or a generic, message that gets sent to a segment that represents your entire file. In other words, it includes people from various geographic segments, with various buying habits, etc. They are not representative of any one particular segment. At the same time, you also should include an alternate control with this same general message sent to one or several of your segments. This way you have a test to see if a more targeted, personalized message can increase response.

6. You send out each message *at the same time*. This is critical—all components of this test must be the same. Remember: keep your tests apples-to-apples and only test one variable at a time. That particular testing strategy we learned earlier in this book applies across the board.

7. When results come in, you can then determine your best offers, your best segments, and what your next marketing plan should be.

Scenario 2

This method is based on using response rates to determine your next steps.

1. You send out your campaign. This can be any one of the offers presented in the last chapter.

2. Based on individualized links embedded in the message, wherein each of your subscribers has a coded tracking link that is completely unique to her, you can find out
   • who opened the message.
   • who clicked on the link (and which links were clicked).
   • what they looked for on the site.
   • how long they stayed on the site.
   • whether they bought something.
   • how much they spent.
   • which specific customers and subscribers responded, based on demographic, geographic, and registration data.

3. Based on the results from the above, you can then divide the various responders based on how they interacted with the site and whether or not they made a purchase. Test specific messages based on these segments.

4. You can then roll out messages. Depending on results of the tests, you will know what messages to send to what segments.

See Figure 13.2 for a chart showing this scenario.

Still another model for sending our personalized messages is the "on-the-fly" communications, also called *dynamic content generation*. An ongoing campaign, or set of communications, that falls under this scenario might run as follows.

FIGURE 13.2 Scenario 2 (simplified)

	Quantity	Open rate	Link 1	Link 2	# of purchases	$ spent
House Mailing	100,000	50%	4%	8%	700	$39,200

Based on unique identifiers and links, purchasers can be selected again and future promotions to them can be customized based on what they responded to here.

You establish a set of business rules based on certain database elements. You then create content around those rules. For example, suppose you run an offline clothing chain of stores, along with an online site that sells the same products. Your goal is to drive traffic to your offline stores. So you create your "what ifs" depending on what your message recipients do. One of the first things you do is break down your customer file by zip code and determine who is within a certain distance to your various store locations. You also split your file by gender so you can determine purchase rates of men's versus women's clothing. You then create your "rules": Those who purchase from the e-mail are immediately sent a thank you and an up-sell or cross-sell message. Those who have purchased in the last three months will automatically get a message showcasing 20 percent off, while those who have purchased six or more months ago will receive messages touting 10 percent off (or vice versa, depending on what you've determined your older and newer buyers best respond to). When the e-mail blast goes out, each recipient gets a personalized message based on when he or she last purchased, where he or she lives, and by gender. And it all happens on the fly as the message is being deployed.

THE RFM MODEL

Now that we understand the various strategies for segmenting and personalizing a house file, what are the points of segmentation that will most likely enhance that file? Many marketers have long used the RFM model—which stands for Recency, Frequency, and Monetary value.

- *Recency.* It's a fact—recency of a transaction plays an integral part in how responsive your customers will be. For instance, if you are selling lower-priced products such as vitamins or magazines, and you just added 10,000 new buyers into your house file, chances are good that those buyers are open and ready to be cross-promoted to. The "get 'em while they're hot" saying rings true here. So, in all likelihood, if you send the new vitamin buyers, for example, a brand new message that promotes a discount on a related product—such as St. John's wort or gingko biloba—chances are that a good number of them will respond.

Magazine buyers will respond similarly. Suppose you get 5,000 new crafts magazine buyers during one month's campaign. The magazine showcases and gives directions for creating a variety of crafts. If you sent out a follow-up message that promoted a complementary magazine specializing in helping craftspeople sell their wares, you would, in all likelihood, glean a higher response rate than if you had waited a month or more to e-mail those same buyers.

- *Frequency.* Selecting multibuyers, or those customers and subscribers who have made some sort of transaction *multiple times,* also will increase response. Getting back to the online vitamin store example, the customers that make the most purchases on an ongoing basis are, of course, your best customers. You'll also find that they're the best prospects for your promotional efforts as well. Again, if you have the technical abilities, you can segment a house file based on number of times purchased (2x, 3x, 4x, and more), and by what products were purchased. Sending out messages based on a combination of these criteria can dramatically enhance your results.
- *Monetary value.* Yes, it's true—the more your customers spend with you, the more likely they are to spend again. Whether you are promoting a high-dollar set of products or a less costly set, you can determine how profitable each and every one of your customers is. This also goes back to the lifetime or long-term value assessment. A customer who regularly spends $200 per year with you, year after year, is ultimately going to garner you more profits than the customer who spends $500 with you after one campaign, and then is never seen again.

Capture the Right Information

Most e-mail marketers capture information at the point of sale (on the Web site). In order to capture the *right* information that will help you with your internal e-mail marketing efforts, you need to make sure you are collecting, at a minimum, the following data points:

- *Full name* Include first, last, middle
- *Gender*
- *City, state, and zip*
- *Category of interest* If you sell books, what genres are your new customers interested in? If you sell camera equipment, what types of photography do your customers enjoy? If you are running an online business-to-business

customer/vendor matching service, then what types of business products do your customers normally need to purchase? And how frequently?

That is the minimum amount of information that you should be collecting from the new members of your database. And whether or not you can segment based on any of these properties, think in terms of the future: one day, you will. And it will only improve what you are doing now.

Personalization

At least with the above information you can personalize somewhat. You can begin every communication with a "Dear Joe," or "Dear Ms. Samuels." It is this type of personalization that sets the tone and lays the groundwork for future enhancements. The more that you can personalize your internal house e-mails, the more effectively you will communicate with your customers and subscribers, and the higher the odds that they will respond.

After that initial database is collected and you have some usable customer information, that information grows based on transactions. For instance, as time goes on and your e-mailed communications are tracked and measured, you can add:

- Number of times purchased
- Average dollar amount spent with each purchase
- Category of purchases (if you offer products across multiple categories)
- What type of offer did your customers respond to that first brought them to your Web site, i.e., how did you acquire them?

WHAT MAKES A CUSTOMER RESPOND?

As we have seen here, personalization and customizing offers and messages both play a key role in customer response. Why?

It's based on a number of factors, really. Some of them are in combination with other components of the offers themselves.

They get the right product at the right time. Suppose that you have tested and analyzed your house file based on what they buy and what they *don't* buy after receiving a series of offers throughout the year. Based on that analysis, you've determined that a select segment of your file always purchases your top-of-the-line cable knit sweater in December. However, that is the *only* time that they buy. What do you do? You only send them a promotion in or around December and you skew it such that the main heart of the e-mail promotes a new style of your cable knit sweater. This way, you are saving time and deployment costs in not sending "wasteful" advertising to a segment that will not respond to anything else. You also are creating more value in the eyes of those customers, because you are not bombarding their inboxes with unnecessary messages.

They are social buyers. A certain segment of your customers will make purchases based on the "everybody else is buying it," or the *fad* mindset. You can determine this by analyzing your past purchasers based on what in-style products were promoted at certain times, and who responded. If tracked over several promotions such as this, you can gauge who your most likely social buyers are.

For instance, suppose you are a marketer for an online toy store. Suddenly, hula hoops come back into style. You send out a promotion to your house list and have a strong segment that buys the hula hoops. Your subsequent promotions advertise other timely and popular offers. You can then do a cross-select to determine who, of that first segment, continues to respond to those types of offers. You then can customize your future campaigns to that select group and only e-mail offers of toys, products, and games that are experiencing a surge in popularity at that particular time.

There is a true perceived value. Keep in mind that *value,* in this sense, does not necessarily mean less costly, a "bargain," or even *cheap.* It simply means that customers are ready and willing to respond because they have a desire or need for the product, they have an overall sense of perceived quality, and the product meets their criteria as far as cost and features. If they receive an e-mailed message from you, their favorite seller of _____, and it promotes this particular product—again, at the right time—then they are yours. With this in mind, you can determine, through a historical analysis of your purchasers' behavior, who your bargain hunters are, who your spendthrifts are, and who's in between. You then can custom-tailor your messages to each segment accordingly.

Determine the Various Purchase Points

In order to bring it all together, you must formulate a plan in order to figure out what variables will help you better serve and communicate with your customers. Let's review the basic necessary components to your plan.

Timing. If you send out a weekly newsletter, for example, you may have a tenth of your customers respond every week, a tenth may respond once a month, a tenth may respond once every six months, and yet another tenth may only respond around the December holidays. The remaining 60 percent of the file never respond and are completely inactive. What do you do with them?

There are two schools of thought here. One school says to simply purge these nonresponders from your file, because it costs a good bit of money to send messages to them. After all, why waste this time and money?

The other school says that this segment responded at some point (i.e., when they first signed onto your file) and that there is hope. Split this segment off, says this school, and test various customized offers to it. If you are aggressive with these efforts (but not overly so), one day you will hit pay dirt.

What they're buying. Deliver true value based on what your customers are buying. Once you have the segmentation and database solutions in place, there is no excuse for you to deliver any other kind of communications.

Suppose you have 100,000 customers on your database, and 15 percent of them are buyers of products in the $200 and up price range only. Another 45 percent purchase only in the $25 to $50 price range. Of the remaining 40 percent, 10 percent buy the $10 products and 30 percent buy across all prices. Of course, based on this knowledge that you have about your customers, you will create custom campaigns for them, according to what they buy. (The $200 folks will receive only your most expensive offers, the $25 to $50 purchasers will receive only product promotions covering that particular price range, etc.) This is just one simple example of how you can segment, and thereby personalize, your audience based on what they're buying. There are plenty of other ways. What makes sense for your business?

Who is buying? This is where response is based on things other than *when* an offer was sent or *how much* or *what type* of products was purchased. Many marketers, for instance, segment their house file simply on gender. An upscale menswear site, for example, may have gift buyers who are women; yet the majority of their best customers are probably made up of the end users—the men. A home decorating products site, however, may target and hence draw in more women than men buyers.

Best customers also may be segmented by where they live, based on the needs of their region or by their proximity to offline stores.

Additionally, as we've seen, they can be segmented by how long it has been since they last purchased, or, in the case of content subscribers, when they "expired" from a file.

How they click. With all of the above in mind, you can see the potential for hundreds of different ways to split your list. The bottom line is that, in most cases, it would behoove you to test a variety of offers. But it goes beyond the final sale. Because one of the beauties of e-mail messages are the embedded links, or unique URLs, you also can measure which links have the highest response. In other words, you can assign a unique link for every product that you promote within a certain message and can measure simple *interest* in addition to purchase rates. Figure 13.3 shows how past buying habits were used to choose which new offers would be sent.

For instance, if you learn that a customer always clicks on a particular offer, do something with that information. If it's always a sale item, send them your discounted offers. If you sell music online and they always click on the alternative music selections, customize your subsequent messages. Use that intelligence and make it work for you.

WHAT TO TEST?

Given all of the information we've learned in this chapter, following are some sample tests that an e-mail marketer can use when deploying his or her house file:

- *Control*—A general e-mail promotion, promoting a sampling of products or services. Sent to a random group of 5,000 customers across the file.
- *Coupon or special sale offers*
  - To random group of 5,000
  - To previous responders (5,000) of lower priced offers

FIGURE 13.3 Using Past Buying Habits to Choose Future Offers

Customers (based on what they have responded to in test)	Quantity	Offer
$45–$100 buyers, no special offer	3,300	Higher dollar offer, emphasis on quality and value. No discount
$25–$44 buyers, no special offer	7,202	Low and mid-priced offers, again with no special incentive
$45–$100 buyers with coupon offer	5,281	Discount, summer savings theme.
$25–$44 buyers with coupon offer	9,682	Same

Responders can be split in a hundred or more ways. This is a simplified example. Most likely, there will be crossover between segments. Most e-mail marketers will make the higher-paid, no discount (thereby higher revenue) offer pull any and all of the crossover names.

- *Frequency* (Example: four promotions per month)
  - To random group of 5,000
  - To 5,000 more frequent responders
  - To 5,000 less frequent responders
- *"Just interested" versus paid buyers*
  - General offer to 5,000 clickers (no paid customers)
  - General offer to 5,000 buyers

NEXT STEPS

In order to create a truly optimized house e-mail database, you need to decide what type of information is important. What type will enhance your file? It is this fine-tuned segmentation that we have been focusing on in this chapter that is truly the wave of the future. This customized, multiple message approach will continue to be how marketers grow their lists, as well as their businesses. See Figure 13.4. The one-size-fits all approach, wherein customers receive one generic outbound promotion that is not only irrelevant but of little value, will quickly fall by

FIGURE 13.4 Fine-tuned Segmentation Is the E-mail Wave of the Future

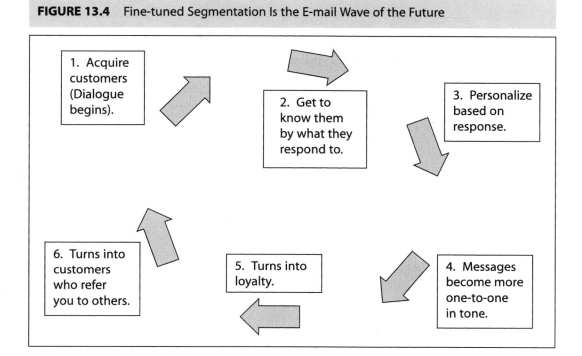

the wayside. We will quickly see that the marketers who truly excel at this level of customization—that is, the ones that can go the deepest as far as customizing and personalizing and optimizing—will be the winners in the end.

So know your customers. Know what they respond to, where they live, what they buy. Know their likes and dislikes and truly "listen" to what they have to say.

That, my fellow marketers, is where true dialogue takes place.

GOLFCOACHCONNECTION.COM GETS ITS RESULTS

The GolfCoachConnection.com team followed up its successful lead generation promotion (strategy, copy, and design were showcased in earlier chapters) with a profitable retention promotion. It is pleased with the results, as shown in Figure 13.5, which compare favorably with previous direct mail promotions, but is eager to parlay its growing expertise with e-mail promotions into much bigger numbers!

FIGURE 13.5   GolfCoachConnection.com's Retention Promotion Results

	Retention promotion results
E-mailed (avid golfers, nonbuyers) quantity:	5,000
Click-throughs	420
CTR	8.4%
Conversions (club orders)	63
Conversion rate	1.26%
Average order	$300
Gross sales	$18,900
Margin ((selling price – shipping, packaging, product cost) × orders)	$6,300
Advertising cost (design)	$2,000
Profit (loss)	$4,300
Profit (cost)/name	$68.25

CHAPTER EXERCISES

1. What does RFM stand for?

2. Take a look at your own business model. List assumptions about which segments of your house file will benefit your future promotions.

CHAPTER 14

Viral Marketing

OBJECTIVES

- Define viral marketing.
- Review its strengths.
- Create strategies for viral-based campaigns.
- Define the top components to achieving success.

What is the least expensive, most cost efficient, and the quickest, most desirable way to get the word out about a business? Word of mouth or referrals, right? This is where your customers, leads, and others who are familiar with your offering become your biggest advocates—so much so that they can't help but recommend you to their friends, family, and/or associates. The hope is that a percentage of *those* friends, pass on even more recommendations, as shown in Figure 14.1. The word will spread farther from there as customers become allies, not to mention friends, partners, and even compatriots.

E-mail is the perfect venue to grow such a chain of events due to its ease-of-use and interactive nature. Look at what happens when someone sends you a great joke via e-mail. What do you typically do? Chances are, if it's good enough for a

FIGURE 14.1 Viral Campaign

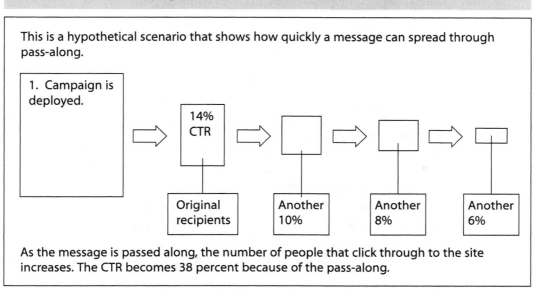

This is a hypothetical scenario that shows how quickly a message can spread through pass-along.

As the message is passed along, the number of people that click through to the site increases. The CTR becomes 38 percent because of the pass-along.

real belly laugh (and not just a chuckle), you *forward* it on to others who, in your estimation, would appreciate the humor. It's as easy as 1-2-3—click *Forward*. Type in the names of your recipients. Click *Send*. Before e-mail, what on earth did we do?

This type of easy "pass along" presents a fantastic opportunity for advertisers who have a message or an offer that is truly extraordinary. Therein lies the challenge: Make it unique. Make it fun, even. If the offer is right and if your original recipients are the right audience for it, then you stand a good chance of achieving marketing bliss.

HOW MANY EYEBALLS?

One reason this method of marketing is often called *viral,* or *organic,* marketing is because of the rate at which a campaign such as this can grow. Think of how a single-celled organism can grow. One cell splits into two. The two cells each split into two more. The four split again. Before you know it, what started out as a single cell has become 3,400.

The same concept applies with a viral e-mail campaign. You send off a stellar promotion to your customer file, or to a brand-new targeted acquisitions list. A percentage of those people will pass that e-mail along to others. *Those* recipients will then forward it on again. It simply mushrooms from there.

Unfortunately, however, this rarely occurs by itself. There are a few things that you need to do to help ensure that it does happen.

VIRAL COMPONENTS

First you need to identify what types of offers and messages can be successful with a viral marketing effort. Not all businesses will get dynamic results either because viral marketing doesn't fit their business model or because their offerings aren't compelling enough to spur viral action.

That is one of the keys to success when it comes to viral marketing. The message and/or offer has to be so unique and interesting that recipients are bound to pass it on. Here are a few examples.

- New Line Cinema created a series of ghoulish (but humorously so) postcards to promote its spooky *Final Destination* film's Web site—<www.deathiscoming.com>. Recipients would receive these animated postcards, which showcased various methods of demise, in their e-mail inboxes. They could then go back to the site and create their own postcards to send to friends and family. The e-mails themselves were creative and highly entertaining. And New Line's goal was accomplished brilliantly—much of the film's ticket sales was attributed to this viral campaign. The movie business is a natural business for this type of offering, which we'll see in the next example as well.
- *Double Parked* was an independent film released by a small producer, Fierce Films. Prior to the movie's release, Fierce Films issued a viral e-mail campaign to just 150 people. Within three days, the e-mail was forwarded 7,000 times. That's right—7,000. How? It was quite simple, really. (For the record, some of the more successful viral campaigns are based on the simplest of setups and principles.) The e-mail read like a summons, wherein the recipients were accused of such mock violations as "works too hard," "fashion crime," and "chronically late." They were then directed to a site where they could create their own fun summons to pass onto their own family and friends. Once they completed them, they were brought to FierceFilms.com, where they viewed the movie's trailer and received more information about the film and cast.
- An Australian-based company by the name of Wotch.com built an opt-in database in the hundreds of thousands with a viral campaign. This company produces small desktop gizmos that are essentially mini-Web browsers in a variety of fun formats. Best of all, they were free and didn't take up much disk space and were fairly easy to forward. Wotch.com made money

from ad space within the browsers themselves. Due to the nature of the attached product that was e-mailed (a combination of toy and desktop tool), the pass along rate was enough to grow the list in just a few short months.

TYPES OF MESSAGE

You can see, based on these examples, how response rates can grow exponentially when a viral campaign is successful. What are some other ways to create enough of a stir as to encourage this "Hey! Take a look at this!" type of forwarding? Let's take a look.

- *Contest entries.* Hypothetical scenario: You receive an advertising e-mail that promotes an offer with a sweepstakes. The contest has as its prize something that you desire, so you enter. Here's the kicker: If you pass the e-mail along, or if you sign up a few friends on the advertiser's site, you'll receive *x* number of additional entries to that beloved sweepstakes with the prize you hold so dear. You get the idea. A sweepstakes can be a popular way to promote your services through e-mail, viral component or not. But add a message to induce pass along and a sweepstakes can definitely encourage this kind of growth.
- *Deep discounts.* In a retail environment, sales and discounts can play a heavy hand in your revenues. With this type of model, you could send out a message with a certain percent discount across select sale items. *And if* your recipient customers sign up or forward the message on to others, they will receive an extra percentage off for every new sign-up.
- *Attachables.* Like Wotch.com and others whose business models are built, at least in part, on advertising revenue, sending a branded executable file can create a viral reaction simply due to the attachment's uniqueness. Office.com once sent a desktop basketball game that could be forwarded. The game was a fun diversion from the everyday workweek and encouraged pass along left and right. And smart thinking on Office.com's part—the desktop game carried the Office.com logo. Just be wary of sending attachments. Many people are not inclined to open them due to the "real" viruses that shut down computers.

TO ATTACH OR NOT TO ATTACH?

Speaking of attachments, these may not be the best things to send to strangers—meaning opt-in prospecting or acquisitions lists. First, many list vendors won't allow attachments due to the fear of *real* computer viruses. And many recipients have that same fear as well, which means that, unless they know who you are, there's a good chance that they won't open the messages.

WHAT MAKES A VIRAL *VIRILE*?

Of course, it takes more than just a few ideas on implementation to create a viral campaign. Every message should also include some, if not all, of the following factors:

- *Urgency factor.* If there is no deadline—a call to "sign up your friends by _____"—the need to share is reduced significantly.
- *Entertainment factor.* The message or offer that has to do with the viral component (such as the death postcards in a previous example) has to be compelling, amusing, different, or fun to your target audience.
- *Ego factor.* At least in part, there will be a certain percentage of recipients who will forward based on the "Hey! Look what I got!" factor. Create messages that appeal to them.
- *"Let me show you" factor.* This camp responds to the recipients who need to share something of significance. They want to help others, or make their day more enjoyable.
- *Value factor.* This is one of the most important factors in any type of e-mail communication, as we've seen previously. Like Office.com's desktop basketball game, make it work for you.

THE TECHNOLOGY

Sure, you say, it all sounds easy. And it definitely sounds worthwhile. However, how do you go about setting up your own viral marketing campaign? Many of the e-mail solutions providers listed at the back of the book can help in that regard. They can help sign up the forwardees, track number of e-mails forwarded, etc.

However, if a professional solutions provider is cost-prohibitive at this time, you can create your own viral campaign relatively easily—as long as you have a Web site and e-mail address of your own, a list of opt-in e-mail addresses, and a solid message. It needn't be fancy. And you may not be able to track your pass-along rate. A compelling offer and inducement to *forward* within your e-mail is all you need to encourage growth.

Or, if you offer a free subscriber newsletter and you want to step up your circulation, encourage pass along next to every article, as well as all over your site. Sometimes just the "asking" does the trick.

Last, whether you offer a newsletter or some other service that is initially free, create a custom landing or "splash" page on your site and drive members of your e-mail list to it. Then encourage them to register people they know on the sign-up form on this page. Offer a downloadable free report, software, or an entry in a contest.

No matter how you choose to implement a viral campaign, be sure to do it with care. Be mindful of the permission factor, and treat any new names with care.

GOLFCOACHCONNECTION.COM ADDS A VIRAL COMPONENT TO ITS HOUSE OFFERS

The marketing team at GolfCoachConnection.com has heard that viral marketing can jumpstart its e-mail marketing efforts to an entire new level. Therefore, it was anxious to test this new tool.

The team assumed that another trait of avid golfers is that they like to show off new equipment and other golfing "finds" to fellow golfers. The GolfCoachConnection.com team decided to capitalize on this trait to help it grow its house list.

So it included a "viral marketing" appeal in its retention e-mail copy to encourage recipients to send the e-mail to fellow golfers:

> "P.S. Send this e-mail to your golfing buddies and you could gain big bucks to spend in the GolfCoachConnection.com Pro Shop! For each friend who registers and buys something in the GolfCoachConnection.com Pro Shop (anything at all!), we'll give you a $10 credit to use in the Pro Shop. Get $10 each for up to 20 friends!"

GolfCoachConnection.com wanted to create the simplest type of viral campaign possible. That is why it simply asked recipients to forward this special offer to friends and family, and gave them incentives to do so.

CHAPTER REVIEW/EXERCISES

1. What can help make an e-mail campaign *viral?*

2. What are some of the top components to creating successful viral-based campaigns?

3. Exercise: Pretend that you run a site that sells children's educational software. You send out a promotion to parents offering a 30-day free trial download of one of your most popular products.

   a. Write the copy and summarize the offer. (Create a mock e-mail promotion.)

   b. How would you encourage a viral component?

   c. If you initially sent out the promotion to 500 people, what do you think your final number of trial downloaders will be?

PART FIVE

Back-End Necessities and Things to Be Mindful Of

CHAPTER 15

Coming in for a Landing

OBJECTIVES

- Define a landing page.
- Look at a few different types of landing pages.
- Review the necessary components.

In all of the chapters in this book, we've focused on the e-mail messages themselves, whether they're acquisitions-based or retention-based. How to write the copy. How to optimize the design. How to segment, test, deploy, and create.

There is a key component that we have thus far not mentioned, however. That component is the very necessary "landing page" on your site. This is also known as a splash, jump, or bounce page—depending on who you talk to.

WHAT IS A LANDING PAGE?

The landing page is the page on your site—the advertiser's site—that is, essentially, part two of the e-mail promotion. Its purpose? It has been specifically designed to help the prospects, recipients, or customers fulfill your call to action, whatever that may be.

Remember this: The landing page is an integral part of the e-mail promotion, no matter what kind of promotion it is. Think of it as a missing, yet very important, piece to the puzzle. Or the answer to a riddle. Or the final act of a great play.

IMPORTANCE OF CUSTOM LANDING

Many e-mail marketing novices automatically drive promotion recipients to the home page of their site, or another page that is already existing. They do this because they feel these pages are salesworthy (or action-inducing) in and of themselves. That may be the case, but the fact is you will achieve a much higher *conversion* rate if you direct people to a custom-created page.

Why? There are several reasons, actually. For one thing, a home page is often too general, and also contains myriad things to distract even the most interested of prospective leads and/or customers. There are usually buttons here, a navigation bar there. Sometimes there are banners and links and other items worth clicking. The problem is when new visitors come from an e-mail click to one of these areas, it makes it very easy to lose them. We'll get into the other reasons why a custom landing page will get you better results in a moment.

A click-through rate is one thing. Yes, we all strive for it because the higher the percentage of click-throughs, the more people we have to convert to what is our ultimate goal. Suppose we send out a prospecting promotion to 10,000 people with an interest in computer software. And suppose 10 percent, or 1,000 people, click through to a generic home page, or other noncustomized page on our site. Based on that, and because it was difficult for people to find the free software, only 10 percent of those 1,000 people end up registering for the offer, which was a free trial download of a very popular product. That is an extremely poor conversion rate for this type of lead generation offer (1 percent of the total names e-mailed, or 10 percent of click-throughs). This is a simple example to demonstrate a very important concept:

A customized landing page that is specific to your e-mail offer and message is a must.

Now let us take a different approach and put that concept into practice. Instead of driving prospects to our home page, we send them to a page that looks a lot like the e-mail where they just came from *and* continues the value pitch described therein even further. And the registration/sign-up form is right there on that page.

What kind of conversion did this one change make? New sign-ups went from 10 percent of click-throughs to almost 70 percent! A huge difference, to be sure.

We'll get into more on tracking and measuring later in this section, but for purposes of this chapter, take a look at the two different scenarios:

1. Test 1: 10,000 messages sent. 10 percent CTR (click-through rate) or 1,000 people who clicked through. 10 percent conversion, or 100 people who signed up.
2. Test 2: 10,000 messages sent. 10 percent CTR or 1,000 click-throughs. 69 percent conversion, or 690 people who signed up.

You can see how the marketer of Test 2 would be happy with those results. But beyond these results, however, take a look at what happens if a third test has a much lower click-through, but because of a custom landing page, results are still better than Test 1 with the much-higher CTR:

3. Test 3: 10,000 messages sent. 3 percent CTR, or 300 people who clicked through. 70 percent conversion, or 210 people who signed up.

As you can see, success does not boil down to click-throughs. In most cases, there is an end directive—whether it is a sign-up for a lead generation campaign, a pay-up for a sales offer, or a new subscription to a free publication. Conversion is one of the measuring factors that matter most.

DIFFERENT TYPES OF LANDING PAGES

Now that we've determined the importance of landing pages, let us review a few different types of them. More often than not, their differences are based on the types of offers showcased in the initial e-mails:

Simple Registration

This landing is used for a variety of lead generation offers. It can be as simple as a line or two of introductory or sales text, followed by the registration form itself, as shown in Figure 15.1. Generally speaking, this type of landing page encompasses just one page. It can be used to collect and/or register:

- New subscribers (to a free or paid subscription-based service)
- New users to a site (as in the case of an advertising-based site or a site that makes its money from user interaction with its online vendors)

FIGURE 15.1 Example of a Custom Landing Page

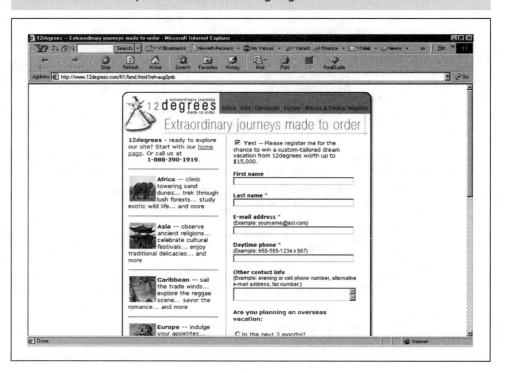

- Sign-ups for a free offer of some sort, including a free report, software trial, Web-based seminar, sweepstakes entry, etc.

Simple E-commerce Landing Page

For online retailers and others that have as their goal to drive sales, this type of landing page gets down to the nitty-gritty of the offer showcased in the e-mail. For instance, Levenger.com drives product sales in its house and outbound e-mail promotions. Typically, it promotes several products within the same e-mail. If recipients click on the product (within the HTML e-mail), they are taken to a specific page on the Levenger site (see Figure 15.2) that tells the recipients all about that particular product. A photo or graphic of the product, some sales copy, and pricing information fill in all of the gaps that the initial e-mail, which is meant more to "tease," leaves out. There is then an easy "buy here" directive, so the sales process, if desired, flows smoothly.

FIGURE 15.2 Levenger E-mail Promotion

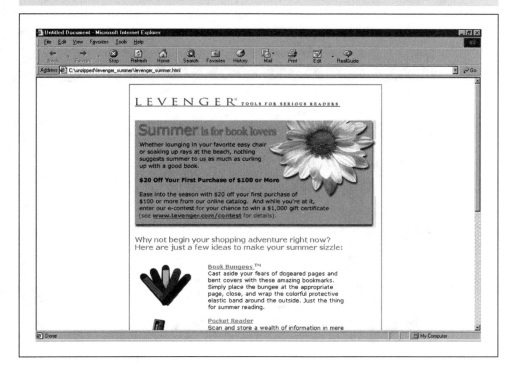

Complex E-commerce Page, or Microsite

Sometimes the promoted products are listed at a price point that requires a more in-depth sales pitch. Or the advertiser's USP (unique selling proposition) is unique, indeed—so unique that it is not an easy story to tell, or *sell,* in just one page. The concept is simple, though it is a bit more complex to develop. The e-mail promotion, which promotes a suite of related products, drives prospects to a landing page. This landing, however, is only page one—essentially a home page—to a number of other related pages. Typically, this extended landing showcases all products and reiterates the offer in the e-mail. If visitors click on one of the products, they are directed to an extended page that lists all of the features and benefits of that particular product, as shown in Figure 15.3. And just like a regular Web site, there usually are multiple layers to a microsite.

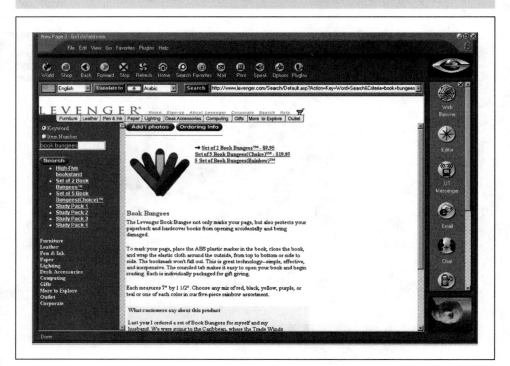

FIGURE 15.3   Landing Page If People Click on the "Book Bungees" on the E-mail

LANDING PAGE MUST-HAVES

No matter what type of landing page you end up developing for your e-mail promotions, there are a few well-tested "rules" to keep in mind. Included are:

- *Be specific.* Think of the landing as the second part of your wonderful, compelling e-mail. If you are promoting registrations for a free online seminar, then your landing page needs to hone in on that seminar and drive registrations to it and nothing else. By the same token, if you are promoting widgets for $1.99, then by all means, showcase those widgets, the special sale, and some compelling sales copy on that landing page. Remain true to the initial e-mail, be as clear and as specific as possible, and leave no room for unanswered questions.
- *Maintain the creative scheme.* If the e-mail that directed people to your landing page was produced in red, white, and blue HTML, then your land-

ing page should follow that same color scheme as closely as possible. If the e-mail had black and white stars sprinkled throughout, then sprinkle them on the landing page, too. If the e-mail was in plain text, you can pretty much create whatever you want. Just be sure to create it using the design specifics from Part Three.

- *Reiterate the offer.* Remember, recipients of the e-mail clicked through to this page because they have an interest. The interest is in your great offer, so sing it out loud and clear. Remind people why they clicked through to begin with. Make it part of your headline at the top of the page.

- *Continue the copy.* Whatever you didn't say in the initial e-mail, say it now. You have more space and time. These people are better prospects and listeners, as a whole, than the sum of all the folks who received the e-mail promotion. Why? Because they were interested enough to click through. So now that you've got them, don't let them get away. Come up with more benefits of your offer, but do not get overly wordy. You just want to be sure that your offer and benefits are crystal clear.

- *Include a final call to action.* This is a given. Before any form or directive that an end user has to complete, there must be a final directive: "Register today with the form below," "Sign up here," "Buy now." Even though it may be obvious to you that your visitors must complete the form in order to get the offer, it may not be as clear to them. Make this call to action sing.

THE FORM

Let us go back to a lead generation form for a moment. What type of information do you capture?

Truly, that depends on your own goals and business needs. Even though you may be just trying to create a house e-mail list for ongoing e-mail marketing, your ultimate goals may require that you collect more than just a set of e-mail addresses at this point.

Just remember that the more you ask for, the more tiresome your sign-up/registration/conversion form will be to your prospects and customers. Come up with your absolute minimum of information that you need to collect, and create your form from there. Most lead generation sign-up forms include

- Name
- E-mail address
- Zip code

Sometimes, they also include a question of some sort, which can be answered with a simple yes or no answer, via a radio button. Such was the case with travel site 12degrees when it ran an acquisitions campaign in which its goal was to build an e-mail list for future marketing. To get people to the landing page, they offered a sweepstakes for a $15,000 trip giveaway. Once on site, the form was very simple and there were just a couple of information-gathering questions, such as "Will you be planning a vacation in the next six months?" As long as you don't bombard your "guests" with too many questions such as these, they can be helpful in determining what kinds of prospects you have on your hands.

A LAST WORD ON LANDINGS

The landing page must be easy to follow and use, over and above the actual sign-up form. If people are unclear about what to do, more likely than not, they'll go elsewhere and forget about your great offer.

One last note: To help alleviate those pesky "unanswered questions," always provide a link to your site's privacy policy. People want to know what you are going to do with their precious personal information. Make sure you address this on your page.

GOLFCOACHCONNECTION.COM CREATES ITS LANDING PAGE

As we've seen in earlier chapters, the GolfCoachConnection.com team has created a compelling e-mail message to open its "sales pitch," but now it needs a strong landing page to "close the deal." In this case, that means convincing golfers who were motivated enough to click through from the e-mail to the landing page to complete the process by signing up for "Golf Tips from Your Golf Coach."

So, the landing page copy must be benefit-oriented and have clear instructions for golfers about signing up. The team also wants to include its privacy pledge to make visitors more comfortable about giving their personal information (a must-have for many Web surfers).

The team does not, however, want the landing page to be so cluttered with text that it discourages golfers from completing the final, crucial step of signing up. The team discussed these concerns with the copywriter and the Web designer, who were able to come up with an attractive solution that would (a) help persuade visitors to fulfill the call to action, (b) be easy for visitors to fill out, and (c) would collect all of the information that the team needed. See Figure 15.4 to view the page that GolfCoachConnection.com thought would meet all its requirements.

FIGURE 15.4 GolfCoachConnection.com Gets a Landing Page

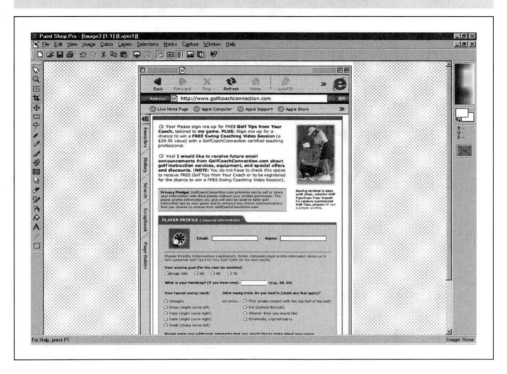

|CHAPTER REVIEW/EXERCISES

1. Which of the following hypothetical scenarios would be better for lead generation?
   a. 50,000 e-mails sent. 14 percent click-through rate. 22 percent signed up to the free offer (converted).
   b. 50,000 e-mails sent. 5 percent click-through rate. 75 percent signed up.

2. Which of the following hypothetical scenarios would be better for profitability?
   a. 20,000 e-mails sent. 5 percent CTR. 2 percent paid an average order of $35
   b. 20,000 e-mails sent. 3 percent CTR. 1 percent paid an average order of $125.

The above two scenarios will help get you in the mind-set of what measurability factors are the most important, as we'll soon see later in this section.

CHAPTER 16

More on Testing, Cookies, and Other Bits and Bytes

OBJECTIVES

- Determine the criteria for deployment frequency.
- Determine testing strategies.
- Define cookies and determine how they can help an e-mail campaign.

Those of us who have been part of successful e-mail campaigns know firsthand what a wonderful feeling it is to reach or exceed our goals and expectations. Excellent results tell us that we've done an excellent job.

Sometimes, however, we think we're doing a fine job, only to find that our response rates don't seem to agree. We have all our "ducks in a row"—compelling copy, an eye-pleasing and quick-to-download design, a solid group of house or acquisitions lists that we've successfully used before . . . but the results are disappointing.

"How can this happen," we ask ourselves, "We just used this list last week/ month/quarter!"

That is where the problem comes in. Often, we are overzealous with our e-mail marketing efforts. We find a prospecting list that brings us double-digit click-through rates and we want to use it again and again. Unfortunately, unlike broadcast advertising—radio and television—frequency does *not* create better results. When you "hit" a list of the same people over and over again, and the duration between hitting them is not long enough, your response rates are bound to fall off.

The same goes for your own house list. We think to ourselves, "This group of people is really interested in my offer. After all, they signed up for it themselves! I need to promote to it as much as possible." Wrong. Use this philosophy and you'll be dead in the water before you know it.

This is probably common sense to many of you. However, there are a good number of new e-mail marketers that unfortunately make this mistake. How do you prevent this from happening? And how do you determine the optimum number of times to deploy your promotions, whether they are acquisitions or retention-based? In a word—test.

SETTING UP TIMING TESTS

There are three things to test with regards to timing:

1. How often (within a certain period of time)
2. Best days of the week
3. Best times of the day

How Often

If you're using an opt-in acquisitions list that you've rolled out to (i.e., e-mailed the entire file) with success in the past, then send the same message (copy and design, if applicable) to it, only this time break it up into segments. Each segment will be e-mailed at a different time. Remember what we learned earlier about only testing one variable at a time? In this case, the variable is the deployment time. Therefore, absolutely *everything else must remain the same*—the offer, the message, the subject line, the copy and design.

Use a statistically significant number for each segment—5,000 is the number to strive for. Your original rollout is your control by which your other tests are measured. Your scenario may look as follows and results will look like those in Figure 16.1.

As you can see, it may be a month before you start seeing decent returns. Then again, depending on your business model, Test 1's results may be good enough for you. Every business is different. This is another reason why testing can yield such valuable results—you may very well find that giving your recipients a week's break, or even just a few days' break, is enough for you to meet your business goals.

FIGURE 16.1 Comparing Time Tests for Efficiency of Returns

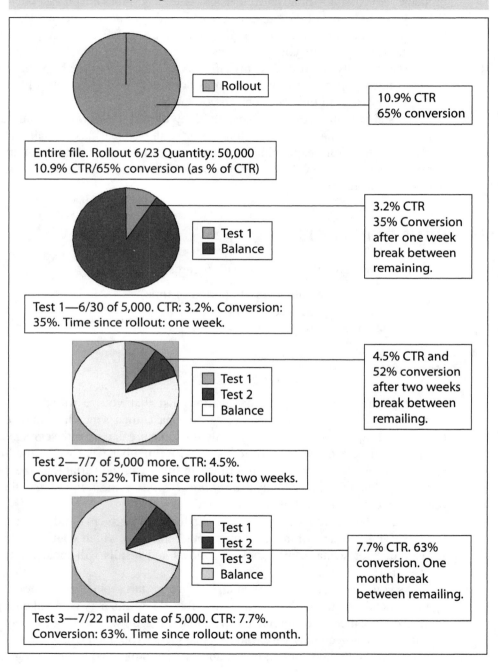

You can apply this same test to your own house list to see how often your newsletter (or whatever your regular house communication is) should come out. Split your house file into statistically significant segments and deploy, using the same strategy. If your newsletter promotes paid products, your strongest indicator will be your paid conversions—how many people ended up buying when they received the newsletter once a week? Twice a month? Once a month? Your results may surprise you.

Keep in mind when you're dealing with extremely large universe lists, it may never be necessary to test timing such as this. You may have four million names to e-mail and if you only send out promotions of 20,000 or fewer once a month or so, you can continue to e-mail "fresh" names for quite some time. You simply tell your list vendor to suppress all previous orders. Then, once you've gone through the entire list, months will have gone by and you can start all over again.

Best Days of the Week

Depending on who you talk to, some days of the week are better than others. Marketer A may find that Tuesdays are optimum for her, while Marketer B may find that Fridays work best. Therefore, this is definitely worth testing for *your* business.

Basically, the test can be set up the same way as for the previously seen frequency test. Use the same offer, same message, same list. Again, the difference is in the day the e-mail goes out. My advice is to send out the various segments within the same week, to account for any holidays or other extraneous elements that could affect results. By the way, there will *always* be factors that affect your testing that are beyond your control. Account for them by always knowing that your results are not going to be 100 percent accurate, but will be a good indication of where you should go.

Your weekday test and results may look like this (where there is no original rollout—only a series of tests):

Test 1—Day: Monday. Quantity: 5,000 List: Q. Message/Offer: B
    CTR: 3.2%, conversion: 3.5% (paid consumer offer).
Test 2—Day: Tuesday. Quantity: 5,000. List: Q. Message/Offer: B
    CTR: 4.6%, conversion: 4.1%.
Test 3—Day: Wednesday. Quantity: 5,000. List: Q. Message/Offer: B
    CTR: 4.8%, conversion: 4.3%.
Test 4—Day: Thursday. Quantity: 5,000. List: Q. Message/Offer: B
    CTR: 5.6%, conversion: 5.6%.
Test 5—Day: Friday. Quantity: 5,000. List: Q. Message/Offer: B
    CTR: 7.8%, conversion: 8%.

Results like these may seem counter-intuitive to some businesses, especially those that target other businesses. (After all, Friday is the end of the work week and the scenario above has this day as the best day.)

Obviously, your best mail times can be set up in this same manner. Just be sure that all segments go out on the same day.

MAKE ASSUMPTIONS

When you get your final results on clicks and conversions, think about what broad assumptions you can make about these results, and then drill down from there. For instance, suppose the last test is for an online clothing retailer. It was trying to determine which day of the week is best to send out its weekly newsletter that promotes its sale items. Perhaps Friday was the best day because recipients were already in the weekend mind-set and were ready to shop. Or perhaps the promotion was tied into a promotion at the retailer's offline stores, where recipients could go over the weekend.

REMAIL STRATEGY

It's important to not wear out a message or offer. Just because a certain promotion gleaned a 20 percent CTR months, or even weeks, ago does not mean that you can use it again and again, even if you've determined that you can get great results if you mail x number of times per month.

This is one reason why you should continually test new offers, messages, and other variables. If you have a winner during one campaign, make that the control. During the next campaign, test your control against another promotion wherein you have changed a variable, be that the copy, the design, the subject line, etc. The goal is to always have a fresh, "unweathered" control. It takes more work, but the results are well worth it and cost-effective.

COOKIES FOR ADDITIONAL TESTS
AND ENHANCEMENTS

What is a cookie and how can it help an e-mail marketer? A cookie is a stored file—it can be a text file or an image file. A text file cookie is more complex, and contains a unique identifier of some sort. Often, though, a cookie is an invisible graphic, or GIF image, posted somewhere on an HTML e-mail or Web page. When a recipient or visitor opens up the page, that graphic is "served" from the site that is hosting it, so you can count the number of times a particular e-mail or page was opened, if it was sent in HTML.

You can tell other things as well. A cookie can tell you where on your site your visitors are going. You can tell which specific products they are interested in (because of where they visit). You can even have a good idea whether or not your viral component is working, due to the number of times an e-mail has been opened. If it is an extraordinarily high percentage of your initial messages sent, chances are your "forward this e-mail" call to action is being followed.

Creating a Cookie

If you want to add a cookie to your e-mail, you can only do it if your e-mail is produced in HTML. An HTML e-mail, as we've seen, is much like a Web page. To create the most elementary type of cookie, you only need to create a tiny (one pixel) image in a GIF format, give it a name (e.g., e-mailtrack.gif) and have it match your background. If the background color of your e-mail promotion is white, make your GIF graphic white. If it's blue, make it blue.

You can also store cookies on your site, to see where people might go after clicking through. For instance, you may name the cookie stored on your landing page "landing1.gif" and give different names to any other pages that they could possibly go to. They will all have the same referring URL, meaning that when you review your server log files, or your tracking software report, you will be able to tell how many times a visitor opened a message, how many clicked through, and how many visited alternate pages after the landing page. It can be very worthwhile information.

How Cookies Enhance Testing Strategies

If you want to just test subject lines, a cookie can be a valuable tool. For instance, many e-mail recipients will only open up a promotion with a catchy subject line. Many others will hit "delete" before ever opening an e-mail . . . simply based on the subject line. A subject line, as mentioned in Chapter 9, is an integral piece of the e-mail marketing puzzle. A great subject can grab an audience and can set them up for the dynamic promotion that lies ahead. A lousy one can . . . well, you get the picture.

Keep this in mind when testing various subject lines and messages. You can also test who the message is *from* because the "from" field is also seen by the recipients before they open the message. Just remember to look beyond click-throughs. Review the following example, which tested three different messages, each with a unique subject line.

Subject Line Test

Test 1—Subject Line A. Message A. Standard copy and lists.
CTR: 6%. Conversion: 50%.
Test 2—Subject Line B. Message B. Standard copy and lists.
CTR: 5.5%. Conversion: 62%.
Test 3—Subject Line C. Message C. Standard copy and lists.
CTR: 7%. Conversion: 63%.

If you were to measure your results by just click-throughs and conversions, Test 3 would be the winner, right? Let us dig a little deeper to see what the "open rate" was for each of these, based on the number of times the embedded cookie was called up for each version.

Test 1—Subject Line A. Message A. Standard copy and lists.
CTR: 6%. Conversion: 50%. Open rate: 66%
Test 2—Subject Line B. Message B. Standard copy and lists.
CTR: 5.5%. Conversion: 62%. Open rate: 43%
Test 3—Subject Line C. Message C. Standard copy and lists.
CTR: 7%. Conversion: 63%. Open rate: 39%

Now let's do that math to see what the numbers break down to, if we were e-mailing 5,000 people with the three tests above.

Test 1—3,300 opened. 300 clicked through. 150 converted.
Test 2—2,150 opened. 275 clicked through. 171 converted.
Test 3—1,950 opened. 350 clicked through. 221 converted.

Yes, Test 3 had the highest click-throughs and conversions, but look at the open rate of Test 1! Results such as these would urge a retest, this time creating a new message wherein the subject line from Test 1 is combined with the body message of Test 3. This is how great promotions are made. By the same token, if you set up a similar test for your landing pages, you can determine which landing is the most effective in inducing people to fulfill the final call to action (rather than going to other areas of the site).

Bottom line: Use cookies to help your testing strategies. But use them wisely, always striving to make your prospects' and customers' privacy top priority.

A FINAL WORD ON TESTING

Make that *two* words, actually: Test again. One-time results should not necessarily be used as the basis for all future promotions. That goes for whether you are testing timing issues, messages, lists, or any kind of creative. That is because results change over time. List subscribers move in and out of the list. Messages become stale. Dramatic offers become commonplace, industry-wide.

CHAPTER REVIEW/EXERCISES

1. What are the best days of the week to send out an e-mail promotion?
   a. Monday.
   b. Wednesday.
   c. Thursday.
   d. Need to test it.

2. What is a cookie, as far as e-mail promotions go?
   a. A sweet snack.
   b. A text or image file that is stored.
   c. A bug on your hard drive.
   d. A type of software used to create tests.

3. Take a look at the following scenario. Then answer the questions that follow.

   Mary Smith had to test two different variables. The first was how often she should send out her company's newsletter to her house file. The second was what the title should be. (This would be posted in the "From" area before recipients even opened the message.)

Test A—How often?
Test 1a—One week apart. Quantity: 5,000. Same list, message, offer.
   CTR: 2.9%, conversion: 33%.
Test 2a—Two weeks apart. Quantity: 5,000. Same list, message, offer.
   CTR: 4.6%, conversion: 50%.
Test 3a—One month apart. Quantity: 5,000. Same list, message, offer.
   CTR: 3.9%, conversion: 44%.

Test B—Name of newsletter
Test 1b—Name X. Message X. Same subject, copy and lists.
   CTR: 4.9%. Conversion: 65% of click-through. Open rate: 50%
Test 2b—Name Y. Message Y. Same subject, copy and lists.
   CTR: 7.5%. Conversion: 62% of click-through. Open rate: 23%
Test 3b—Name Z. Message Z. Same subject, copy and lists.
   CTR: 5%. Conversion: 53% of click-through. Open rate: 34%

   i. What is the optimum number of times per month this marketer should send out her newsletter?
   ii. What is the newsletter name winner?

iii. What recommendations would you make with regards to name and message?

iv. What combination of frequency and title and message would you use?

Answers:

i.   Two weeks apart

ii. Name *X*

iii. Perhaps Mary could test the copy from Name *Y*, Message *Y*, because click-throughs were higher. Test it with her winning name, Name *X*, against the control.

iv. She should next roll out every two weeks to Name *X* until she has a winner.

CHAPTER 17

The Last Word: What It All Adds Up To—Tracking and Measuring Your Results

OBJECTIVES

- Define ROI.
- Determine best methods to track and measure campaign results.
- Learn how to best apply these results.
- Review various tracking procedures.
- Review sample reports.

One of the best things about marketing with e-mail is that you can track and measure your results. You can then apply whatever lessons you've learned on offer, message, timing, etc., to future successful campaigns.

As we've seen in this book, however, there are several key measurement tools. Success is not solely determined by the click-through. Conversion is key. And, as we saw in the last chapter, even open rates have their importance.

Depending again on your business model, you need to look at all of these areas. In addition, you need to look at your campaigns from a profitability standpoint, and how well they measure up to your ultimate goals. And that means you probably need to look at ROI.

ROI: THE ULTIMATE MEASUREMENT

ROI means return on investment. For the most part, it refers to paid offers; but even lead generation offers ultimately sell *something* of monetary value. Your job, in either case, is to help keep costs down and profits up.

A simple formula for ROI (for a paid call to action e-mail promotion) follows:

First calculate costs. Remember, your deployment costs can include any or all of the following:

- List costs
- Creative costs
- Extra deployment costs
- Tracking costs
- Miscellaneous

Total campaign costs ÷ total e-mails sent = Cost to e-mail/recipient
Total campaign costs ÷ # of recipients who clicked through = Cost per click
Total campaign costs ÷ # of people who bought = Cost per converted customer

Then calculate revenue:

Total revenue ÷ # of converted customers = Revenue per customer

Then calculate ROI:

Total revenue − Total costs = ROI in dollars
ROI in dollars ÷ Total costs × 100 = ROI percentage

Let us apply this formula and look at two different companies. One is a retail site that sells product in its acquisitions promotions as well as in its internal house newsletters. The other is a high-end e-mailed newsletter that applies lead generation practices to its acquisitions campaigns and then attempts to convert these new leads in follow-up internal campaigns. In other words, you're tracking two different marketers, and two completely different ways of marketing through e-mail.

Scenario 1—Retail Site

Goal: To drive prospects to buy products on the site. After they buy, they become part of the house file for future e-mail marketing through promotional newsletters.

Plan: E-mailed 50,000 opt-in list prospects a promotion that showcased this site's $35 fall sweater. Total costs, including lists, creative, and miscellaneous: $15,000.

Results: 2,500 people clicked through (5 percent CTR). Of those that clicked through, a total of 75 (or 3 percent) bought the sweater. So we have a $6 cost per click, $200 cost per conversion. Total revenue: $2,625.

Was this cost-effective? Determine the ROI using the ROI formula:

ROI in dollars: $2,625 − $15,000 = −$12,375
ROI % = −$12,375 ÷ $15,000 × 100 = −82.5% ROI.

So this was not a profitable scenario. However, for this particular marketer, she may have been willing to lose money on the front end in order to bring people into her house file. She would then have those customers for future cross-selling and up-selling efforts down the road.

Let's look at another paid scenario, before moving onto the lead generation campaign:

Goal: Again, to drive prospects to buy products on the site. After they buy, they become part of the house file for future e-mail marketing through promotional newsletters.

Plan: E-mailed 50,000 opt-in list prospects a promotion that showcased a $275 product, but this higher price was not in the initial e-mail (this is sometimes a deterrent). Total costs, including lists, creative, and miscellaneous: $15,000. (So the product pricing is higher than the last scenario, but the total costs are the same.)

Results: Because the product showcased was so attractive, and the price wasn't listed, the click-through rate was still high. 3,000 people clicked through (6 percent CTR). Based on a dynamic landing page, of those that clicked through, a total of 60 people, or 2 percent of those who clicked through, bought the product. So we have a $5 cost per click, $250 cost per conversion. Total Revenue: $16,500.

Was this cost-effective? Determine the ROI using the ROI formula, we see the following:

ROI in dollars: $16,500 − $15,000 = −$1,500
ROI % = −$1,500 ÷ $15,000 × 100 = 10% ROI.

So we have a small, yet still profitable, ROI.

Scenario 2—Paid Newsletter—Business Site

Goal: To drive prospects to the site for lead generation. After they sign up, they become part of the house file for future e-mail marketing to get them to convert to their higher dollar products.

Plan: E-mailed 75,000 opt-in list prospects a promotion that presented an offer for a free industry research report, the type of which is tremendously valuable to this group of prospects. The ultimate goal is to get leads to eventually purchase a $695 high-quality business newsletter. Total costs for acquisitions, including lists, creative, and miscellaneous: $30,000.

Results—acquisitions. Because this was an offer for something free that had such a high value to this list, 7,500 people clicked through (10% CTR). Of those who clicked through, a total of 4,875 or 65 percent signed up for the report. So we have a $4 cost per click, $6.15 cost per conversion. Total Revenue: $0 at this point.

Results—conversion efforts. With this type of scenario, converting to the point of profitability takes time. Therefore, listed below are results of subsequent conversion efforts:

Effort 1: E-mailed immediately after sign-up. Offer: Newsletter at "special discount rate" of 10 percent off. Results: 0 paid.

Effort 2: E-mailed one week after sign-up. Offer: Newsletter at same discount rate, but with an "urgency" note that this offer goes away by a certain date. Results: 5 people made a purchase. Revenue: $3,037.50 (after 10 percent discount).

Effort 3: E-mailed two weeks after Effort 2. Offer: Newsletter with no discount ("we told you so") but features the many benefits to the paid subscription. Results: 10 people made a purchase. Revenue: $6,950.

Effort 4: E-mailed three weeks after Effort 3. Offer: Newsletter with a special "summer discount" of 10 percent again. Results: 22 people made a purchase. Revenue: $13,761 (after 10 percent discount).

Effort 5: E-mailed three weeks after Effort 4. Offer: Last chance discount of 10 percent. Results: 30 people made a purchase. Revenue: $18,765 (after 10 percent discount).

As you can see, by the time Effort 5 concluded, this company was in the black. But remember—this was nine weeks after the initial e-mail was sent *and* is a stepped-up example for demonstration purposes. Most of the time, you'll find that higher dollar offers, such as this one, take longer to convert and hence longer to reach profitability. Months, at times, and sometimes close to a year may pass before this offer reaches profitability. What you have to determine is how long it is before you need to:

- Generate revenue
- Break even
- Generate profits per campaign

This last example also doesn't take into account that a certain percentage of registered leads will unsubscribe with each effort. That is why you shouldn't over-load these leads with an abundance of e-mails.

Was this cost-effective? Determine the ROI using the ROI formula, we see the following:

ROI in dollars after Effort 5: $42,513.50 (total revenue) − $30,000 = −$12,513.50
ROI % = −$12,514 ÷ $30,000 × 100 = 41.71% ROI.

So this was another profitable scenario, but *over time*.

Other Things to Track

Aside from click-throughs, conversions, and ROI, track open rates (with the use of cookies) and pass-along rates (many e-mail solutions providers can help in this regard). Reports that show all variables and all measures of response can get quite complex and time-consuming to read. To combat that, break up your reports into manageable segments, or categories.

Use the worksheet in Figure 17.1 as a guide for your own tracking results.

THE FUTURE

We learn new things every day in this arena—the tremendously exciting and rewarding e-mail marketplace. What's next?

As we've already seen, rich media e-mails are quickly gaining momentum as an industry powerhouse in terms of their ability to send dynamic content. Video, audio, and e-commerce–enabled e-mails are only part of the scenario. Full-feature

FIGURE 17.1 Worksheet for Tracking Your Results

Campaign number	Mail date	Message	# of e-mails Sent	Total Cost	Cost per e-mail	% Click-throughs	% Conversion	# of Click-throughs	# of Conversions	Average order $	Total revenue	ROI

"commercials," the likes of which we've seen elsewhere are coming down the pike, once bandwidth speeds are no longer an issue.

Wireless providers, such as those that give us cell phones and personal digital assistants, also may play a role in future e-mail marketing. Alert services, special coupons that pop up when you walk by a certain store, may very soon become mainstream.

GOLFCOACHCONNECTION.COM LOOKS TOWARD THE FUTURE

Except for the assistance of its regular list broker and two list vendors, the GolfCoachConnection.com marketing team successfully planned, developed, and executed its first acquisition and retention e-mail promotions using in-house resources only.

Past experience with traditional direct mail helped a great deal, but the team also encountered a number of situations that it hopes to handle better in the future, possibly through outsourcing, when it moves on to larger promotions.

The team would like to be able to track pass-alongs of its e-mail promotions to other prospects, for example, to measure the effectiveness of its viral marketing efforts. It also lacked a database solution that would help it segment its house file with greater precision, or integrate buying patterns and other data, for highly targeted, personalized e-mail promotions.

E-mail marketing proved to bit a little more complicated than the team first anticipated, but definitely worth it!

CONCLUSION

All of this innovation and growth make this an exciting time to be a marketer in this medium. I hope you'll be able to walk away from this book ready to take on the new challenges of what is about to take place. It's sure to be a fun and wild ride, and I'm so glad you've been able to take it this far. Just wait until you see how far you can go!

Now, without further ado, it's time to review some of the most effective e-mail campaigns from your fellow e-mail marketers. As you read this, these seasoned professionals are creating e-mail marketing "best practices" with what they have learned—*and* what they were willing to share. My sincerest appreciation and thanks goes out to all of them for their generosity.

|CHAPTER REVIEW/EXERCISES:

1. What is ROI?

2. Consider the following scenario:
   a. Acquisitions paid promotion: 10,000 e-mails sent. $2,500 total cost.
   b. 6% CTR, 4% conversion.
   c. Order size: $50 per paid order.
   Calculate ROI. Is this profitable?

3. Now using the following scenario, calculate ROI at steps (d), (e), and (f).
   a. Acquisitions lead generation promotion: 100,000 e-mails sent. $35,000 total cost.
   b. 14% CTR, 75% conversion to lead generation offer. $0 revenue.
   c. Six follow-up efforts over six months.
   d. Month 3: Total revenue = $18,500. Calculate ROI at this point.
   e. Month 4: Total revenue = $32,000. Calculate ROI.
   f. Month 5: Total revenue = 46,000. Calculate ROI.

TRAVELNOW.COM

Company: TravelNow.com
<www.TravelNow.com>
TravelNow.com is an online travel company providing air, rail, auto, cruise, and hotel reservation services. It has been in business since 1995 and started as an online hotel reservation company.

Objective: Drive holiday cruise bookings. Additionally, it wanted to build brand and name recognition and hopefully future travel bookings by staying in touch with its customers and building relationships

Offer: "Here's the Deal . . . Holiday Cruises" was the subject line. The main feature, the one that gets most of the action, offered a Texaribbean cruise at a special price in this edition of the newsletter.

Format: HTML only. If recipients can't read HTML, they are sent a link and instructions for them to cut and paste the site URL into their browser, and they can see the newsletter on the site. Each special goes to its own landing page, giving details of the special—11 specials/11 landing pages. See Figure CS.1 for a sample landing page. TravelNow.com sent out about 250,000 Here's the Deal newsletters and about 10,000 each of the five specialty newsletters. It experimented with the creative on Here's the Deal—more photos, less specials—though the overall look will remain the same. TravelNow.com added the title of the special to the subject line. Originally the subject line only read "Here's the Deal." Now it gives a clue about what the deal is! That helped response rates.

Lists Used: TravelNow didn't segment Here's the Deal—it went to everyone on the opt-in list. For the specialty newsletters, it analyzed the click-through patterns

FIGURE CS.1   One example of a TravelNow.com newsletter in HTML.

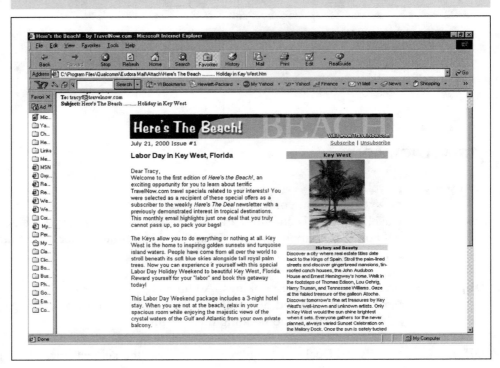

and, based on that analysis, asked customers if they would like to receive the specialty newsletter that TravelNow.com finds reflects their interests. The sending is done in-house. TravelNow.com used UnityMail to send and it used its own copy and creative.

Results: For the Texaribbean special, the click-through rate was .6 percent. For the newsletter overall, the click-through percentage was 4.8 percent. Conversion was approximately .4 percent. Conversion on the whole newsletter was .05 percent. Average sale was about $2,500.

Other: TravelNow.com continues to fine-tune its e-mail program. It has a person dedicated to managing it and is continuing to learn and integrate what it learns into what it does with the program.

12DEGREES

Company: 12degrees
<www.12degrees.com>
12degrees is an Internet-based, custom travel site for independent travelers. It develops overseas itineraries for its customers, including airfare, accommodations, and all ground services. Service is delivered by connecting customers with travel guidebook writers and destination specialists who consult with customers to provide truly unique and rewarding travel experiences. 12degrees' target is upscale, highly educated, time-strapped consumers, aged 35 to 65. See Figure CS.2 for an example of how 12degrees seeks to reach this audience.

Objective: The objective of the e-mail campaign was customer acquisition. There was no specific quantity in mind during the planning of the campaign, but 12degrees

FIGURE CS.2   12degrees trip offer.

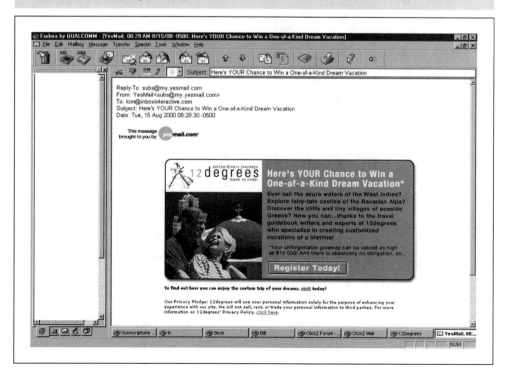

knew, based on research, that it should expect a 4 to 5 percent click-through. It was aiming for more than that, based on great creative and proper list selection! The sales cycle for the product is quite long (from a few weeks to many months), so acquiring the customer (i.e., obtaining their e-mail addresses and permission to communicate with them) is a critically important first step and an important investment.

Offer: 12degrees' core competency is custom travel—what better offer than a free custom travel package? Register on the site and win a custom-designed trip for two, with a value up to $15,000. Average sale is about $7,000 to $8,000 per person, based on a 10 to 14 day overseas trip.

Format: Text and HTML. 12degrees tested both long and short versions of e-mails. Long, but well-written copy, consistently delivers better results, although a short version just outperformed the long in the most recent test! In general, 12degrees thinks that short copy is not as compelling because the 12degrees offering is not an easy story to tell in few words.

Lists Used: 12degrees has a small in-house list that was used and it also rented lists based on recommendations of the companies hired to consult with on its e-mail marketing strategies (Metaresponse and Inbox Interactive, Inc.). Recommended lists were those from YesMail, Postmaster Direct, and DeliverE. It tested all travel selects.

Results: To date, approximately 54,000 e-mails were delivered, divided almost equally between short and long versions. Reported here are results for approximately 30,000 mailings.

CTR overall is above 6 percent; it varied by length of copy and one list performed better than the other two.

List A
Short version: 5,000; 5.32% CTR
Long version: 5,000; 6.5% CTR

List B
Short version: 5,000; 6.5% CTR
Long version: 5,000; 7.56% CTR

List C
Short version: 5,000; 8.7% CTR
Long version: 5,000; 7.34% CTR

Conversion rates as a percentage of CTR averaged more than 50 percent for all versions combined. As a percentage of total quantity mailed, registered users represented 4.3 percent.

List A

Short version:	48%
Long version:	30%

List B

Short version:	64%
Long version:	42%

List C

Short version:	77%
Long version:	82%

INCHORUS UNICEF

Company: UNICEF
<www.unicef.org>
UNICEF is an organization created by the United Nations General Assembly to advocate for the protection of children's rights, to help meet their basic needs, and to expand their opportunities to reach their full potential. Much of their work involves gathering and sharing information, resources, and education to promote the well-being of children throughout the world. See Figure CS.3.

Objective: To build awareness for the release of the 7th Annual Progress of Nations Report and press conference to UNICEF's in-house e-mail list.

Offer: The e-mail offer was a free copy of UNICEF's 7th Annual Progress of Nation's Report. The e-mail was sent out two days prior to the official press release as a strategic measure to build awareness of the press conference and report release. Indications are that it worked, because once the e-mail became available, the press conference speaker asked that it be shown for the opening of the actual press conference.

Format: Rich Media—graphics, animation, and sound. Link to home page for donations. Landing page was the report itself, but was made operational on the day of the press conference (i.e., it was not available when the e-mail was sent out, prior to the press conference). No testing of variables or subject head.

FIGURE CS.3 UNICEF promotes the well-being of children around the world.

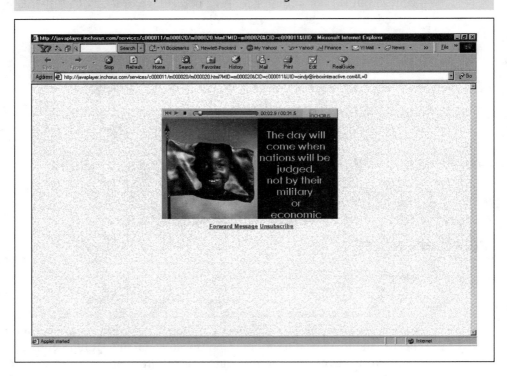

Lists Used: E-mailed approximately 36,000 addresses on the in-house list. No segmentation; Inchorus did the initial e-mailing. UNICEF continues to e-mail this themselves on a discretionary basis to new donators, interested parties, etc. This e-mail was sent all over the world to many, many remote places and areas where one would wonder if the technical infrastructure is really available to support text mail, let alone rich media e-mail. But our results were very good—there were very few delivery problems and lots of very positive feedback. The world really is wired—we proved it!

Lists Used: House file

Results:
sent: 35,819
failures to send: 18
unsubscribes   1303
view rate of successful delivery   36.77%

# of forwards: 709
Average elapsed time: 330.57 seconds
Average total length of rich media message played: 32.35 seconds
Average length of rich media message played: 28.32 seconds
Average # of times rich media message is played: 1.14
URL clicks to home page: 4431
Click-through rate per view: 43.76%
16%
Unique click-through rate per unique view; 31.71%
No conversion measured—offer was free.

REALAGE.COM

Company: Real Age, Inc.
<www.realage.com>
RealAge's business is based on providing personal, highly relevant health and lifestyle information. It does this in the form of assessments that people can take for free. Based on the assessment, they get highly targeted and relevant tips, information, and offers from advertisers and from RealAge.com. Revenues come from advertisers and from its e-store.

Objectives: The Tip of the Day shown in Figure CS.4 was about hair loss and included an ad for American Express travel services. The objective was twofold; continue building the relationship with RealAge and build brand for American Express. The Tip of the Day e-mail is intended for retention for Real Age and for producing revenues for the sponsor. Real Age gets 3,000 to 4,000 customer service calls/inquiries a day generated by the Tip of the Day e-mail.

Offer(s):   Retention: Hair Today, Gone Tomorrow (hair loss tip)
Branding: Fly, Drive, Cruise, Relax, Laugh, Schmooze; Find it at the Real Age Travel Center.

Format: HTML. Real Age formats in three versions so the e-mail promotions work with all e-mails, including AOL. Short, excellent writing worked best. Sometimes it used a landing page, sometimes the e-mails directed recipients to the advertiser's site. In this Tip of the Day, there are two landing pages; one for "more information on this tip" and one for the American Express travel offer.

Lists Used: The segmenting and deployment took place in-house. Tip of the Day was not segmented.

Results: 1,056,237 of this tip were sent out. Tip of the Day averages 2.5 percent "clicking on something;" Real Age has had ranges from .5 to 25 percent, but those aren't typical. One higher rate was for a skin care advertiser. If click through on an advertiser's spot was measured, 7 to 10 percent response rates on a targeted e-mail were gleaned.

With a compelling offer, Real Age experienced conversions of up to 25 percent. If the offer is of the value-added, branding, traffic-building type, conversions were lower. The advertiser spot in the hair loss Tip of the Day received a low conversion—maybe .1 percent—because it was for brand building. There was no incentive or call to action.

CATALOG CITY

Company: CatalogCity.com
              <www.catalogcity.com>
              CatalogCity.com is an online aggregator of hundreds of catalogs that sell every-
thing from gifts to hobby supplies, apparel to tools. Using one online shopping cart, shoppers can shop from literally hundreds of catalog merchants.

Objectives: Four e-mail campaigns are discussed. One was targeted for acquisition and
used a purchased list and two different offers; the other was targeted for retention and used the house file and two different offers.

Offers: *Acquisition* (purchased list, mailed to 250,000):

1. Enter a sweepstakes to win a trip to Pebble Beach, FL. See Figure CS5.b.
2. $10 off and enter sweepstakes. See Figure CS.5a.

Retention (house file, mailed to 500,000):

3. No offer and enter sweepstakes. See Figure CS.5d.
4. $10 off and enter sweepstakes. See Figure CS.5c.

Format: All four e-mails are text. The acquisition e-mails are shorter than the retention e-mails; it found that its house list responds better to longer, fuller
e-mails so the retention e-mails are longer. It tested by varying the subject
line and offer (results below).

Lists Used: House file and purchased list. Used a list broker who in turn used lists from
Cool Savings, Yesmail, 24/7, and others.

Results: *Acquisition list click-through:*

1. Sweepstakes with no offer: average c.4.0%
2. $10 offer with sweepstakes: average c. 4.5%

House list click-through:

3. No offer and sweepstakes: average 4.0%
4. $10 offer and sweepstakes: average 5.0%

Acquisition list conversion rates (% of click-throughs that purchased)

1. Sweepstakes with no offer: average 2%
2. $10 offer and sweepstakes: average 2%

House list conversion rate:

3. No offer and sweepstakes: average 12%
4. $10 offer and sweepstakes: average 20%

Average $ amount produced was about normal: $70 to $85, with variation for gift-giving seasons.

See Figure CS.6 to see an offering page for Catalog City.

FIGURE CS.5   Catalog City e-mail campaigns.

---

a. Acquisitions with Sweepstakes and Offer

```
From: Chris Flannery <ChrisF@catalogcity.com>
To: "'cindy@inboxinteractive.com'"
<cindy@inboxinteractive.com>
Subject: FW: CatalogCity.com can save YOU $10 off gifts for Dad
Date: Wed, 26 Jul 2000 08:18:06 -0700
X-Mailer: Internet Mail Service (5.5.2650.21)


-----Original Message-----
From: subs@my.yesmail.com [mailto: subs@my.yesmail.com]
Sent: Wednesday, June 07, 2000 9:06 PM
Subject: CatalogCity.com can save YOU $10 off gifts for Dad
------------------------------------------------------------
This message is brought to you by YesMail. We appreciate
your membership. To modify your member profile, please see
"Member Services" below.
------------------------------------------------------------
CatalogCity.com gives you easy access to the world's best
products. As the number one online shopping mall, we bring
you hundreds of your favorite catalogs all in one convenient
place. June at CatalogCity.com is all about dads, grads,
weddings, golf at Pebble Beach, and saving YOU money.

*** You Can Win a Pebble Beach Golf Getaway! ***

In celebration of great fathers everywhere, CatalogCity.com
is giving you the chance to win a trip for two to beautiful
Carmel, California -- including a stay at The Lodge at
Pebble Beach and a round of golf at the world-renowned
Pebble Beach course. All you have to do to enter is click
on the link below or enter it into your browser.

http://catalogmart.ym0.net/re3.asp?C=10074&P=14361&E=00000
```

No purchase necessary to enter or claim prize. A purchase does not increase your chances of winning. Must be legal resident of USA or Canada (excluding Quebec) 18 or older. Void where prohibited. Complete rules at CatalogCity.com through 6/30/00.

*** $10 off your next order of $75 or more! ***

CatalogCity.com is giving you $10.00 off your next purchase of $75.00 or more from your favorite catalogs by 6/19/2000. Just enter the special coupon code FDHTEN when you check out, to receive your $10.00 Off. (Discount cannot be combined with any other offer)

*** Don't Forget Father's Day is June 18th! ***

Finding the perfect Father's Day gift doesn't have to be a chore. We've selected a wide range of the best items for Dad from hundreds of your favorite catalogs to make finding him the perfect gift easy on you. Whatever Dad's interests are, or for the man who has everything, we can help. Check out our special Father's Day gift store at:

http://catalogcity.ym0.net/re3.asp?C=10074&P=14362&E=00000

*** Bargains galore! ***
From clearance items to white sales, our Outlet Center is filled with extraordinary values from your favorite catalogs -- 20-60% off everything!
Visit our Outlet Center for more money saving offers at:

http://catalogcity.ym0.net/re3.asp?C=10074&P=14363&E=00000

Plus remember to use your $10 off discount when you buy before June 19th. And don't forget to enter for your chance to win a Pebble Beach Golf Getaway sponsored by CatalogCity.com. You could be the lucky winner!

http://catalogmart.ym0.net/re3.asp?C=10074&P=14361&E=00000

Happy Shopping!
              Your friends at CatalogCity.com

b. Acquisitions, No Offer

From: subs@my.yesmail.com [mailto: subs@my.yesmail.com]
Sent: Wednesday, June 07, 2000 9:06 PM

(continued)

Subject: Enter to Win a Pebble Beach Golf Getaway at CatalogCity.com
----
This message is brought to you by YesMail. We appreciate your membership. To modify your member profile, please see "Member Services" below.

CatalogCity.com gives you easy access to the world's best products. As the number one online shopping mall, we bring you hundreds of your favorite catalogs all in one convenient place. June at CatalogCity.com is all about dads, grads, weddings, golf at Pebble Beach, and saving YOU money.

*** You Can Win a Pebble Beach Golf Getaway! ***

In celebration of great fathers everywhere, CatalogCity.com is giving you the chance to win a trip for two to beautiful Carmel, California -- including a stay at The Lodge at Pebble Beach and a round of golf at the world-renown Pebble Beach course. All you have to do to enter is click on the link below or enter it into your browser.

http://catalogmart.ym0.net/re3.asp?C=10883&P=14361&E=00000

No purchase necessary to enter or claim prize. A purchase does not increase your chances of winning. Must be legal resident of USA or Canada (excluding Quebec) 18 or older. Void where prohibited. Complete rules at CatalogCity through 6/30/00.

*** Don't Forget Father's Day is June 18th! ***

Finding the perfect Father's Day gift doesn't have to be a chore. We've selected a wide range of the best items for Dad from hundreds of your favorite catalogs to make finding him the perfect gift easy on you. Whatever Dad's interests are, or for the man who has everything, we can help. Check out our special Father's Day gift store at:

http://catalogcity.ym0.net/re3.asp?C=10883&P=14362&E=00000

****** Bargains galore! ******

From clearance items to white sales, our Outlet Center is filled with extraordinary values from your favorite catalogs -- 20-60% off on everything! Visit our Bargain Center for more money-saving offers at:

http://catalogcity.ym0.net/re3.asp?C=10883&P=14363&E=00000

Plus remember to enter for your chance to win a Pebble Beach Golf Getaway sponsored by CatalogCity.com. You could be the lucky winner!

http://catalogmart.ym0.net/re3.asp?C=10883&P=14361&E=00000

Happy Shopping!
Your friends at CatalogCity.com

c. Retention with Offer

From: Chris Flannery <ChrisF@catalogcity.com>
To: "'cindy@inboxinteractive.com'"
<cindy@inboxinteractive.com>
Subject: FW: CatalogCity Is Giving You $10 Off
Date: Wed, 26 Jul 2000 08:19:35 -0700
X-Mailer: Internet Mail Service (5.5.2650.21)

-----Original Message-----
From: catalogcity@clickaction.net
[mailto:catalogcity@clickaction.net]
Sent: Wednesday, May 31, 2000 2:31 PM
To: chrisf@catalogcity.com
Subject: CatalogCity Is Giving You $10 Off

Dear Chris Flannery,

Easy Access to the World's Best Products

This June CatalogCity.com is all about Dads, grads, weddings, golf at Pebble Beach, and saving money when you shop the world's leading online shopping mall. If you don't wish to receive these e-mails in the future, you can scroll to the end of this message and follow the simple instructions to remove yourself from our list.

*** You Can Win a Pebble Beach Golf Getaway! ***

In celebration of great Fathers everywhere, CatalogCity.com is giving you the chance to win a trip for two to beautiful Carmel, California -- including a stay at The Lodge at Pebble Beach and a round of golf at the world-renowned Pebble Beach course. All you have to do to enter is click on the link below or enter it into your browser. Then fill out the simple registration form that follows and you'll be entered for a chance to win.

(continued)

http://www.you-click.net/GoNow/a13223a21108a46741193a6

No purchase necessary to enter or claim prize. A purchase does not increase your chances of winning. Must be legal resident of USA or Canada (excluding Quebec) 18 or older. Void where prohibited. Complete rules at CatalogCity.com through 6/30/00.

*** $10 off your next order of $50 or more! ***

As a special thank you, CatalogCity.com is giving you $10 off your next purchase of $50 or more from your favorite catalogs by 6/19/2000. Just enter the special coupon code FDETEN when you check out to receive your $10 off. (Discount cannot be combined with any other offer)

*** Don't Forget Father's Day is June 18th! ***

Finding the perfect Father's Day gift doesn't have to be a chore. We've selected a wide range of the best items for Dad from hundreds of your favorite catalogs to make finding him the perfect gift easy on you.
http://www.you-click.net/GoNow/a13223a21108a46741193a0
Whatever Dad's interests, or if he's a man who has everything, we can help.
Check out these special selections.

*** Sports Pop ***
Is Dad a sports buff? Then he's sure to love a gift that helps him get the most from his favorite activity -- from golf to lounging around in the backyard.

http://www.you-click.net/GoNow/a13223a21108a46741193a2

*** Gadget Daddy ***
How about the latest and greatest gizmo or a time-proven tool to keep Dad amused and help him get the job done right?

http://www.you-click.net/GoNow/a13223a21108a46741193a3

*** Sophisticated Dad ***
If Dad's a man who prefers the finer things in life, then he'll appreciate the tasteful items we've selected for Sophisticated Dads.

http://www.you-click.net/GoNow/a13223a21108a46741193a4

*** Special Offers! ***

As a shopper we're sure you appreciate knowing about great values and special offers. Here are a few we thought you'd enjoy. Every month CatalogCity.com will bring you new offers. Or, you can check our Web site any time to see what's hot.

*** Get Free Shipping (up to $20) at Alsto's Catalog! ***

Alsto's Handy Helpers, a fantastic catalog filled with useful items to make living easier, is giving you Free Shipping (up to $20) from their catalog store at CatalogCity.com until 6/21/00. Just enter the special code DG01401 when you check out to receive your Free Shipping.

http://www.you-click.net/GoNow/a13223a21108a46741193a5

(Please note this offer cannot be used in conjunction with the CatalogCity.com offer posted above.)

*** Bargains galore! ***

From clearance items to white sales, our Outlet Center is filled with extraordinary values from your favorite catalogs -- 20-60% off everything!
Visit our Outlet Center for money-saving offers at:

http://www.you-click.net/GoNow/a13223a21108a46741193a1

Plus remember to use your $10 off discount when you buy before June 19th. And don't forget to enter for your chance to win a Pebble Beach Golf Getaway sponsored by CatalogCity.com. You could be the lucky winner!

http://www.you-click.net/GoNow/a13223a21108a46741193a6

Happy Shopping!
Your friends at CatalogCity.com
===
visit us at www.catalogcity.com

d. Retention, No Offer

From: catalogcity@clickaction.net
[mailto:catalogcity@clickaction.net]
Sent: Thursday, June 01, 2000 8:31 PM
To: chrisf@catalogcity.com
Subject: CatalogCity brings you Gifts for Dad
Dear Chris Flannery,
~~~~~~
Easy Access to the World's Best Products
~~~~~~

(continued)

This June CatalogCity.com is all about Dads, grads, weddings, golf at Pebble Beach and saving money when you shop the world's leading online shopping mall.

*** You Can Win a Pebble Beach Golf Getaway! ***

In celebration of great Fathers everywhere, CatalogCity.com is giving you the chance to win a trip for two to beautiful Carmel, California -- including a stay at The Lodge at Pebble Beach and a round of golf at the world-renowned Pebble Beach course. All you have to do to enter is click on the link below or enter it into your browser.

http://www.you-click.net/GoNow/a13223a21116a46741193a3

No purchase necessary to enter or claim prize. A purchase does not increase your chances of winning. Must be legal resident of USA or Canada (excluding Quebec) 18 or older. Void where prohibited. Complete rules at CatalogCity.com through 6/30/00.

*** Don't Forget Father's Day is June 18th! ***

Finding the perfect Father's Day gift doesn't have to be a chore. We've selected a wide range of the best items for Dad from hundreds of your favorite catalogs to make finding him the perfect gift easy on you. Whatever Dad's interests are, or if he's a man who has everything, we can help.
Check out these special selections.

http://www.you-click.net/GoNow/a13223a21116a46741193a0

***Special Offers! ***

As a shopper we're sure you appreciate knowing about great values and special offers. Here are a few we thought you'd enjoy. Every month CatalogCity.com will bring you new offers. Or, you can check our Web site any time to see what's hot.

*** Get 10% off at Alsto's Catalog when you spend $100! ***

Alsto's Handy Helpers, a fantastic catalog filled with useful items to make living easier, is giving you 10% off when you spend $100 from their catalog store at CatalogCity.com until 6/21/00. Just enter the special code DG01402 when you check out to receive your 10% off.

http://www.you-click.net/GoNow/a13223a21116a46741193a2

(Please note this offer cannot be used in conjunction with the CatalogCity.com offer posted above.)

```
*** Bargains galore! ***

From clearance items to white sales, our Outlet Center is
filled with extraordinary values from your favorite catalogs
-- 20-60% off everything!
Visit our Bargain Center for money saving offers:

http://www.you-click.net/GoNow/a13223a21116a46741193a1

Plus remember to enter for your chance to win a Pebble Beach
Golf Getaway sponsored by CatalogCity.com. You could be the
lucky winner!

http://www.you-click.net/GoNow/a13223a21116a46741193a3

Happy Shopping!
Your friends at CatalogCity.com
==================================================
visit us at www.catalogcity.com
```

FIGURE CS.6 Catalog City offers one-stop shopping from many catalogs.

INTERNATIONAL QUILT STUDY CENTER (NONPROFIT)

Organization:

International Quilt Study Center
<www.ianr.unl.edu/quiltstudy>
The International Quilt Study Center is a nonprofit organization dedicated to scholarship and nurturing the appreciation of quilts as art and cultural history. The IQSC was created to encourage the interdisciplinary study of all aspects of quiltmaking traditions and to foster preservation of this tradition through the collection, conservation and exhibition of quilts and related materials. The Center's mission is twofold:

1. To study those persons past and present who have practiced the tradition, plus the objects they have made and the materials they have used.
2. To collect, conserve, and exhibit quilts and associated textiles.

The University of Nebraska and private donations have supported this mission by building a state-of-the-art storage facility and establishing the International Quilt Study Center.

Objective: The goals of the International Quilt Study Center e-mail retention program are to build support and awareness for the Center, encourage return visitors, encourage memberships, encourage participation in activites, promote access to information available on the site and at the Center, and encourage fundraising. The organization uses e-mail to increase outreach and memberships, both nationally and internationally.

Offer: The IQSC has established a monthly e-mail program called "Quilt of the Month." It highlights a quilt from the Center's collection and other news, information, or updates for members. IQSC staff and board of directors brainstorm to identify a topic that is interesting to the membership. The Center's collection has many important historical quilts in it and typically the Quilt of the Month focuses on one of them.

Format: The e-mail gives a brief description of the quilt of the month and provides a link to a landing page showing the quilt. It may also contain updates and additional links to places on the site. The e-mail is text; the landing page is HTML, one page long. There is no segmentation of the list; the same e-mail is sent to all list members. The University of Nebraska hosts the site and the International Quilt Study Center in the Textile, Clothing, and Design Department of the University send the e-mails each month. Approximately 500 are sent out each month, and the list is growing.

Lists Used: The first e-mail sent introduced the Quilt of the Month program and was delivered to the Center's existing group members and Center visitors who had signed the guest book. Visitors to the Center from Australia who signed the guest book were sent a Quilt of the Month e-mail and in one day 45 other sign-ups for the list were received from Australia! Viral marketing came into play and the information about the Quilt of the Month e-mail became known to the Australian quilting community and the IQSC benefited from the response!

Results: The IQSC has been very pleased with the response to the Quilt of the Month e-mails and the positive effects it has had on membership and awareness of the Center and it mission. The IQSC does not at this time measure click-throughs or conversion, but knows from the increase in list names (about 70 new names are added to the e-mail list each month), that the e-mail program is working to expand awareness and membership for the Center. See Figure CS.7 for a sample e-mail.

FIGURE CS.7 The Quilt of the Month e-mail highlights awareness of quilting and raises funds to promote and preserve the art.

```
Subject: IQSC Quilt of the Month

Date: Wed, 02 Aug 2000 10:09:43 -0500

From: Alta Ottoson <aottoson@unlnotes.unl.edu>

Reply-To: aottoson@unlnotes.unl.edu

To: QOM@crcvms.unl.edu

The International Quilt Study Center is proud to announce
the newest addition to our Quilt of the Month program.
Continue on to

http://www.ianr.unl.edu/quiltstudy/Exhibitions/
QuiltoftheMonth/QM_0215.html

to see our latest installment.

For the past month, the International Quilt Study Center
has been busy preparing an annual report for the National
Endowment for the Humanities (NEH). As you may recall, the
IQSC was awarded a $450,000 challenge grant from the
National Edowment for the Humanitites in 1998. As a recipient
```

(continued)

of this grant, NEH will match every $4 donated to the Center with a gift of $1 until the year 2002. Your support during this period has had a large impact toward reaching our fund-raising goal.

For more information on the NEH Challenge Grant visit our site at

http://www.ianr.unl.edu/quiltstudy/Press/98News/98_16.html

Alta E. Ottoson

Textiles, Clothing, and Design Department

International Quilt Study Center

402/472-6549

AOTTOSON2@unl.edu

MONDERA

Company: Mondera
<www.mondera.com>
The Mouawad Company, a legend in the fine jewelry industry, owns Mondera.com. The company has specialized in high-end luxury goods and fine jewelry manufacturing for 110 years. In that time, the Mouawad Company has grown from a small workshop to an international luxury fine jewelry and watch business. Mouawad Boutiques are located in more than 50 cities around the world including; Paris, Munich, London, Jeddah, Beirut, Tokyo, and Bangkok. The company also owns the Swiss luxury watch brands Robergé and Trebor that combine the finest elements of high style and quality. Most designs are created in the Paris office, known as Mouawad Creations, although each of the company's six factories around the world has its own design team.

Objective: The company goal for the e-mail program is to initiate a relationship with potential customers and strengthen the relationship with current customers. Special features and offers also are used in the e-mails to encourage click-throughs to the site and conversion. E-mails are sent weekly.

Offer: The offer is an invitation to attend an exclusive online Web cast previewing the season's new jewelry. See Figure CS.8 to see the invitation. Promoting this as an "insider event" lifted response rates, compared to the company's "regular" e-mails.

Format: An HTML invitation; text version also is available.

Lists Used: The company has two main sources for lists—the company site and partner sites. On the Mondera site, visitors can sign up directly or can opt-in when registering for sweepstakes, shopping, etc. On partner sites such as Yahoo, The Knot, and Main Floor, customers can opt-in as part of various promotions. No segmentation was used; FloNetwork deployed the mailing.

Results: Approximately 40,000 e-mails were sent. Click-throughs of those who registered for the event were 5.58 percent. Attendance for the event—which

FIGURE CS.8 Mondera has a style show on the Internet.

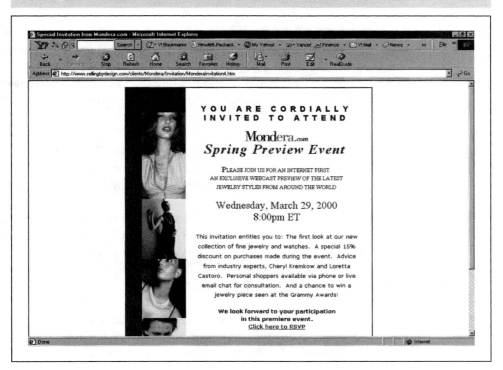

occurred on a specific day and time—was more than 1,000 people (approximately 2.5 percent of recipients).

Mondera reports that in general, short, clear, creative subject lines are more effective in getting customers to open e-mails, especially during peak competitive times, like holidays. Also, for their e-mail subscribers, subject mattered more than offer. For example, estate and bridal themes outperformed gift or watch themes, even when the latter were accompanied by coupon codes.

SPORTS CAPSULE

Company: SportsCapsule
<www.sportscapsule.com>
Sportscapsule is an online video service that enables kids and their families to view, edit, enhance, and save personal sports video over the Internet. Sportscapsule offers players and their parents an easy and inexpensive way to capture and share precious moments in their athletic activities. Simply by submitting videotapes in any format to Sportscapsule, any team or personal sports footage can be transferred to CD-ROM or streamed over the Web, allowing viewers to see the games on their home computers. Sportscapsule users can then clip and save favorite moments from any computer, without the need of additional computer software or hardware. They also can add music, graphics, sound effects, and live calls by acclaimed sportscasters such as Chris Berman or John Madden. After the *sportscapsule* has been completed, the highlights can be shared with teammates, friends, or family worldwide.

Objective: The campaign objective was customer acquisition. The biggest obstacle facing the company is educating individuals about the service and how it works. The free trial offer was intended to help overcome possible reluctance.

Offer: Free Trial Offer—send in a video and try the service for free for one video. A consumer will send in a tape and Sportscapsule will digitize the footage and send it back on CD-ROM, ready for editing (the original tape gets sent back, too). Then a consumer can edit the video and create highlights for seven days for free. It is a 7-Day Free Trial.

Format: HTML and text versions were used. Each e-mail for each segment had slightly different copy; the one geared toward teens had a fun, cool approach, as seen in Figure CS.9. The text for parents was more of a "preserve precious

FIGURE CS.9   SportsCapsule offers a free trial to introduce customers to its service.

FIGURE CS.9   SportsCapsule offers a free trial to introduce customers to its service.

memories" approach. The subject lines and copy reflected these differences in copy, but the copy length was essentially the same. The free offer was the same and the landing page was the same. The landing page was an ordering page.

Lists Used: Two main segments were used: (1) teens who play sports and (2) parents whose kids play sports. The segmentation and sending of the e-mail was provided by its solutions vendor, Meta Response. 30,000 were sent in the first mailing; 200,000 in total over the month of September.

CHIPSHOT

Company: Chipshot.com
<www.chipshot.com>
Chipshot.com is no longer in business, but they did have successful e-mail promotions. It was the Internet's largest retailer of custom-built, tour-quality golf clubs. Its innovative PerfectFit customization technology enabled consumers to configure a set of golf clubs that fit a golfer's physique and style of play. Customers could take advantage of the flexibility and convenience of the Internet to purchase customized, high-quality, low-priced golf clubs delivered to their doorstep. See Figure CS.10 to see a Chipshot page.

Objective: Drive revenues by introducing a new line.

Offer: The e-mail announced new Chipshot brand golf clubs.

FIGURE CS.10   Chipshot.com offers golfers a variety of equipment for their game.

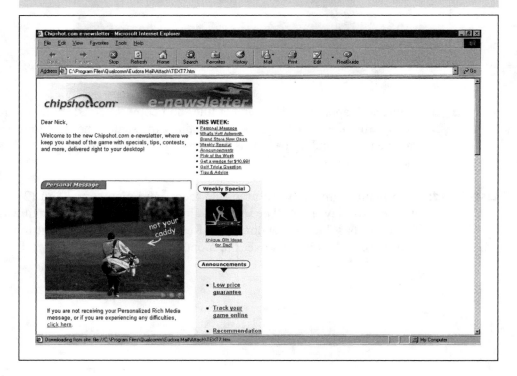

Format: Multimedia in Flash, personalized. It is very dramatic with audio and visual effects. 25,000 of the company's members received the multimedia campaign; 33,000 received HTML or text. There was no customized landing page. Chipshot segmented the database and Dynamics Direct deployed the campaign.

Lists Used: In-house list was used, segmented into roughly two halves to test multimedia versus HTML/text presentation.

Results: CTR was 14.7 percent for the multimedia versus 13 percent for the HTML or text version. Conversion was 11.6 percent for the multimedia versus 8.7 percent for the HTML or text. Another metric that it used was revenue generated/e-mail. For this e-mail, it saw a 98 percent increase in the revenue/e-mail (meaning the average order per e-mail) compared to revenues generated by the HTML or text presentation. Average order size also increased with the multimedia presentation, from $22.20 for an HTML or text order to $29.30 for the multimedia e-mail.

ONEMADE

Company: OneMade, Inc.
                <www.onemade.com>
                OneMade, the marketplace for all things handmade, is the world's online art and craft neighborhood dedicated to serving people with a passion for handmade products. Craftspeople and artists of all mediums—from silver and gold, to needle and thread, to clay and wheel, to paint and brush, are here. Show organizers, guilds, associations, and other nonprofit groups supporting artisans are here. So too are wonderful art and craft retailers—boutiques, gift shops, and galleries. OneMade provides global access to everyone in the art and craft community, creating an equal opportunity marketplace and the primary center for learning, sharing, and making new friends, as well as for developing new business relationships that have no geographic boundaries.

Objective: Drive traffic to bid on the four items featured, as well as create bidding on other items in the same categories. See Figure CS.11. The concept is to promote specific items in order to cross-sell and/or up-sell to other similar items. There were two ceramic items, one jewelry item, and a home furnishings item.

Offer: Charity Auction—proceeds from the sale of the four items were donated to Make-a-Wish Foundation, bidding started at $1.

Format: HTML—no text and no AOL. 12,000 nonsegmented e-mails were sent. The company did the mailing in-house using Aureate software. OneMade consistently experiences better response using HTML rather than text; for example, the company cites a 26 percent response rate to an HTML e-mail, and a 10 percent response on a text form of the same e-mail. No custom landing pages were used. The shopper was linked directly to the category listing the item.

Lists Used: For this campaign OneMade used a list from a broker. The company recently hired an agency to serve, track, and measure campaigns and will use lists recommended by them, in addition to the sources they research and identify.

Results: OneMade didn't measure click-through in this e-mail. Measured instead were the number of bids the items received, compared to average number of bids. Average number of bids is in the 5 to 6 range; these featured items received anywhere from 20 to 45 bids, 4 to 9 times the average. The company believes that the charity factor had an impact on the results, but, in addition, because

FIGURE CS.11 OneMade drives visitors to sites and pages that offer a variety of handmade art and products.

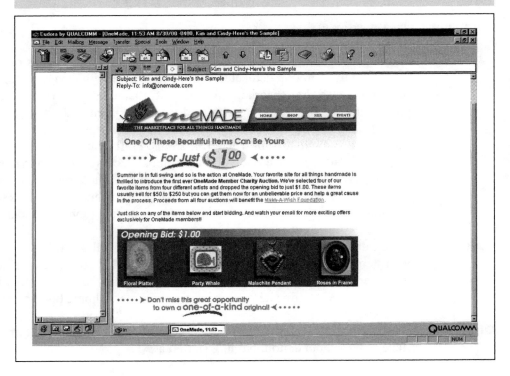

bidding started at $1, the "bargain" perception played a very important role in response. Because one of the objectives was to cross-sell and/or up-sell to other similar items, the amount of bidding on other items in the same categories as the charity items also was measured. Each category recorded at least a 100 percent increase in the number of bids over average. OneMade's average dollar amount per sale is $50–$100. The order size generated by this e-mail campaign was within that average.

ESOFT INC.

Company: eSoft, Inc.
<www.esoft.com>
eSoft sells VPN (Virtual Private Network) and firewall Internet security appliance products.

Objective: Lead generation. Visitors had to register in order to get the paper.

Offer: eSoft uses a two-step process—offering a free white paper (PDF) in exchange for registration on the site. The registration is a Web lead form, which triggers an auto response acknowledging receipt of the registration and the white paper. A sales rep then follows up with a call.

In this case study, the e-mail subject head was: "Protect Your Network with Interceptor from eSoft." A free white paper was offered and the brief e-mail copy discussed key features of the product. The offer was:

(Read below to receive a Free Firewall Fundamentals Guide!)

eSoft does a lot of testing, but finds that white papers are very effective. The paper on firewalls has produced good results, as has the one on VPNs. The target market is IT decision makers in small-sized to medium-sized businesses. Because there is a lot of priority in that segment on security issues related to the Internet, an educational paper on topics related to these priorities is very attractive. See Figure CS.12 to see how eSoft sold to this group's security concerns.

Format: The format for this e-mail was text, but the company also has tested HTML. This case study includes two tests: (A) testing two lists and (B) testing HTML versus text. Each test mailing was 5,000 each.

List Test
Test A used a list with the old paper; Test B used a list with the new paper. Both lists are from the same source.

FIGURE CS.12   eSoft wants to address the B2B market's goal of safe Internet use.

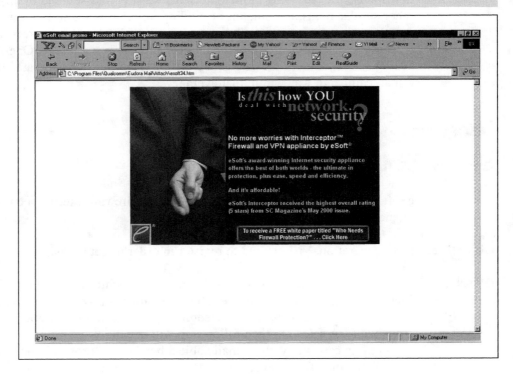

HTML versus Text Test

The message and offer were the same, just the mail format was different. 5,000 of each format were sent.

Segmentation and sending were outsourced. The e-mail length is usually the same—short—although the paper itself is four to six pages long. The white paper is changed when response slips; when the paper changes so does the copy and subject line. The landing page varies by white paper.

Lists Used: E-mail addresses are rented from opt-in, outside lists

Results: Click-throughs:
List A—Old paper: 222 or 4.4%
List B—New paper: 311 or 6.2%

HTML: 201 or 4.0%
Text: 216 or 4.3%

Conversion rates (% of click-throughs that signed up for the offer)
List A—Old paper: 27.93%
List B—New paper: 40.84%

HTML: 31.34%
Text: 26.85%

Response rates (% of people sent to who signed up)
List A—Old paper: 1.24%
List B—New paper: 2.54%

HTML: 1.26%
Text: 1.16%

The company is still learning and tests continually. It is experimenting now with a series of papers, rather than just one, on firewalls to see if the response rate is affected. eSoft tests new lists, too. The most common problem found with lists is that they tend to be too consumer oriented and do not produce enough B2B interest. Figure CS.13 shows the two choices used.

FIGURE CS.13 eSoft tests two versions of an e-mail.

Test A:

```
From: ITworld.com [mailto:itworld@msgexpress.net]
Sent: Thursday, August 24, 2000 9:44 AM
To: ncurtiss@esoft.com
Subject: Free Firewall White Paper

*************************************************************
A message to ITworld.com newsletter readers from eSoft

Protect Your Network with Interceptor from eSoft
**(Read below to receive a FREE white paper on firewall
security!)**
eSoft's award-winning FIREWALL & VPN appliance offers the
ULTIMATE in protection, PLUS ease, speed and efficiency.

And it's AFFORDABLE!

Interceptor also offers real-time alerting, spam filtering,
Web site filtering, reporting tools and much more!
```

(continued)

eSoft's Interceptor just received the highest overall rating (5 STARS!)from SC Magazine's May Issue.

Click here for a FREE Firewall and Network Security White Paper

http://www.esoft.com/info/of1_71t000824.cfm

Thanks for your time.
eSoft, Inc.
888.903.7638 (press 4 for sales)

Test B:

From: ITworld.com [mailto:itworld@msgexpress.net]
Sent: Thursday, August 24, 2000 9:27 AM
To: ncurtiss@esoft.com
Subject: Firewall Fundamentals (A Free Guide)
****
A message to ITworld.com newsletter readers from eSoft
****

Protect Your Network with Interceptor from eSoft

(Read below to receive a Free Firewall Fundamentals Guide!)

eSoft's award-winning FIREWALL & VPN appliance offers the ULTIMATE in protection, PLUS ease, speed, and efficiency. And it's AFFORDABLE! Not only does Interceptor contain the fundamental components of a robust firewall, it also offers real-time alerting, spam filtering, Web site filtering, reporting tools and much more!

eSoft's Interceptor just received the highest overall rating (5 STARS!) from SC Magazine's May Issue.

Click here for a Free Firewall Fundamentals Guide

http://www.esoft.com/info/off2a_71t000824.cfm

Thanks for your time.
eSoft, Inc.
888.903.7638 (press 4 for sales)

FULL SPECTRUM LENDING

Company: Full Spectrum Lending
(Subsidiary of Countrywide Home Loans)
5220 Las Virgenes Road
Calabasas, CA 91302
Jeremy Bachmann, VP Internet Marketing
818-871-4741
<www.fullspectrumlending.com>
Countrywide Home Loans is a 30-year-old company, a member of the Fortune 500 and Forbes 500, and among the top home lenders in the United States. The company has an extensive loan-servicing portfolio and a very large base of current customers. One challenge is bringing these customers into an online relationship, as well as developing new business with them. Much of the company's business is wholesale. Countrywide buys mortgage servicing rights from banks and other lenders, so B2B is a very important segment of the business.

Full Spectrum Lending, a subsidiary of Countrywide, serves consumers who for various reasons don't qualify for a traditional or conforming loan. At any time, approximately 10 to 20 percent of consumers may fall into this nontraditional or subprime category. This is a mortgage niche that has been largely ignored online and includes debt consolidation, home equity loans, and refinancing to reduce monthly debt payments. See Figure CS.14 to view Full Spectrum's offerings. E-mail is central to the transaction in this segment to keep the company name and the subject at the top of the consumer's mind, as well as to build trust, which is very central to creating a sale in this market. A retention e-mail campaign is targeted to these consumers who need home loans for refinancing or debt consolidation. Full Spectrum Lending offers these services and distributes a quarterly e-newsletter which includes information and special offers to targeted prospects.

Objective: The objective is to increase loan applications from among visitors drawn to the Full Spectrum Web site and to convert them to a borrower, with cross-selling and brand building also important. Each month, the last campaign's statistics are reviewed to develop the goals for the next campaign.

Offer: The offer is a free analysis of how much a consumer could save in monthly payments through a Full Spectrum loan. To receive the analysis, prospects complete a simple interactive form. With the information gathered on the

FIGURE CS.14 Full Spectrum offers mortgage services online.

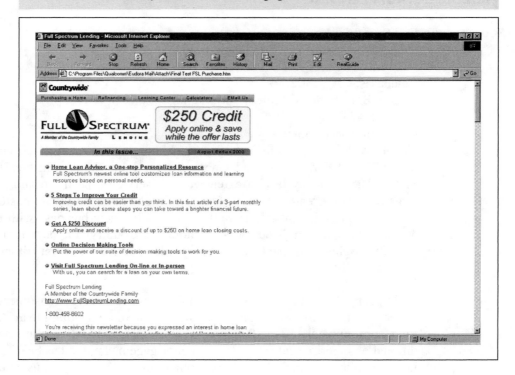

form, the prospect's financial position is analyzed and recommendations are made. If the prospect chooses to subscribe to the newsletter, they receive monthly updates on products and special offers along with educational articles. There's often a considerable lag time before a consumer is ready to apply for a loan, so the newsletter helps Full Spectrum Lending stay in touch.

Format: HTML and text. Approximately 75,000 to 80,000 e-mails are sent quarterly. Segmentation is completed in-house, but the company outsources the sending functions. The company decides what information goes in the newsletter based on the profile of the customer. These campaigns are focused on providing value-added information and tips to the audiences, helping to bring them back to the sites, and keeping the name, products, and services fresh in their minds. For example, someone without a pet isn't going to receive an offer for pet insurance. The e-newsletters promote special promotional offers, such as special discounts for completing a loan application online, or its Mortgage Independence Day contest, which gives prospects the chance to win several months' worth of mortgage payments.

Lists: Lists are developed internally from selected prospects, customers, and business partners. Buying external lists hasn't been successful for Full Spectrum.

Results: HTML tends to always far outperform the text mailers. Writing so customers can scan the e-mail quickly improves responses as does making it easy for them to find what they're looking for. CTR is 12 to 14 percent on average. Conversion rates are 2 to 3 percent on average. The average refinance loan amount is $130,000. Interestingly, e-mail campaigns produce a higher average refinancing amount than that generated by Full Spectrum's offline campaigns.

GURU.COM

Company: Guru.com
615 Battery Street
San Francisco, CA 94111
419-693-9500
<www.guru.com>
Launched in November of 1999, Guru.com offers a meeting place for independent professionals ("gurus") and hirers seeking their expertise, usually for short-term projects. The company offers free membership to gurus that provides them with access to hirers, posts an online resume, and offers business tips and special offers. Hirers also register for free and then pay to post projects to which gurus apply to provide services.

E-mail is an essential element of its overall marketing mix, which includes mediums like referral programs, online banners and newsletters, as well as mass advertising mediums and PR.

Guru.com actively uses e-mail to acquire new members, known as gurus, and new hirers—those who contract with a guru to complete a project. The company prospects for both audiences.

Guru.com calls retention e-mails "install base" marketing and considers it to be a very critical function.

Communications with gurus and hirers is almost exclusively by e-mail. The company finds it to be a very efficient and cost-effective way to stay connected, to identify its best customers, and to learn about its member gurus and hirers. This case study deals with retention e-mails.

Objective: Retention campaigns always have three goals:

1. To develop and improve loyalty
2. To incent or encourage specific behaviors (posting a project or creating a profile, for example)
3. Keeping members informed of new product offerings

Specifically, this campaign objective was to encourage profile creation.

Offer: The company focuses initially on offering free registration for both gurus and hirers. The second offer would encourage members to "take the next step" with Guru.com, such as creating a profile for gurus or posting a project for hirers. Occasionally Guru.com makes an offer to encourage a specific action. An example of an incentive that worked well was a drawing for free DSL service for a year if the member posted her or his profile. This offer was tested against a drawing for a free vacation, and results found that the relevancy of DSL service to the gurus' solo businesses was the key to a higher response. The free DSL drawing, as shown in Figure CS.15, is the specific offer examined in this case study.

Format: Personalized plain text. More than 350,000 members were sent the e-mail in the course of three months. Segmentation and sending is outsourced in order to leverage the vendor's experience and opt-out capture capability. The supplier provides an opt-out suppression safety net so that Guru.com never e-mails a customer who has chosen to opt out.

Lists Used: House file.

Results: Click-throughs were more than 5 percent and the conversion rate on that offer was about three times that of some previous conversions. Relevancy is very important. What a company offers in the e-mail needs to solve a problem for the recipient. Guru.com uses a small part of its budget to test continually, establishing a control group and comparing results. Novelty, newness, and the ability to stand out plays a very important role in the success of e-mail in conversion.

FIGURE CS.15 Guru.com wants both experts and hirers to use its site.

Dear [insert name of guru],

What do you miss most about working in a "real" office?
Is it the commute? Not likely. The free office supplies?
Perhaps. How about that trusty T-1 line? Now there's
something that could make any guru nostalgic.

If it's the need for speed that's got you down, you'll be
happy to learn about our newest promotion here at Guru.com.
Create a Guru Profile and you'll be automatically entered to
win FREE DSL for a year!

> http://info.guru.com/Key=3558.EgfPMD.B.TW376

Remember, your Guru Profile is a free online resume that
makes it easy for hiring companies to find you in our
database. It's a great way to market your skills and line
up cool gigs. Now, it's also your chance to win free DSL for
your office at home.

So what are you waiting for? Create your profile today and
enter to win. To get started, click here:

> http://info.guru.com/Key=3558.EgfPMD.B.TW376

Yours in speediness,

Team Guru.com

If you choose not to receive these messages simply click
here:

> http://info.guru.com/opt-out/Key=3558.EgfPMD.v46UY

or e-mail us with a subject of "unsubscribe" and we'll take
you off the list as quickly as possible. Please include this
entire message in your reply.

Message-Id: <20000531085706.99DE992C.0.-1-3558@info.guru.com>
Customer Id: ppd@-pd.com - To Approve Sending this message,
visit:

https://results.eclassdirect.com/asp/approve/checkmsgid.asp?MsgId=20000

531085706.99DE992C.0.-1-3558@info.guru.com

NATURE'S DISTRIBUTORS

Company: Nature's Distributors, Inc.
<www.naturesdistributors.com>
Nature's Distributors is a 15-year-old direct mail marketer of vitamins and dietary supplements. The veteran direct mailer uses e-mail campaigns to implement many of the basic practices it has developed in its direct mail business, but the company also makes adaptations according to what it knows about its digital customers. For example, visitors to the site do not come from the company's existing base for the most part, but rather are arriving at naturesdistributors.com as the result of searches by search engines. Also, the demographic for the company's online customer is completely different from that of its established direct mail customer; the e-commerce customer tends to be younger than the company's direct mail customer and wants to operate more independently and quickly to browse and order. The case study described here is the company's first experience with using e-mail to acquire customers.

In the planning stages is a retention e-mail program to help build relationships and increase repeat business with existing customers. A retention e-mail program is in development. Nature's Distributors has one of the highest reorder rates in the vitamin/supplement industry, so implementation of a retention program is expected to produce very good revenues as well as reduce expenses associated with a direct mail or telephone order.

Objective: Test for driving customer acquisition and revenues.

Offer: Three for Free (see Figure CS.16 to view the offer):

a. NO PURCHASE NECESSARY—a FREE 12-issue subscription to an exclusive 28-page newsletter called The Healthy Cell News just for registering on the site. Each month's issue contains in-depth reports on today's most potent natural therapies, a Q&A section with nutritional expert Dr. Decker Weiss, and money-saving opportunities.

b. A first order of $75 or more, was rewarded with a FREE 30-capsule (60 mg.) supply of its top grade ginkgo biloba in addition to everyday Free Gift offers.

c. An extra bonus: FREE shipping on the first order—regardless of size.

The company knew it wanted to offer a free 12-month subscription to its 28-page newsletter to encourage new registrations. Each month the newslet-

FIGURE CS.16 The major draw of the three free offers was a free newsletter subscription.

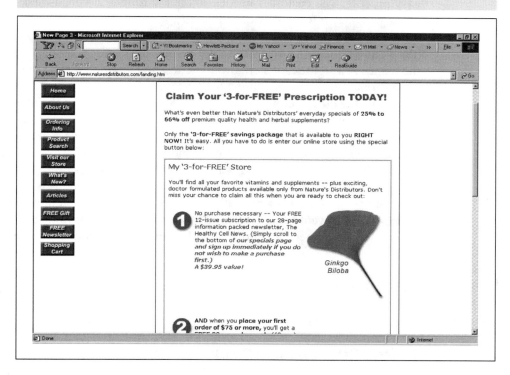

ter offers in-depth reports on today's natural therapies, a Q&A section with nutritional expert Dr. Decker Weiss, and money-saving opportunities. Analysis of the click-throughs indicates that this offer is what pulled, though two other offers were also included—a free gift and free shipping. The company's historical data indicates that free gifts and free shipping are effective in increasing revenues. The expense of these incentives is enabled for the company due in large part to the economies associated with taking an order online versus direct mail or over the telephone.

Format: HTML and text; custom landing page.

Lists Used: A testing sample of 5,000 received the e-mail. No segmentation; deployed by a third party solutions provider. Good categories for Nature's Distributors are health and fitness categories.

Results: 3.56 percent opened the e-mail and went to the landing page. 32.6 percent of those click-throughs signed up for the free subscription, which wasn't a real easy process. The customer needed to click through two pages and then fill out a personal information questionnaire in order to receive the free subscription. 20.6 percent of those who signed up for the free subscription have placed an online order so far, and the results are still coming in. Capture of the names is a significant step toward generating additional revenues, even if the customer didn't buy anything the first time. It is too soon to determine if, over time, the customer acquired by this campaign will order above or below the average order size.

Nature's Distributors believes that key to the effectiveness of any e-mail campaign is the creation of a user-friendly Web site. If customers cannot quickly figure out how to find what they want and how to order it, the best e-mail in the world will not drive revenues. Contrary to current "e-commerce thought" concerning personalization, Nature's Distributor e-commerce customers doesn't want the transaction "personal"; they want to be able to figure out what they need and order it with a minimum of interaction and time.

CHAPTERS ONLINE INC.

Company: Chapters Online Inc.
<www.chapters.ca>
Chapters Online Inc. is a Canadian e-commerce company that operates <www.chapters.ca> and <www.villa.ca>, both leading Canadian destinations for online shoppers. The Chapters.ca Web site features millions of book, music CDs, videos, DVD software, and video game titles as well as digital downloads and consumer electronics. The Villa.ca Web site features Canada's largest online inventory of home and garden products. Both Web sites' wide selection of products are priced in Canadian dollars with a unique focus on products of interest to Canadians.

Objective: This retention campaign was targeted to previous Chapters Online technology buyers. The campaign objective was to see if an e-mail promotion would be effective in driving purchase of higher ticket technology products and to test landing page presentation format.

Offer: The subject line read "An Affordable New Palm." In the body of the e-mail was a limited-time gift with a purchase offer—a free Road Scholar CD including eleven software applications that transform the Palm m100 into a powerful learning tool. See Figure CS.17 to view the e-mail message.

Format: 7000 plain-text e-mails were sent. Time constraints prevented development of HTML versions. A solutions provider managed the e-mail project including sending and reporting. Chapters Online provided the list, which was a segment of the company's customers who had previously purchased technology products from Chapters Online. Two different landing pages were designed to test the concepts of "one item on a page" and a "boutique of related items."

Results: Overall click-throughs were more than 20 percent. The landing page showing only the single item generated three times the sales of the boutique page presentation. Typically, conversion on this type of item (higher price point) is *very* low, so these results were excellent for the company. Average order size was $229, the price of this Palm.

FIGURE CS.17 Chapters Online lists reasons to purchase a Palm m100.

Item page:
http://www.chapters.ca/ELECTRONICS/details/default.asp?UPC=662705365909
Palm Place boutique: http://www.chapters.ca/Electronics/Spotlight/PalmPlace
Sample text e-mail:

```
-----Original Message-----
From: Chapters.ca TechTalk
[mailto:Chapters.ca-TechTalk@new.chapters.ca]
Sent: Thursday, August 10, 2000 3:52 PM
To: june@chapters.ca
Subject: An Affordable New Palm

Dear June Macdonald,

Have you ever thought about buying a Palm, but didn't
because you believed it was too expensive?

If you have, do we have some great news for you. Palm Inc.
has just launched the new Palm m100. It's a cool looking,
*affordable* handheld organizer that makes it easy to keep
track of addresses, phone numbers, appointments, to-dos, and
more.
```

(continued)

The Palm m100 is now available at Chapters.ca. AND IF YOU ORDER IT BEFORE SEPTEMBER 30, 2000, YOU'LL RECEIVE A FREE ROAD SCHOLAR CD.

The CD is packed with eleven software applications that'll transform your Palm m100 into a powerful learning tool.

To order your Palm m100, go to:
http://new.chapters.ca/cgi-bin1/flo?y=eDy30iDoK0Gf0xgGK
We expect the Palm m100 to be one our hottest sellers. It's sleek and stylish with curvy edges, a double hinged flip top, and funky removable front plate.

It weighs only 4.4 ounces and features a Note Pad application that captures handwritten notes and attaches them to an alarm that'll alert you of important appointments or tasks. Plus, there's a HotSync cable for connecting and sharing data between a desktop computer and your handheld. For Macintosh users, Mac software is included in the box--with a free adapter.

The Palm m100 even comes with an infrared port that will allow you to beam info to other Palm users. But what it doesn't come with is an expensive price tag.

In fact, IT HAS THE LOWEST INTRODUCTORY PRICE FOR A PALM PDA.

You won't believe how organized your life will become. Take advantage of the Free Road Scholar offer and your Palm m100 today! Go to:

http://new.chapters.ca/cgi-bin1/flo?y=eDy30iDoK0Gf0xgGK

Sincerely,

Suzanne Ethier
Business Unit Manager - Electronics
Chapters Online Inc.
"We're open if you are"
To REMOVE your name from this and all nonorder related e-mail, please send a blank e-mail to:

mailto:remove-techtalk@new.chapters.ca

To SUBSCRIBE a different address from the one above, please send a blank e-mail to:

mailto:subscribe-techtalk@new.chapters.ca

SOFTWARE AND SOLUTIONS PROVIDERS

L-Soft

<www.lsoft.com>
L-Soft International, Inc.
8100 Corporate Drive, Suite 350
Landover, MD 20785-2231
301-731-0440
800-399-5449
301-731-6302 fax

Founded in 1994, L-Soft is a provider of e-mail list and e-mail delivery solutions. L-Soft's Web-enabled technology offers an extensive portfolio of products and services that provide list management and delivery alternatives for electronic newsletters, discussion groups, and personalized direct e-mail campaigns. Products and services include: LISTSERV®, e-mail list management software that was one of the original e-mail list managers and is still widely used today; LSMTP®, high-volume e-mail delivery software that was released in 1996 and allows large e-mail list workloads to be carried on modest hardware; ListPlex® and EASESM, e-mail list hosting services that provide customers with access to L-Soft's expertise and technology without hardware, software, or personnel investment. L-Soft is privately held and has offices in Landover, Maryland, and Stockholm, Sweden.

e2 Communications

<www.e2software.com>
6404 International Parkway, Suite 1200
Plano, TX 75093
972-931-7000

Dallas-based e2 Communications is an Application Services Provider (ASP) offering technology and consulting services for e-communications planning, implementation, and reporting. Using a patent-pending technology called Adaptive Sequenced Messaging (ASM), e2Mail Center clients have the ability to devise e-mail "branches" and "tracks" that adapt and change based on recipient behaviors (e.g., whether or not they responded to previous offers). This feature allows the marketer to create sequenced, personalized messages, and address both inbound and outbound messaging, all with a great deal of flexibility.

Roving Software, Inc.

<www.roving.com>
117 Kendrick Street
Needham, MA 02494
781-444-6160
781-444-6155 fax

Roving Software Inc.'s award winning Constant Contact™ products deliver e-marketing solutions for small and medium e-businesses. Constant Contact™ Opt-In Builder is a tool for customer acquisition that collects e-mail addresses from Web site opt-in, targets e-mail by opt-in interest groups, and creates and delivers e-mail campaigns. Constant Contact™ Customer Builder is a tool for customer retention and collects customer e-mail addresses from e-commerce data, targets and personalizes e-mails with order history, creates and delivers e-mail campaigns to customers, and integrates with top small business commerce server platforms.

DoubleClick Sweepstakes

<www.sweepstakes.doubleclick.net>
DoubleClick
450 W. 33rd Street
New York, NY 10001
212-683-0001
212-287-9267 fax

Originally founded in 1998 as Flashbase, the company was acquired by DoubleClick Inc. in 2000 and renamed DoubleClick Sweepstakes. The service offers marketers automated solutions for acquiring new customers using the popular sweepstakes promotion vehicle. DoubleClick's sweepstakes service enables creation of a customized online sweepstakes, rewarded registration form, or rewarded survey, in a matter of minutes. Entries are stored in an online database accessible in real time and integrated direct marketing tools allow marketers to launch targeted, permission-based e-mail campaigns and track the results. DoubleClick Inc. is a provider of comprehensive global Internet advertising solutions for marketers and Web publishers. Global Headquarters is in New York City with more than 30 offices around the world.

Pivotal Corporation

<www.pivotal.com>
300-224 W. Esplanade
North Vancouver, British Columbia, CA V7M 3M6
604-988-9982
877-748-6825
604-988-0035 fax

Pivotal Corporation provides Microsoft-based software solutions that provide integrated applications for managing enterprise e-business functions, targeted to mid-sized and large-sized companies. The company's Pivotal Relationship product lets users share information for targeting prospects, building marketing campaigns, forecasting sales, and tracking orders. The company also offers consulting, implementation, support, and training services. Pivotal software solutions are designed for Web, wireless, and hosted deployment and are provided on a flexible license, lease, or subscription basis.

Message Media, Inc.

<www.messagemedia.com>
6060 Spine Road
Boulder, CO 80027
303-440-7550
888-440-7550
303-440-0303 fax

Software Solutions—UnityMail
<www.messagemedia.com/sc/unitymail/>

UnityMail is e-mail marketing software that allows companies to manage their own e-mail marketing system. Linked directly to a database, UnityMail can send individualized, targeted e-mail campaigns, with trackable URLs, to customers and prospects. UnityMail performs all standard e-mail list server functions such as reliable high throughput e-mail delivery, bounce management, discussion lists, announcement lists, and easy unsubscribes. Integrated with relational databases such as Oracle or SQL Server, UnityMail can perform unique functions such as targeted e-mail (filtering and data segmentation), personalized e-mail, dynamic content editing, trackable URLs, and campaign sequencing.

Software Solutions—MailKing
<www.messagemedia.com/solutions/mailking/>

MailKing, recently acquired by MessageMedia, is a powerful e-mail merge software tool for Windows that creates a form letter and merges personalized data into each letter. It allows users to open most popular databases directly, filter data into targeted e-mail lists, and then send personalized e-mail to members of the lists. MailKing opens contact databases directly with no importing and individually addresses the e-mail along with merging personal data into the message body.

Solution Provider Services

MessageMedia also offers full-service advanced e-messaging solutions in a comprehensive suite of services that includes information delivery, e-commerce services, permission-based direct marketing, ongoing customer communications, and real-time customer feedback solutions. Founded in 1994, MessageMedia's customer portfolio includes global clients from the financial services, publishing, direct marketing, retailing, and software and electronic commerce. The company's UnityMail product (described above) is offered as a software component for both business clients and Application Service Providers (ASP).

BoldFish

<www.boldfish.com>
471 El Camino Real, Suite 110
Santa Clara, CA 95050
408-236-3620

BoldFish provides software and services that allow organizations to e-mail–enable their customer database for high volume outbound e-mail campaigns. BoldFish integrates seamlessly with an organization's Web site, database, and existing IT infrastructure to provide enterprise-class capabilities for reaching customers in a responsive, personal way. Key features include: personalized message creation, high-speed delivery, efficient management of bounced e-mail with automatic retry for soft bounces and removal of addresses for hard bounces, campaign response rate tracking, and detailed reports for each campaign.

Marketing Communications Systems

<www.networkmcs.com>
1044 Pulinski Road
Ivyland, PA 18974
215-675-2000

Marketing Communication Systems, Inc. (MCS) is an Application Services Provider (ASP) offering direct marketing services for e-communications as well as for offline direct marketing campaigns. MCS clients manage entire nationwide marketing campaigns, including all online and offline advertising and direct marketing, within a customized Web-based application. MCS is one of five companies in the Communications Concept Group; other companies include: Communication Concepts, Inc.; Mail-Guard; Database Marketing Concepts; and Pacific Communication Concepts, Inc. The CCG companies provide complete direct marketing services including Internet-based database management and merge/purge services, print and letter shop services, list brokerage and management, and disaster recovery services.

FloNetwork

<www.flonetwork.com>
260 King Street East
Toronto, Ontario, CA M5A 1K3
800-793-6320
416-369-1100
416-369-9037 fax

FloNetwork Inc., formerly Media Synergy, is an e-marketing Application Service Provider (ASP) specializing in permission-based online direct marketing and e-communications. Services include comprehensive hosted applications and services for managing permission-based e-mail messaging campaigns, including designing e-mail messages, building and managing address lists, testing and deploying campaigns, real-time tracking, and reporting and analysis of results.

Responsys.com

<www.responsys.com>
2225 E. Bayshore Road, Suite 100
Palo Alto, CA 94303
650-858-7400
888-219-7150
650-858-7401 fax

Responsys.com is an Application Services Provider (ASP) offering a secure, Web-hosted application called Responsys Intereact for online direct marketing. The software allows marketers to create, launch, and manage permission-based e-marketing campaigns. Features include tools for dynamic personalization of e-mails, multi–e-mail support, list and data management, powerful response rules, flexible campaign execution, response management and tracking, real time reporting, analysis, and open architecture for easy integration.

Bigfoot Interactive

<www.bigfootinteractive.com>
521 Fifth Avenue, 5th Floor
New York, NY 10175
646-227-7400

Bigfoot Interactive is a direct e-marketing company providing campaign management using its Generation eNetwork. The company offers seamless integration of e-mail marketing applications and services, personalization applications, e-strategy consultation, opt-in list services, and creative services including rich media, and high volume e-mail delivery. Privately held, the company was founded in 1997.

Digital Impact

<www.digital-impact.com>
177 Bovet Road, Suite 200
San Mateo, CA 94402
650-356-3400
650-356-3410 fax

Digital Impact is a solutions provider for e-mail campaigns, delivering millions of e-mail messages a month for Internet marketers. One of the company's services, Email Exchange (EMX), offers marketers cobranded e-mail opportunities, an approach that pairs noncompeting advertisers' messages together in the same e-mail and sends it to a recipient who has opted-in to interests in both advertisers' categories (babies and cooking for example). Over 17 million names and 46 companies are involved in the EMX program. Other Digital Impact services include Mass Personalization Engine (MPE) which performs full assembly, delivery, and analysis of millions of messages; and Adaptive Intelligent Marketing (AIM), a methodology that optimizes marketing based on the results of successive campaigns. The company was founded in 1997 and is headquartered in San Mateo, California.

Innovyx.com

1600 Fairview Avenue East, Suite 300
Seattle, WA 98102
206-336-3003
206-336-3002 fax

Dialogue 1to1™ is Innovyx's Enterprise Dialogue Management (EDM) solution, a rapidly growing category of Internet-based marketing systems using e-mail, the Web, and database tools to automate one-to-one communications with individual customers. Dialogue 1to1 provides all the tools needed to create and deliver customized, e-mail–based direct marketing, and customer communications; to generate direct response and feedback from users; and to measure and manage the ongoing one-to-one relationship with each individual customer. The company is privately held with offices in Seattle.

Socketware, Inc.

<www.accucast.com>
1776 Peachtree Street N.W., Suite 500 South
Atlanta, Georgia 30309
404-815-1998
877-815-1998
404-815-1993 fax

Founded in 1997, Socketware is a software solutions provider specializing in customized e-marketing products and services. Socketware's flagship product, Accucast, is software that enables organizations to launch permission-based e-mail marketing campaigns with customization and personalization features that deliver media-rich content to the recipient's inbox, in any language. Accucast is available as a hosted (ASP) platform (Accucast Accelerator) or as a software solution (Accucast Enterprise) for in-house implementation. Socketware provides services across several industries including transportation, retailing, technology, and telecommunications companies.

ClickAction Inc.

<www.clickaction.com>
2197 East Bayshore Road
Palo Alto, CA 94303-3219
650-473-3600
650-325-0873 fax

ClickAction, Inc. is a provider of e-mail marketing and e-messaging services that offer a comprehensive, Web-based campaign management solution. ClickAction Email Relationship Management (ERM) is a comprehensive service that enables marketers to conduct targeted permission-based e-mail campaigns, collect and profile customer data, and access real-time results in an entirely Web-hosted environment. The service easily integrates with legacy databases, advancing the real-time management of customer data across all channels. ClickForward is a new service, launched to offer viral marketing technology. ClickAction has developed thousands of e-mail campaigns across many industries including major food manufactures, retailers, and technology suppliers.

RICH MEDIA

Dynamics Direct

<www.dynamicsdirect.com>
22736 Vanowen Street, Third Floor
West Hills, CA 91307
818-348-0494 ext. 223
818-348-0501 fax

Dynamics Direct, Inc. is an individualized rich media marketing company that combines technology with the successful methods of direct marketing to produce and deliver highly targeted, customized e-mail. The company's patent-pending Dynamic Individualization™ product enables marketers to use database information and rich media technology to deliver e-mail that has customized sound to accompany streaming video. For example, customers can actually hear their own names as part of a multimedia message.

InChorus.com

<www.inchorus.com>
2041 Mission College Boulevard, Suite 259
Santa Clara, CA 95054
408-566-6000

Founded in 1996, and originally named Softlink, inChorus.com is a Silicon Valley–based software and rich media e-mail services company. Using sophisticated voice and graphics compression technology, inChorus.com delivers rich media messages bringing voice, animation, sound, and graphics to e-mail marketing, advertising, and personal e-mail. Messages are delivered to recipients as file attachments. Through the use of the free inChorus media player (which can be automatically packaged with the message), recipients are able to experience the message on any Windows or Macintosh system. InChorus provides software solutions or complete e-mail marketing campaign services including creative, delivery, and tracking.

Indimi

<www.indimi.com>
555 Madison Avenue
10th Floor
New York, NY 10022
212-833-8718

Indimi (Internet Direct Marketing Intelligence) is a media company that develops online consumer and business-to-business brands by using e-mail and the desktop to deliver news, information, and product and service offers across many categories. The Infobeat division produces a consumer brand e-newspaper that each week delivers personalized e-mails to subscribers who have opted-in and have created their own profiles. Other Indimi consumer brands include MessageMates.com and Tooned.com, which are two eCard sites; and ScreenMates.com, a site that offers downloadable screensavers. Indimi's AdTools offers Internet marketers technology that creates and delivers multimedia presentations to these brand audiences by presenting a window, customized to the client's brand, that contains a short video clip. The video presentations have small file sizes, offer two-way communication and do not require plug-ins. Indimi is headquartered in New York, with offices in Boston, Denver, Los Angeles, and London.

RadicalMail

<www.radicalmail.com>
4086 Glencoe Avenue
Marina Del Rey, CA 90292
310-578-6725
310-306-0126 fax

RadicalMail provides Internet marketers with highly customized and interactive technologies that deliver streaming audio and video to the inbox. Radical-Mail features include: ultralight java applets that eliminate the need for plug-ins or third party software, e-commerce that can be transacted without leaving the body of the e-mail message, and encoding for multiple speeds to ensure that recipients receive the media optimized for their bandwidths. Using no executable files, lengthy downloads or plug-ins, RadicalMail creates a seamless, quality experience for the recipient. RadicalMail's reporting capabilities provide marketers with more than 40 distinct data points on user behavior and interaction.

MindArrow Systems

<www.mindarrow.com>
<www.ecommercials.com>
101 Enterprise Drive, Suite 340
Aliso Viejo, CA 92656-2609
949-916-8705
949-916-8713 fax

MindArrow Systems is a global provider of interactive marketing automation solutions. A public company that was founded in March 1999, MindArrow comprises three integrated business units: eComStudio, providing design and production services; eComNetwork, providing servers and routers that ensure fast, secure, e-mail delivery; and eComTracker that monitors all campaign components and produces online, real-time reporting. The company's patent-pending technologies enable marketers to deliver targeted, rich media content, including high-quality video and audio, as an e-mail message or Web-page download. Called eBrochures and eCommercials, they are actually ultrathin Web browsers with built-in, high-quality video and graphics that are delivered in an e-mail as a self-playing attachment. These attachments are completely independent of browser or e-mail software—no players, plug-ins, or streaming is required.

AudioBase Inc.

<www.audiobase.com>
116 West 23rd Street, Suite 500
New York, NY 10011
646-375-2233
646-375-2235 fax

AudioBase Inc. is an ASP-based solution, delivering streaming audio in an ultra light, cross-platform player. AudioBase's Integrated Content Engine (ICE) creates multimedia presentations, ads, promotions, and destination pages, as well as content that can be rotated by recipient with varying presentations. In addition, individuals' voices can be recorded with a conventional phone call and standardized or customized prompts, then published to the Web for listening. AudioBase does not require plug-ins (for most browsers), software downloads, or installations by the recipient and can play while graphics are still loading. If recipient-initiated audio is desired, clicks and/or mouse-overs start the audio. Services include strategic campaign development and production; hardware and software integration; project management; and hosting on fast, scalable infrastructure.

bluestreak.com, Inc.

<www.bluestreak.com>
P.O. Box 3399
Newport, RI 02840
401-341-3300
401-841-5643 fax

Founded in 1999, bluestreak.com, Inc. is a technology-based marketing company providing rich media and interactive solutions and services for Internet marketers. The company offers four main groups of services:

1. eBanners provides customer interactive ads, not just simple messaging.
2. On The Fly (OTF) provides a Web-based interface for marketers that allows integration of rich media with creative content.

3. Real Time Aggregate Data Analysis and Response (RADAR) provides noninvasive online targeting that eliminates cookies and tags while still matching content to recipients.
4. Streaking Media creates a full-scale multimedia experience instead of an automated GIF.

Based in Rhode Island, the company also has offices in San Francisco, Chicago, and Boston.

LIST BROKERS, VENDORS, AND SUPPLIERS

MetaResponse Group

<www.metaresponse.com>
901 Martin Downs Boulevard
Palm City, FL 34990
561-219-9422
561-219-0365 fax

MetaResponse Group® is an Information Marketing organization that provides campaign direct marketing consulting, targeting, list brokerage, management, and delivery services for online campaigns, as well as for traditional offline direct mail campaigns. The Florida company services business-to-business, high-technology, and consumer marketplaces across many industries. Core competencies include e-mail and direct mail list acquisition, e-mail sponsorship placement, and e-mail transmission, tracking, and reporting.

NetCreations, Inc.

<www.netcreations.com>
<www.postmaster.com>
379 W. Broadway, Suite 202
New York, NY 10012
212-625-1370
212-274-9266 fax

NetCreations, Inc specializes in opt-in e-mail address list management, brokerage, and delivery services. Through its PostMasterDirect.com service, NetCreations sends e-mail messages on behalf of more than 1,500 direct marketing clients, ranging from large companies to small retailers. PostMasterDirect.com has a network of targeted opt-in e-mail addresses in more than 3,000 topical lists and with 10 million names. The company's double–opt-in system ensures that no e-mail address will be added to list without the user's knowledge or consent.

TargitMail, a division of GTMI, LLC

<www.targitmail.com>
155 Commerce Way
Portsmouth, NH 03801
888-467-7709
603-766-8300
603-766-8263 fax

TargitMail.com, a division of GTMI, LLC, was founded in 1997 to provide permission-based, e-mail database marketing services. In early 1998, work began on patent-pending software called "electronic Targeted Opt-in Messaging" or eTOM. This software provides marketers with powerful tools through which to query databases, launch highly targeted marketing campaigns, and track results by using a Web-based interface. Features include: password protected, unlimited 24/7 queries; campaign delivery scheduling and past campaign tracking; comprehensive data profiles; real-time response tracking; and reports and multimedia capabilities. TargitMail.com has explicit consent from every person in the database—currently nearly 12 million individuals—to send promotional e-mails to them. Future development will include the TargitMailDIRECT, a self-service e-mail marketing center and various branded reseller interfaces.

YesMail

<www.yesmail.com>
222 S. Riverside Plaza, Floor 17
Chicago, IL 60606
312-423-5000
312-423-5070 fax

Founded in 1995 as WebPromote, and currently owned by CMGI, YesMail was one of the first permission-based e-mail marketing companies. With an opt-in database of more than 11 million, YesMail provides technologies that target customers, personalize messages, deliver campaigns, track and analyze results, customize responses, and generate real-time reports. CMGI, Inc., with 70 companies, represents one of the largest and most diverse networks of Internet companies.

24/7 Media Inc.

<www.247media.com>
1250 Broadway, Floor 28
New York, NY 10001
212-231-7100
212-760-1744 fax

24/7 Media is a global Internet, media, and technology company with a network of quality content sites that as a whole deliver more than 3.3 billion ad impressions per month on more than 4,000 Web sites worldwide. 24/7 Media offers three main groups of services: 24/7 Mail, one of the largest permission-based e-mail databases available with more than 20 million profiles; 24/7 Technology Solutions, offering comprehensive ad-serving solutions across multiple platforms; and 24/7 Connect, an ad management and reporting system, that seamlessly delivers ads to Web sites worldwide. 24/7 Mail offers a comprehensive suite of end-to-end e-mail communications solutions including list acquisition and administration, ad sales and serving, subscription management, advanced list hygiene, customer service, 24 hours a day/7 days a week account management, Web-based reporting, rich media formats, and a guarantee of uninterrupted service.

Rubin Response Services

<www.rubinresponse.com>
1111 Plaza Drive
Shaumburg, IL 60173
847-619-9800 ext. 139
847-619-1228 fax

Rubin Response Services (RRS) is one of the largest U.S. direct marketing firms and mailing list brokers available with access to more than 35,000 lists including business, consumer, high-tech, international, and alternative media. Rubin Response Services provides list recommendations for thousands of mailing programs each year and manages more than 300 mailing lists for its clients. Services also include extensive direct marketing consultation and support for both offline and online campaigns.

Penton Media Inc.

<www.penton.com>
<www.pentonlists.com>
1100 Superior Avenue
Cleveland, OH 44114
216-931-9265
216-696-6662 fax

Penton Media, Inc. is a diversified media company offering online and off-line marketing related products and services in several vertical markets. In addition to list brokerage, Penton Media produces several industry trade magazines, Web sites, trade shows, and conferences. Among the industries served are broadband Internet; retail natural products and foods; manufacturing; electronics; design/engineering; management; aviation supply chain; government/compliance; mechanical systems/construction; and leisure/hospitality markets.

BulletMail

<www.bulletmail.com>
Waterville Valley, NH
603-236-3628 telephone and fax

Established in 1997, BulletMail provides companies with opt-in e-mail lists for online direct marketing campaigns. The company maintains more than 100 lists organized by topic and includes thousands of BulletMail members who have registered to receive e-mail offers personalized to their interests. List topics include shopping, business, travel, hobbies, lifestyles, money, finance, Internet, computing, software, business-to-business, entertainment, sports, and electronics.

The XactMail Network
(owned by Venture Direct Worldwide)

<www.xactmail.com>
<www.venturedirect.com>
60 Madison Avenue
New York, NY 10010
212-655-5231
212 576-1129 fax

XactMail™ is a service of VentureDirect Worldwide, Inc., a $100 million direct marketing company with more than 16 years' experience in traditional direct mail. XactMail™ draws on significant experience in database marketing, list segmentation, and appending to identify the best target audience for each mailing. With more than 40 million names, XactMail™ technology maximizes segmentation opportunities and tracks the response of every e-mail.

VentureDirect Worldwide is a Manhattan-based marketing company providing both online and offline media services. Online services in addition to XactMail include:

- B2BfreeNet, <www.b2bfreenet.com>, which integrates a search resource with targeted direct mail
- Ad-Venture Network, <www.ad-venture.com>, an advertising network of more than 2000 Web sites
- Free Forum Network, <www.freeforum.com>, a free-offer shopping portal with 22 channels
- VentureDirectOnline, <www.venturedirect.com>, an online media planning and buying service

Offline media businesses managed by Venture Direct include List Management, List Brokerage, Inserts, B2BFreeMail (Card Pac Publishing), and Print Media.

eDirect.com

<www.edirect.com>
6601 Park of Commerce Boulevard
Boca Raton, FL 33487
888-239-3831
888-811-3069 fax
561-999-4545
561-999-4670 fax

eDirect.com is a subscription-based ASP offering online direct marketing services. Its opt-in e-mail database numbers in the millions and covers a wide variety of categories. eDirect.com uses a double–opt-in procedure for all of its database entries that sends a confirmation e-mail to verify that the subscriber wants to receive information pertaining to the topics that the subscriber selected. After receiving an affirmative reply, eDirect confirms the authenticity of the record by matching it against the company's consumer database of 175 million individual consumers, before adding the record to eDirect's file.

Kroll Direct Marketing

<www.krolldirect.com>
666 Plainsboro Road, Suite 540
Plainsboro, NJ 08536
609-275-2900 ext. 108
609-609-275-6606 fax

Kroll Direct Marketing is a full-service list brokerage, and list management and Web-based services company with a ten-year history of marketing programs with mailers and marketers worldwide. Services include list brokerage, list management, international lists, and Web-based services such as enhancements to e-mail lists, online data management, and electronic newsletter broadcasts. The *Publibase International Executive Masterfile* produced by Kroll Direct contains international B2B lists of more than 2.5 million unduplicated names and is one of the largest global publishers' databases available.

Walter Karl

<www.walterkarl.com>
1 Blue Hill Plaza
Pearl River, NY 10965
845-732-7055
845-620-1885 fax

Walter Karl, Inc. is a division of Donnelly Marketing, an *info*USA Company, and one of the nation's largest providers of data for B2B and B2C marketing solutions. The Walter Karl division has provided list management, list brokerage, and related direct mail services for offline marketers for nearly 50 years. Through its WK Interactive group, online marketing services are offered that integrate traditional direct marketing with new and emerging e-marketing strategies.

Pinpoint Media

<www.pinpointmedia.com>
1400 E. Hillsboro Boulevard, 2nd Floor
Deerfield Beach, FL 33441
954-725-6455 ext. 101
945-725-7990 fax

Pinpoint Media is an e-media management company offering advertising agency services to online businesses. Services include e-campaign strategy development and planning, media buying and creative services, campaign tracking, optimization, ROI reporting, and e-promotion opportunities such as list rentals, newsletter sponsorships, and e-viral campaigns. The company has more than 11,000 list owners and 22 million opt-in e-mail addresses in more than 500 categories.

List Services Corporation

<www.listservices.com>
6 Trowbridge Drive
P.O. Box 516
Bethel, CT 06801-0516
203-791-4454
203-778-4299 fax

List Services Corporation (LSC) was founded in 1980 as a direct marketing list management firm. The company expanded in 1981 to include list brokerage services and again in 1985 to include a data center specializing in list maintenance, database development, list enhancement, merge/purge, regression analysis, modeling, custom programming, and other direct marketing services. LSC specializes in very targeted list development and list brokerage services.

Worldata

<www.worldata.com>
3000 N. Military Trail
Boca Raton, FL 33431-6375
800-331-8102
561-241-7257 fax

Worldata is a direct marketing and information company with services for both online and offline marketers. List management and brokerage, database marketing, merge/purge services, and response analysis for both B2B and B2C markets are provided in the Direct Marketing/Postal division. The Interactive Marketing division offers opt-in e-mail list brokerage and management, e-mail transmission, and tracking. In 1995, the company founded WebConnect, an ad placement division of the company that targets, places, and tracks advertising.

e•PostDirect

<www.epostdirect.com>
Blue Hill Plaza, 16th Floor
Pearl River, NY 10965-3104
800-409-4443
914-620-9035 fax

Incorporated in 1998, e•PostDirect's is an online one-to-one marketer offering scalable e-mail solutions that can create and deliver personalized e-mails to targeted recipients in multiple formats. Services include list brokerage, creative services, and rich media presentations using e•PostDirect's proprietary software, Visual Mail; transmission of e-mails; capture of the order or direction to a Web site; tracking; and report generation. Services are delivered using advanced database technology integrated with delivery at T3 speed and 24/7 support.

21st Century Marketing

<www.21stcm.com>
1750 New Highway
Farmingdale, New York 11735-1512
631-293-8550
631-293-8974 fax

A 23-year-old company, 21st Century Marketing is a direct media organization specializing in postal and e-mail lists. The company offers list brokerage services, database development, and list management, plus a full range of data processing services, including merge-purge, modeling, and customer profiling. 21stezone.com from 21st Century Marketing provides e-services including search engine optimization and e-mail address appending, e-mail list brokerage, management, and fulfillment.

American List Council

<www.amlist.com>
88 Orchard Road, CN-5219
Princeton, NJ 08543
800-ALC-LIST
908-874-4433 fax

American List Council, Inc. (ALC) is the world's largest independent database brokerage and management company. The company's Impower.net division grew out of ALC Interactive, a company formed in 1996. Impower.net develops, maintains, and mines proprietary, managed, and licensed electronic databases by applying direct marketing methods, techniques, and disciplines. It produces and delivers targeted Internet-based direct marketing campaigns and promotions with TransAct!, a cost-per-action-based direct response Internet network. ACL supports thousands of clients—including more than 300 blue chip clients—in nearly all business categories. Headquarters is in Princeton, New Jersey, with sales and account management offices in New York City, New England, and northern California.

IDG List Services

<www.idglist.com>
508-370-0823

IDG Communications List Services is a full service list management and brokerage division of International Data Group, a media, research, and exposition company specializing in the Information Technology sector. IDG List Services has two division:

1. List Management Division, which manages subscriber lists; and trade shows, expositions, conferences, and customer databases
2. Brokerage Division, which specializes in promotion and list research

E-development.com, Inc.

<www.e-development.com>
<www.e-target.com>
1806 South Alpine Road, Suite F
Rockford, Illinois 61108
888-399-6313
815-399-3018
815-399-5713 fax

E-target.com, from E-development.com, Inc., is an opt-in e-mail marketing firm whose network of newsletter publishers and e-mail list owners reaches millions of consumers. With more than 400 newsletters, e-zines, and direct e-mail lists, E-target.com's network consists of more than 15 million opt-in subscribers, making the network one of the largest of its kind. Marketers can target audiences by age, gender, interest and other demographic information, with permission-based e-mail campaigns.

A

Accessibility, 80–81
Acquisition campaign, 102
    costs, 4, 29–30, 133–34
    definition, 26
    from line, 94
    goals, 27–29
    opt-in lists, 18–19
    prospect lists for, 6
    return-on-investment, 190–91
    strategy, 31–33
    target leads, 4
    testing strategies, 64–74
Acquisitions phase, contact cycle, 5
Alignment, 108–11
Asterisk, 124
Attachments, 165
Audience
    appeals, 39–40
    assumptions, 39–40, 45
    customer profile, 36–38, 45
    definition of, 8
    target, 36–38, 54–55, 101
Auto-billed trial offer, 44–45

B

Balance, 53, 113–15
Banners, 118
Benefits
    body copy, 97
    emphasis on, 101
    from line style, 92
    offer, 101
Body copy, 90
    benefits, 97
    offer, 97
    proof, 99
    rules, 99–100
    sample, 98
    unique selling proposition, 97
Bounce page, 11

Breakeven point, 31
B2B, 42
B2C, 42–44
Budget, 29–33
Business
    books, 42
    free gift offers, 42
    tools, 42
Business-to-business (B2B), 42
Business-to-consumer (B2C),
    42–44

C

Call to action
    copywriting, 90, 100, 101
    design tips, 118–20
    landing page, 177
    rich media, 127
Campaign
    acquisition, 102
    benefits, 3–4
    budget, 30–33
    costs, 190
    customer paid, 12
    goals, 27–29, 101
    review of, 85
    strategy, 31–33
    success measurement tools, 9,
        12, 190–95
Cancellation policies, 60
Capitalization
    in body copy, 99
    overuse, 115
    purpose, 124
Carrot, 100
Cash discount, 45
Catalog, 43
CD-ROM giveaway, 42
Clickable text, 8
Click-through rate (CTR), 101
    definition of, 9
    determination of, 28–29

landing page and, 172–73
    return on investment, 190–93
    statistical significance, 53
    tracking, 69
Close, 87, 100
Communication
    coupon offers, 148
    direct, 3–4
    executive, 140
    forms of, 4
    holiday promotions, 146–47
    members-only club offers, 148
    newsletters, 145–46
    paid customer, 143
    registered leads, 144
    registered subscribers, 143–44
    retention, 142–49
    special offers, 146–47
    timing issues, 142–44
    update announcements, 148–49
    users, 143–44
    welcome message, 144–45
Competition, 85
Compiled list, 9
Complementary products, 43
Confirmed opt-in, 22, 50
Connection principle, 108–11
Contest entries, 165
Continuation, 53
Contrast, 113–15
Control, 158
Conversational tone, 88
Conversion, 134–35
    definition of, 9, 26
    landing page and, 172–73
    lead-to-sale rate, 28
    return-on-investment, 190–93
    tracking, 69
Cookie, 184–85
    creation of, 185
    definition of, 9
    testing strategies and, 185–86
Copy
    body, 90, 97–100

Copy, *continued*
　　landing page, 177
　　samples, 60–61
Copywriting
　　call to action, 90, 100, 101
　　close, 87, 100
　　conversational tone, 88
　　features/benefits, 86–87
　　format, 85–87
　　foundation, 83–84
　　from line, 90, 94
　　grammar, 88–89
　　greeting, 85–86
　　introduction, 90, 95–97
　　product excitement, 89
　　promise, 86, 87
　　prospect knowledge, 84–85
　　punctuation, 89
　　repetitive statements, 88
　　subject line, 90, 91–93
　　tease, 86
　　techniques, 101
　　unique selling proposition,
　　　　87
Cost of goods, 139
Cost-per-thousand, 9
Costs
　　acquisition, 29–30
　　dedicated prospecting
　　　　promotion, 4
　　deployment, 190
　　fulfillment, 139
　　list, 29–30
　　retention, 4, 137–39
Coupon offers, 45, 148, 158
CPM, 9
Creative scheme, 176–77
Creativity, 6
Credit card, 44–45
Cross-pollination, 54–55
Cross-selling, 9, 135
CTR. *See* Click-through rate
Cultural tie-ins, 93
Customer
　　base, 27
　　communication with, 3–4
　　contact cycle, 5–7
　　development goals, 27–29
　　dialogue, 77–81
　　existing, 26–27
　　paid, 12, 143
　　profile, 36–38, 45, 84–85
　　relationship with, 6, 7, 12,
　　　　77–81
　　response, 155–58
　　rewards, 139–40
　　tiers, 27
　　unsubscribe option for, 22

D

Database marketing, 12
　　definition of, 10
　　retention strategy, 135–36
　　segmentation, 151–53
Datacard, 56, 59–60
　　components, 60–61
　　example, 56–59
Data collection
　　changes in, 22
　　data points, 154–55
　　methods, 61
　　privacy policy, 19–21
Data mining, 151
Dedicated prospecting promotion,
　　4
Deep discounts, 165
Deployment
　　costs, 190
　　definition of, 10
　　frequency, 180–81
　　tests, 65
Design, 105–6
　　alignment, 108–11
　　balance/contrast, 113–15
　　banners/headers, 118
　　download time, 116
　　font, 125
　　HTML rules, 116–20
　　layout, 108–11
　　links, 118–20
　　proximity principle, 106–8
　　repetition principle, 111–13
　　reverse text useage, 118
　　rich media, 126–28
　　space useage, 117–18
　　special effects, 124
　　text blocks, 116–17
　　text promotion, 120, 122–24
　　tips, 115
Dialogue, 77–81
Direct communication, 3–4
Direct response marketing, 10
Discounts, 45
Domain name, 10
Double opt-in, 18, 22, 50
Download
　　definition of, 10
　　speed, 116
Dynamic content marketing, 10, 12,
　　152–53. *See also* Segmentation

E

E-commerce page, 174–76
E-mail addresses. *See* List

E-mail customer contact cycle,
　　5–7
E-mail reports, 43
Early-bird discount, 45
Ego factor, 166
80/20 rule, 27
Emotions, 83–84
Emphasis, 99
Entertainment factor, 166
Exclusive club, 140
Executable files, 127
Existing customer, 26–27
Exit, 149

F

Fad mindset, 156
Features/benefits, 86–87
Feeder product, 42–43, 134
Font, 125
Freebie seekers, 41
Free gift offers, 41–44
Free product, 42–43
Free registration, 42
Frequency, 154, 159
From line, 90, 94
Fulfillment costs, 139
Full-blown format, 149

G

GIF, 10
Goals
　　identification of, 27–29
　　timeframe, 29–30
Graphical interchange format, 10
Grammar, 88–89
Graphic images, 10, 11
Greeting, 85–86
Grouping, 107–8

H

Hard bounce, 10
Headers, 118
Headline, 85–86
Holiday promotions, 147–48
Hotline names, 55
House file, 36
　　creation of, 134
　　splits, 156–58
　　tests, 158–59
HTML
　　definition of, 10–11
　　design rules, 116–20

HTTP, 11
Hyperlink, 8, 11
Hypertext markup language, 10–11, 116–20
Hypertext transfer protocol, 11

I

Interactivity, 4
Internet Service Provider (ISP), 15
Introduction, 90, 95–97
Introductory offers, 45

J

Joint photographic experts group, 11
JPEG, 11
Jump page, 11

K

Keycode
  assignment of, 71–72
  creation of, 67–71
  definition of, 11

L

Landing page, 68
  definition of, 11, 171–72
  e-commerce, 174–76
  form, 177–78
  importance of, 172–73
  links, 178
  purpose of, 171–72
  rules, 176–77
  simple registration, 173–74
  viral marketing, 166–67
Layout, 108–11
Lead. *See also* Prospect
  communications, 144
  conversion rate, 28, 134–35
  definition of, 11, 26
Lead generation campaign
  free gift offer, 41–44
  landing page, 173–74
  registration, 177–78
  return on investment, 192–93
  sales offer, 44–45
  timeframe, 4
Leads-to-sale ratio, 28
Let me show you factor, 166
Lifetime value, 28
  definition of, 11
  retention strategy, 136–39

Limited-time use, 44
Link
  body copy, 99
  definition of, 11
  design tips, 118–20
  keycodes in, 67–69
  redirect link, 66
  tests, 65
List
  brokers, 52–54, 61–62
  categories, 54–55
  cost of, 29–30
  datacard, 56–61
  data collection, 19–21
  minimum orders, 60
  opt-in, 18–19
  pricing methods, 9, 52, 55
  selects, 55, 60
  test strategies, 52–54, 59–60, 62, 65
  updates, 62
  usage, 61
  vendors, 51–52, 61–62
Loss leader, 42–43, 134
Loyalty program, 139–40
LTV, 11, 28, 136–39

M

Market segmentation. *See* Segmentation
Matter-of-fact style, 91–92
Members-only club offers, 148
Message
  role of, 81
  test, 65
  viral marketing, 165, 166
Microsite, 175–76
Monetary value, 154
Multiple gifts, 43
Mystery gift, 43

N

Newsletters, 145–46
Nonexecutable files, 127
Nth, 54

O

Objections, 83–84
Objectives, 40–41, 45
Offer, 101
  audience appeals, 39–40
  audience assumptions, 39–40, 45

body copy, 97
customer profile, 45
definition of, 11
development, 47, 48
free gift, 42–44
importance of, 39
lead generation, 41–45
objectives, 40–41
paid, 30–31
primary, 39, 45
promotional objectives, 45
sales, 44–45
secondary, 39, 45
testing strategy, 65
trial, 44–45
types of, 39, 41–45
Online chats, 42
Opening statement, 95–97
Open rates, 9, 193
Opt-in
  confirmations, 22
  definition of, 11
  list. *See* List
  solicitation procedures, 15
Opt-out
  definition of, 11–12
  solicitation procedures, 15
Organic marketing. *See* Viral marketing
Overhead, 139

P

Paid campaign
  budget, 30–33
  definition of, 12
Pareto's Principle, 27
Pass-along, 13, 163, 193
Perceived value, 156
Permissions, 11, 14. *See also* Opt-in
Personalization, 93
  definition of, 12
  RFM model, 155
  welcome message, 145
Presentation, 78–79
  introduction, 79–80
  tools, 10–11
Primary offer, 39, 45
Privacy, 11–12, 14–22
Privacy policy, 19
  elements of, 21
  example, 20
  landing page links, 178
  link to, 22
Privacy seal organizations, 21
Product
  details, 145

Product, *continued*
  discount, 45
  timing, 155–56
Promise
  body copy, 97–100
  copywriting, 86, 87
  opening statement, 95–97
  subject line approach, 92
Promotions. *See* Campaign
Proof, 99
Prospect
  acquisition, 26
  communication with, 3–4, 144
  conversion rate, 28, 134–35
  dedicated promotion, 4
  definition of, 26
  dialogue, 77–81
  goals, 27–29
  knowledge of, 84–85
  opt-in lists, 18–19
  sales momentum, 83–84, 86
  solicitation procedures, 15–22
  unqualified, 41
  unsubscribe option for, 22
Proximity principle, 106–8
Pull, 12
Punctuation, 89, 124
Purchase points, 156–58
Push, 12

Q

Quantity discount, 45
Question style, 92

R

Rapport, 84–85
Recency, 153–54
Redirect link, 66
Registered leads, 144
Registered subscribers/users, 143–44
Registration page, 173–74, 177–78
Relationship marketing, 12
Remail strategy, 184
Reminders, 140, 145, 177
Repetition
  principle, 111–13
  tips, 115
  usage rules, 113
Repetitive statements, 88
Reports, 43
Retention campaign
  communications, 142–49
  costs of, 4, 137–39
  from line, 94

goals, 27–29
  target leads, 4
Retention marketing, 134–35
Retention phase, contact cycle, 5–6
Retention strategy
  database marketing, 135–36,
    151–53
  lifetime value analysis,
    136–39
  loyalty programs, 139–40
  segmentation, 135–36,
    150–60
Return on investment, 12, 190–93
Revenue, 190
Reverse text, 118
RFM model, 153–55
Rich media, 126–28
ROI, 12, 190–93
Rollout, 53
  definition of, 12
  results, 74

S

Sales
  campaign, 4
  momentum, 83–84, 85–87
  offers, 44–45
Secondary offer, 39, 45
Seeding, 85
Segmentation, 4. *See also* Database
  marketing; Dynamic content
  marketing
  database, 151–53
  definition of, 12
  fine-tuned, 159
  retention strategy, 135–36
  RFM model, 153–55
Select list, 55, 60, 65, 66
Seminars, 42
Service bureaus, 51–52
Service details, 145
Shipping, 44
Social buyers, 156
Soft bounce, 10
Space, 115, 117–18
Spam
  definition of, 12, 15
  example of, 16–17
  opposition to, 15, 17
Special effects, 124
Special offers, 139, 146–47, 158
Specifics, 176
Splash page, 11, 166–67
Statistical significance, 53–54
Subject line
  benefits, 92

construction, 85–86
  copywriting, 90, 91–93,
    101
  cultural tie-in, 93
  direct approach, 91–92
  personalization, 93
  question, 92
  teaser, 92
  test, 65
Subscriptions, 85
Sweepstakes, 44

T

Target audience, 26, 101
Target marketing, 4, 12
Teaser copy, 86
Teaser format, 92, 149
Terminology, 8–13
Testing, 6
  acquisitions, 64–74
  cookies for, 184–86
  deployment, 65
  house file, 158–59
  lists, 59–60, 62, 65
  keycodes, 67–72
  message, 65
  remail strategy, 184
  result reports, 72–74
  retest, 72, 786–87
  rules, 71–72
  selects, 65, 66
  statistical quantities, 72
  timing issues, 181–84
  variables, 71
Testing phase, contact cycle, 5
Text blocks, 116–17
Text promotion
  creation of, 122
  design, 120
  formatting tips, 122–24
Timing issues, 156–57
Timing tests
  assumptions, 184
  best days of week, 183–84
  comparisons, 182
  how often, 181–83
Token gifts, 43
Tracking system, 119, 120
  methods used, 66, 67–71
  open rates, 193
  pass-along, 193
  return on investment,
    190–93
  rich media, 127, 128
  worksheet, 194
Trial offers, 44–45

U

Unique selling proposition, 87, 97
Universal resource locator, 13, 67–69
Universe, 52, 60
Unsolicitated e-mail. *See* Spam
Unsubscribe option, 145
Update announcements, 148–49
Up-selling, 12, 135
Urgency factor, 99, 166

URL
    definition of, 13
    keycodes, 67–69
User communication, 143–44
USP, 87, 97

V

Value factor, 156, 166
Vendor, 65, 66
Viral marketing, 162–67

components, 164–65
definition of, 13
message components, 166
message types, 165
technology, 166–67

W

Webcasts, 42
Welcome message, 144–45
Whitepapers, 42